Sleeping Rough in Port-au-Prince

P9-DDI-802

Florida A&M University, Tallahassee
Florida Atlantic University, Boca Raton
Florida Gulf Coast University, Ft. Myers
Florida International University, Miami
Florida State University, Tallahassee
University of Central Florida, Orlando
University of Florida, Gainesville
University of North Florida, Jacksonville
University of South Florida, Tampa
University of West Florida, Pensacola

J. Christopher Kovats-Bernat

Sleeping Rough in Port-au-Prince

AN ETHNOGRAPHY OF
STREET CHILDREN AND
VIOLENCE IN HAITI

University Press of Florida

Gainesville · Tallahassee · Tampa
Boca Raton · Pensacola · Orlando
Miami · Jacksonville · Ft. Myers

Copyright 2006 by J. Christopher Kovats-Bernat
Printed in the United States of America on acid-free paper
All rights reserved

A record of cataloging-in-publication data is available from
the Library of Congress.
ISBN 978-0-8130-3009-8 (cloth)
ISBN 978-0-8130-3302-0 (pbk.)

First cloth printing, 2006
First paperback printing, 2008

The University Press of Florida is the scholarly publishing
agency for the State University System of Florida, compris-
ing Florida A&M University, Florida Atlantic University,
Florida Gulf Coast University, Florida International University, Florida State University, University of Central Florida,
University of Florida, University of North Florida, University
of South Florida, and University of West Florida.

University Press of Florida
15 Northwest 15th Street
Gainesville, FL 32611-2079
http://www.upf.com

For Addison and Ella
As you grow, may you come to understand
that your lives are inextricably linked to
the lives of children everywhere
And for Dina, whose love sets me free

Bay kou, bliye. Pote mak, sonje.
[The one who strikes, forgets. The one stricken, remembers.]
—Haitian proverb

Contents

Illustrations

Tables

Preface

At the 2003 meeting of the American Anthropological Association held in New Orleans and organized around the theme of "(Un)Imaginable Futures: Anthropology Faces the Next 100 Years," I chaired a panel that featured papers that dealt with emerging anthropologies of violence and childhood. In the introduction to that session, I suggested that as ethnographers are increasingly pressed into research in postcolonial, postoccupation, postwar states, what they may well expect to encounter are populations with high fertility rates and low life expectancy—the offshoots of cultures of prolonged poverty and conflict. So as anthropology moves into its next generation, our research fields are getting ever more violent as the states that contain them struggle with the political challenges and power contests of the new millennium; and our informants are getting ever younger. We might go so far as to say that the anthropology of violence and the anthropology of childhood are the primary anthropologies of both the here and now and of the foreseeable future. If this is truly the case, and the data suggests as much, then it is surely time for us to pay closer attention to that which passes from the mouths of babes. Put another way, its time for us to get to work.

My purpose in writing this book is to call attention to the lives and words of street children in Haiti. My reason for doing so is that what they do and what they say can offer anthropology a fresh perspective—one that truly originates on the ground—on the causes and consequences of poverty and violence. It is my hope that the reader will agree that the children discussed in the pages that follow are far more than passive victims of social, economic, and political processes gone awry. Rather, these children are active and determined social beings whose ability to survive on the street is wholly dependent on their differential abilities to express themselves through their agency in creating social, cultural, folkloric, economic, and political relations among themselves and with the larger civil society of which they indeed are a part. This is not to say that Haiti's street children are not victimized; to be sure, they routinely are—by the economy, the police, passersby, reckless drivers, drug gangs, stray dogs, and each other. But what makes their lives far more meaningful for anthropology is their ability to survive in a world bent to their victimization through the establishment of networks of social support and exchange that permit them critical cultural space to act in a world in which they otherwise would not be able.

Over the past decade anthropologists have been contributing to an ever clearer understanding of the intersection of childhood and violence, and the work that has leveraged against this problem before my own has in no small way helped me to better understand the meaning of the lives of children I have come to know in Haiti. It is with deep gratitude that I first acknowledge the work of Philip Kilbride, whose ethnographic study of street children in Kenya with Enos Njeru and Collete Suda opened up a world of possibilities for my own research. Both Dr. Kilbride and an anonymous knowledgeable reviewer (to whom I am equally grateful) contributed a great deal to the revisions of the manuscript that led to this book, and I believe that the finished product is all the better for them. If the reader should find this book a good one, these estimable scholars are in no small way responsible. Carolyn Nordstrom and Jeff Sluka, both pioneers of the kind of ethnography that I am sure will define the discipline of anthropology in the next century, also offered their encouraging support of my work.

I appreciate the opportunity that John Byram, Susan Albury and the editorial staff at the University Press of Florida have given me to bring my decade of research with street kids in Haiti to published fruition. The stories that these children have to tell is far too important to remain locked in my field notes, and I am pleased that John and his press found my presentation of those stories worth putting in print.

My colleagues in the Department of Sociology and Anthropology at Muhlenberg College have offered me a wealth of assistance and support without which I may never have completed this book: Bill Abruzzi, Tammy Lewis, and Janine Chi. My conversations with Amber VanDerwarker and Greg Wilson, both archaeologists in the department, sparked fresh ideas about the street and children, and helped me navigate through what sometimes seemed to be conceptual dead ends. I also thank Tracy Kline for taking on the critical minutiae throughout the revisions process. Two of my brightest students, Tara Trudnak and Adam Schieffer, also deserve my thanks for the thorough background research that they did in support of this project.

The research that formed the basis of this book would not have been possible without a generous grant from the Wenner-Gren Foundation for Anthropological Research. I am also indebted to the Bureau of Ethnology at the National University of Haiti for providing me with research affiliation as well as access to their resources and facilities. I wish to acknowledge as well the assistance of the Aristide Foundation for Democracy, the Haitian

National Police, and the staff at the Prison Juvénile-Sous-Fort for the access and liberties that they granted me as I conducted my research.

My arrival in Haiti for the first time in 1994 found me a stranger in a strange land, but the friendship and support of many there helped me to eventually regard Haiti as home. I owe a debt of appreciation to the staff, teachers, and especially the children of Lafanmi Selavi and Centre d'Action for their openness and their trust. Early in my research, Jean-Bertrand Aristide and Mildred Trouillot-Aristide opened many doors for me as well, and for that I am grateful.

During nights in Port-au-Prince when fear and loneliness may have otherwise gotten the better of me, I was fortunate to have good friends with whom to share conversation, political arguments, conspiracy theories, and not a little bit of rum: Paisley Dodd, Jennifer Cheek-Pantaleon, Roger Lyons, Eleanor Louise Snare, and Eric Wafer. I am grateful to Richard Morse, Madame DePradines, and the staff of the Hotel Oloffson who provided me with a safe place to live, eat, drink, work, and sleep. It was on the balcony of that beloved and hallowed place that I came to know the late Professor Harold Courlander (on his last and my first visit to Haiti), who I thank for reminding me that anthropology can still craft legends out of men.

Of all the friends that Haiti has given me, none compares to Jean-Role Jean Louis. Whether in his role as confidante, field assistant, or friend, Jean-Role represents what every citizen of every nation, and certainly what every friend, should aspire to be: informed, knowledgeable, diplomatic, honorable, loyal, and incorruptible. I have traveled with Jean-Role into Haiti's darkest and brightest places, and without him I could never have begun my work, nor would I ever have made it home. I am unsure of how to thank someone for such a thing, so I will simply say that I will always remember.

There is no way for me to adequately express my appreciation of the sacrifice, patience, and trust that my family has extended to me. Gini, Jennifer, Karl Jr., Rich, Sandy, Julie, and Anton have given to me far more, I fear, than I have returned.

No one is more deserving of my appreciation than my best friend and partner, Dina, who has stood steadfastly by my side even at those times when the choice to do so could have broken her heart. Though too young to yet understand, I thank Addison and Ella as well, simply for seeing the world in a way that I long to remember.

While they will never know the full extent of their impact on my life and my work, I thank the boys and girls of Port-au-Prince who offered me their stories, their secrets, their dreams and more than frequently their protections, for which they never asked for anything in return; especially, Niksyon, Josier, Laronce, Floreal, Gregoire, Mati Ren, Dezalin, Blak Lovli, Ti Amos, Bèl Marie, Tifrè, Gito, Claudette, Lajounou, Dèjwi, Ronel, Nadès, Michel, and Selejeur.

Finally, I thank Gèdè, for always showing up just when I needed him.

Abbreviations

ADTB	Anti-Drug Trafficking Brigade
AFD	Aristide Foundation for Democracy
AGU	Anti-Gang Unit
BLTS	Bureau de Lutte contre le Trafic des Stupéfiants
BRIC	Bureau de Recherche et d'Identification des Criminel
CARE	Cooperative for Assistance and Relief Everywhere
CBTPA	Caribbean Basin Trade Partnership Act
CIMO	Compagnie d'Intervention et de Maintien de l'Orde
FADH	Forces Armées d'Haïti
FRA	Front de Résistance de l'Artibonite
FRAPH	Front Révolutionnaire pour l'Avancement et le Progès d'Haïti
GIPNH	Groupe d'Intervention de la Police Nationale d'Haïti
HASCO	Haitian-American Sugar Company
HDI	Human Development Index
IBESR	Institut du Bien Etre Social et de Recherches
ICRC	International Committee of the Red Cross
IPSF	Interim Public Security Force
MINUSTAH	United Nations Stabilization Mission in Haiti
MOPRADD	Mouvman Revandikatif Ayisyen pou Devlopman ak Demokrasi
OAS	Organization of American States
PNH	Police Nationale d'Häiti
SAG	Service d'Investigation et de Recherche Anti-Gang
SAS	Small Arms Survey
SIN	Service d'Intelligence Nationale
UN	United Nations
UNDP	United Nations Development Program
UNICEF	United Nations Children's Fund
UNMIF	United Nations Multinational Intervention Force
USAID	United States Agency for International Development

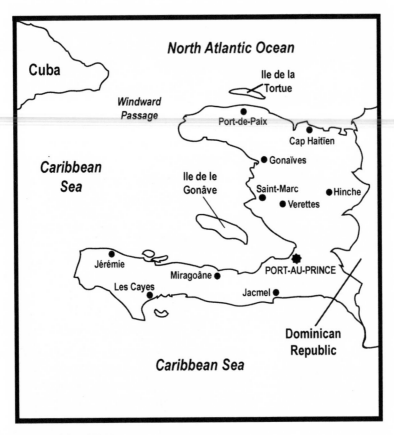

The Republic of Haiti

Metropolitan Port-au-Prince, Haiti

Shaded regions correspond to the author's primary fieldwork sites.

KEY:

1. National Palace

2. Hospital

3. Sylvio Cator Soccer Stadium

4. National Cemetery

5. USAID Headquarters

6. U.S. Embassy

7. Iron Market

8. National Cathedral

Sleeping Rough in Port-au-Prince

Introduction

Haiti is the poorest and most volatile country in the Western Hemisphere and has the highest under-five mortality rate in the Americas, making it one of the most inhospitable and unhealthy places in the world for a child to live. Here adolescent morbidity and death threaten from all quarters of everyday life. Diarrhea is the number one killer of Haitian children, a problem attributable to the fact that less than half of them are drinking clean water. This is a place where it is not at all uncommon for children to die of starvation or worse, thirst. Add to this the rampant gun violence and civil terror that has served as the backdrop of everyday life in Haiti for the past half-century, and it becomes immediately apparent that if there is any place in the world in which children have no business growing up, it is in the Republic of Haiti.

But grow up—and thrive, live, and survive—they do. This is an incredibly young country. Half of Haiti's population is under the age of eighteen, many of them working, eating, sleeping, socializing, loving, fighting, killing, and dying on the streets of the combustible capital of Port-au-Prince. To be sure, the challenges to child health and survival in Haiti are far more aggravated for those children who have been displaced from their homes and onto the streets, where they subsist and survive wholly in a world of violence, scarcity, and uncertainty. It is not an easy life, this *vi lari*, this street life. As one boy once told me, "*Blanc*, it is easy enough for anyone to die here."

But to simply regard Haiti's street children as the tragic victims of economic crisis and dissolute political circumstances is to ignore the profound impact that they have had on the developing course of Haitian democratization. To see them solely, as many in Haiti do, as Hobbesian brutes bent to the ruthless task of self-preservation is to deny the abundant evidence of their economic creativity, symbolic productivity, and communal politics that combine to form a rich cultural and social response to the hardscrabble challenges that the street presents. Many do suffer short lives that are every bit as solitary, nasty, and brutish as some perceive, but such is hardly the sum of their lived experience. The question that is begged by the high rates of child morbidity and mortality in Haiti (and throughout the developing world, for that matter) is not simply "How do street children suffer?" but more precisely "how do they negotiate their suffering?" How do street children adapt to their circumstances of scarcity? How do they contribute to the construction of a cultural (that is, symbolic) world that enables them to make sense of their lot? As an ethnographic exploration of street childhood in Haiti, this book draws on the lived experience of poor, displaced children in Port-au-Prince in order to better understand how they are crafting and negotiating their adolescence under extremely difficult circumstances. The aim is to document and interpret how the everyday violence of street life molds and *is molded by* the child who lives and works there. The observations made and conclusions drawn here have emerged over the course of ten years of ethnographic research in Haiti (from 1994 to 2004), with children who are carving their livelihoods and creating rich cultural milieus amid the filth, blight, and gunplay of some of the most destitute and volatile streets in the world.

Whither the Street Child?

Although childhood has been a passing concern of anthropologists since the birth of the discipline, with some recent notable exceptions (Riesman 1992; Amit-Talai and Wulff 1995; Stephens 1995; Morton 1996; Hecht 1998; Márquez 1999; Scheper-Hughes and Hoffman 1997, 1998; Scheper-Hughes and Sargent 1998; DeLauche and Gottlieb 2000; Kilbride, Suda, and Njeru 2001; Schwartzman 2001; Lanclos 2003; Gottlieb 2004), anthropology has not been at the forefront of research on childhood, a subject of relatively limited anthropological concern since it was taken up for the first time as the focus of serious ethnographic consideration in Margaret Mead's *Coming of Age in Samoa,* published in 1928.[1] Since the 1990s however, anthropologists have been steadily building on an exclusive "anthropology of the child." Alma Gottlieb provides a comprehensive history of the development of the anthropology of childhood since the work of Mead in her *The Afterlife Is Where We Come From: The Culture of Infancy in West Africa* (2004), obviating the need to give a full accounting of this history here. In addition to the ever-growing canon in anthropology, a number of scholarly centers and interdisciplinary programs devoted exclusively to the study of children and childhood have been established in the past decade, and the work of anthropologists has been central to their respective missions.[2]

The existing anthropological literature on childhood in the Caribbean is scant at best, and tends to be dominated by psychological models of socialization that subsume childhood into gross considerations of the family and gender construction (Clarke 1957, Chevannes 2001). The fact that such little attention is paid to childhood issues in the Caribbean is surprising, given that the region is demographically quite young—40 percent of the region's population is under the age of eighteen years. Such little social science research with children has been done in the Caribbean that one might go so far as to say that, from a scholarly perspective, we hardly know the child there at all.

Discussions of street childhood in particular are almost nonexistent in the anthropological canon, though there are some outstanding examples of just how much we can learn from displaced children's negotiation and use of urban space (Hecht 1998; Kilbride, Suda, and Njeru 2001; Panter-Brick 2001; Matthews 2003; Olwig 2003). The primary theoretical problem with street child research in anthropology is that ethnographic investigations of children in extremely difficult circumstances tend to begin with discussions of their vulnerability and victimization, to the neglect of their capacities to adapt and transform their social worlds. Such children are typically presented to the reader as characterized by their deprivation of freedom, security, or life without just cause. The introduction of more detailed personal biography and accounts of their everyday lives enter into the analysis only when it may lend some insight into the nature of state formation or larger cultural politics (Stephens 1995; Scheper-Hughes and Sargent 1998). Such top-down perspectives have contributed to oversimplified descriptions of poor and exposed children—from street kids, to child soldiers, to children in pornography—as *merely* victims or exploited objects, their social agency variously ignored or denied in the discourse.

Perhaps no class of children is regarded as less empowered than those millions of children worldwide who live a significant proportion of their lives on the street. As members of a status group discussed exclusively in terms of their assumed universal victimhood, the adolescent actors of the drama unfolding in the social science and public policy literature remain little more than two-dimensional stick figures, their cultural identity and agency obscured to the extent that they become utterly de-historicized, what Eric Wolf (1982) would call a people without history. No mention of how they got there or why, no commentary on what they typically do to subsist and adapt once there. What is still desperately needed is richer ethnographic research into the social experience of poverty, violence, and displacement *from the perspective of the children and youth who live it every day*, children and youth who are not regarded in the text as powerless dupes of global economic policies, nor as ancillary subissues related to gender and motherhood, but as vital cultural actors and valued informants. As an in-depth ethnographic study of the lived experiences and cultural adaptations of street children in one of the most impoverished and volatile countries in the modern world, this book is a contribution to that end. The approach to Haitian street childhood taken by this book is one that regards the children as vibrant agents of social and symbolic processes, producing and reproducing culture, rather than passively absorbing it as a consciousness forged within the context of adult-dominated institutions like the family and the school (indeed, most of the children on the boulevards of Haiti have had limited if any experience with these structures of adult society). Such an approach is in keeping with anthropology's broadening focus on the cultural and social lives of children in the here-and-now: their games, their language, their folklore, their economic practices, their strategies for conflict resolution, their means of reckoning who is friend and who is foe. Street children are thus described throughout this book as I have found them; as empowered social *beings* able to construct meaning and effect change in their world through economic cooperation, social interdependence, political engagement and resistance, and cultural production and reproduction. As such, this book situates children at the center of ethnographic consideration, not on the periphery of an otherwise gerontocratic world. In so doing it frames childhood as both a temporal and spatial site of cultural *being*, and not simply as a liminal space of cultural *becoming*. By focusing in this way on "youth culture" (Amit-Talai and Wulff 1995) rather than on youth psychology or socialization, it is my firm conviction that anthropology can continue to make genuinely substantive contributions to the interdisciplinary field of childhood studies.

Framing the Anthropological Child: Personhood, Self, and Society

A specific goal of this book is to dismantle the false construction of Haitian street children as unsocialized and therefore acultural entities, bent to the dictates of Hobbesian violence and disorder because they have been raised outside the bounds of adult norms and rearage characteristic of domestic life. To do this, I adopt as my theoretical basis a model of adolescent identity that envisions childhood as a distinctly social and symbolic space in which children continuously orient one another to the ever-changing rules of social life through ritual activities, economic exchanges, and symbolic interactions. I assume that no child develops without relating to peers with whom that child will continuously and cooperatively interpret and re-create a cultural universe. I privilege the economic and political relations of Haitian street children as social and symbolic points of departure for this ethnography, as I explore the interconnectedness of these relations with other aspects of Haitian cultural life.

This theoretical approach is akin to that taken up by Helen Morton (1996), whereby childhood is conceived as a composite of subjectively and objectively informed identities. I depart from Morton however by subordinating emotion as a core cause of child identity formation, favoring instead the idea that economic and political relations are at the social and symbolic center of child identity formation. A child participates in multiple spheres of social life often simultaneously, as someone's daughter or son, someone's friend, someone's classmate, someone's coworker. Each social relation in which a child is engaged (kinship, economic, political, sexual) further expands the web of specific responsibilities and obligations expected by society of the child. In its sum, this is the child's "personhood," the social normative of the child's identity, what is "expected" of the child. It derives from the composite of intrinsic rights to which children are entitled by virtue of their status as members of a society, even if those rights are limited to existence and well being. This complex network of social relations often presents children with conflicting obligations, opening up regular opportunities for them to act as agents on their own behalf and to make conscious choices about what each social occasion calls for in terms of expected behavior and demeanor. By measuring public standards of expected status roles (personhood) against a sense of self (with its intrinsic rights and privileges), the child expresses itself as an autonomous social *being*. In this way children are capable of contributing to the construction of their own cultural worlds, setting rules of behavior among themselves, resolving conflicts when they emerge, negotiating their own economy, and regulating the formation of symbolic life among themselves.

From this vantage children can be engaged in a useful theoretical manner by envisioning childhood as the continuously reconstituted product of a dialectic that opposes the *social expectations* of a child's personhood to that child's autonomy and selfhood or *what the child expects*. The result is choice, freedom, and agency, and new opportunities for identity formation. This dialectical approach also acknowledges the fluid and shifting roles that all persons experience as they move through one social context into the next. It allows the anthropologist to explore when children are making choices and how those choices affect and are affected by the tension between personhood and selfhood. It also affords the anthropologist a more sophisticated means to analyze the behavioral and symbolic products that follow.

In locating street-child identity in Haiti, I have identified two primary influences on the personhood of the street child: the larger Haitian civil society including adults in general and "domiciled" or "settled" children (those who are not comported to the street as their "home") and the Haitian state, primarily its economic and legal institutions, including the police and its various quasi military factions. Both the civil society and the state (and the individuals and groups that make up each) construct children's personhood through different lenses, place heavy expectations on what it means to be a "child" in Haiti, and accord certain rights and protections to them.

Of equal significance to street-child identity is the children's own sense of autonomy and selfhood, most often expressed in their economic, political, and occasionally emotional relations with the larger community of street children. This social focus has allowed me to define and collect hard evidence of child identity and agency (through the products of their economic relations, for example) rather than just speculate on their emotional states. These emotional states are nonetheless critical to a full understanding of street-child identity formation, and they too produce tangible effects in the social world. Street children sometimes fall in love, and they express that love both physically and behaviorally. They fear the police and predatory street kids, and manifest that fear in both their actions and their words. The reader will therefore find throughout the chapters that follow an exploration of street children's selfhoods that draws as much on what they do and say as it does on how they feel and why.

The notion of child agency that I develop over the course of the chapters that follow is one in which the autonomy of the child is expressed in his/her relations with adults, domiciled children, other street kids, and the state. Children also comport themselves in relation to public and private space, the Haitian economy, the political process, and social structures of power in willful ways, and these too are expressions of their agency. While a street child's autonomy and will may be deeply subjective, the ethnographic evidence for their existence is explicitly manifest in their speech, their folklore, their ritual behaviors, their social networks, their material productions, their economic exchanges, their strategies for survival, as well as in the accepted norms and taboos that they establish among themselves as a cultural community distinct from that of the larger urban community. It is these traits, expressions, artifacts, and behaviors that I have collected in support of the argument that street children are engaged in a negotiation of their identities, and as such are not passive recipients of a unidirectional process of socialization on the street. The idea that child identity formation is a political process, one informed by a negotiation of power between children and others and one that results in a rich production of youth culture, is one shared by other anthropologists who have done ethnographic work with children

(Riesman 1992, Morton 1996, Hecht 1998, Chevannes 2001, Kilbride, Suda, and Njeru 2001, Lanclos 2003, Gottlieb 2004).

No ethnography of childhood can proceed without a definition of the material and symbolic setting for socialization, and in this case, the street itself is the most significant acculturative terrain upon which the children who live there are hashing out the details of their cultural identity. The "street" in Haiti is here defined as the avenues, boulevards, intersections, plazas, pavements, gutters, and tarmacs that form the exposed and not infrequently dangerous public domain of Haitian urban life. It is regarded as a formative terrain throughout this book, mediating children's interpretations of their natural and symbolic universe through scarcity and violence. This is not to say that the street is an environment that *determines* child identity, but rather is one that delimits the ability of a child to express its agency. No setting for socialization, be it in the family home, the orphanage, the schoolyard, or the street, permits the boundless expression of child (or adult, for that matter) identity. The street may shape a child's personality, it may inform his choices, but it never supplants his ability to engage it, to transform it, or to negotiate his place on it.

The street in Haiti is a profoundly contested social space, and the lifestyles of the thousands of children who have settled it over the past three decades have not only been challenging assumptions about the cultural passivity of children, but also dominant local ideas about appropriate uses of public space. Deviations from social expectations of appropriate use of the street in Haiti (also a concrete expression of street children's agency, as will be seen) has contributed in part to the criminalization of street children that further complicates their comportment to the larger Haitian citizenry.

The danger in emphasizing the agency of street children lies in the erroneous assumption that they are not simultaneously victims of larger political and economic machinations that severely impact their lives, complicate their survival, and place them at higher risk of dying younger and more violently than other children in Haiti or elsewhere. To be certain, it is difficult to recognize Haitian street kids as anything more than victims. In addition to the structural violence of scarcity and poverty, the bodies of many of the children are marked with the evidence of their subjugation to forces of brutality, morbidity, and destruction. Some have crooked limbs of wrongly healed fractures suffered in the more than frequent collisions between car and child that force steel into bone. Many others bear the dimpled scars of bullet wounds and purulent gouges and lacerations suffered in razor fights with other street children. Some of their arms, legs, feet, and faces are marred by the black, corrugated gristle of molten-plastic burns suffered in the darkness of night at the hands of adversaries who have melted down plastic juice bottles onto them as they slept. All of the children on the street spend the better part of their weeks with diarrhea or fever. They are more than frequently arrested by state forces without just charge, beaten by the police and neighborhood "vigilance groups," and routinely denied access to public spaces. To be sure, street children are victims in Haiti; but it is their daily resistance to their victimization through considered, cooperative social action that offers the best evidence of their agency and their humanity. The tension between street-child victimization and agency is at the very core of this book, and it will be explored systematically in the chapters that follow.

As an anthropologist and an ethnographer, I am interested in how childhood and community are conceived in Haiti, and what that means for our assumptions about children and community in general. As such, throughout this text I fix attention on some fundamental questions about adolescent life on the street in Port-au-Prince: What are the factors that contribute to the displacement of children from their homes and onto the street in Haiti? What are the material and cultural conditions of the street that combine to form the social world of street children? What are the physical, cultural, and social hazards to the welfare of street children? How do poverty and civil and political violence affect the ways that street children engage the larger urban community? What is the nature of social relations among street children, and how do these networks contribute to or detract from their survival? How is the status of street children in Haiti revelatory of the ever-changing relations between the state and the civil society?

A Different Kind of Fieldwork

The present dearth of ethnographic projects that focus on street children is due in part to the conditions under which one must work to be with them. There are not many anthropologists who relish working in the kinds of places that street children congregate. Those districts of Port-au-Prince where one can find the vibrant cultural worlds of street youth are among the most decrepit places on earth. The street itself is filthy. Rabid rats and dogs abound, raw sewage pungent with human waste flows through the very gutters adjacent to which street children sleep. The air is rich with the odors of the least developed world; a mix of truck exhaust, concrete dust, smoke, septic water, rotting mangoes, and feces permeate the air.

Violence is ubiquitous in Port-au-Prince. Gunfire barks out in sputters at unpredictable moments, and the air in some sections of town fairly vibrates in anticipation of the next outpouring of brutality. Staccatos of pistol reports break the heavy, tropical air in the crowded marketplaces as often as there is a political issue worth engaging in a shoot-out in the streets, which lately is more often than not. I have been, at various times, present at street shootings, threatened, searched, suspected of subversion, and in the midst of crossfire; none of which are experiences unknown to anthropologists who have worked in dangerous fields in North America (Adler 1993; Bourgois 1990, 1995a, 1995b), Central and South America (Bourgois 1990; Stoll 1993; Hale 1996; Hecht 1998), Europe (Sluka 1990, 1995, 2000; Aretxaga 2000), Africa (Nordstrom 1993, 1997, 2004; Malkki 1995; Robarchek and Robarchek 1998; Besteman 1999) and elsewhere (Tambiah 1992; Daniel 1996; Mahmood 1996). I have argued (Kovats-Bernat 2002) that this kind of field violence is no longer sui generis but characteristic of the instability that anthropologists working in postcolonial states like Haiti should expect to find, and that an ethnographic longing for tranquility in such states derives from a misguided professional nostalgia for the "peace" of the field once guaranteed by colonial force.

Port-au-Prince is dangerous and it is unhealthy, and it is very difficult to do ethnographic work under such circumstances. My own research has been interrupted over the years as often by debilitating bouts of diarrhea and high malarial fevers as it has by gunfire and paramilitary intimidation and threat. The resistance of many anthropologists against working under such circumstances is perfectly understandable. Indeed I was once told by a colleague that perhaps such work should not be done at all, given the limitations placed on ethnographic research methods that the dirt and disorder of places like Haiti present. Nonetheless we would do well to recognize that the very extreme conditions of life on the street in Haiti beg an urgent anthropological question about childhood: what does socialization and child development look like outside the bounds of adult norms and institutional control, and under circumstances that all would agree are the least conducive to child health and survival? The short answer, the reactionary one, is that it looks terrifying and tragic. When in confrontations with other children, street kids will resort to some of the most abhorrent brutalities imaginable. When they are high from sniffing glue, they have a tendency to agitate easily and lash out with razor blades, fists, or rocks. When saddened, they sometimes weep uncontrollably, their bodies shuddering in a way that every time I see it, my already tenuous grasp on the last bit of ethnographic objectivity that I fool myself into claiming is challenged. When ill, some crawl like animals into sewage culverts to suffer in secret, sometimes dying there only to be found days later by their peers in a state that any Vodouisaint would regard as exposed not only to public disgust but to supernatural threats that befall the souls of those who die outside of what is considered to be the proper ritual context. Given these realities it is perhaps understandable that so often Haitian street children are cast as victims, the helpless detritus of a failed economy, devoid of any agency or will to power.

As anyone with field experience in Haiti knows, anthropology done with children there has to be both reflexive and critical. It is all at once arrogant, colonial, and naive to assume that one can or even should treat children solely as objects of research, without ever engaging them on a moral or otherwise humanistic plane. While working with street children in Port-au-Prince, I often acted outside the customary bounds of the objective researcher. I treated and dressed their wounds, I took razor blades from the hands of the aggressive and angry among them, I gave them clothes and money and food when I could. I spoke on their behalf at the juvenile prison, helped to extricate them from hostile territories and associated with members of political organizations that advocated on their behalf. The decision to do these things was a natural extension of a local ethic that demanded it, and as such was an integral part of the participant-observation component of my methodology. But doing ethnography with street children this way presents the researcher with many ethical dilemmas. I paid the kids with whom I worked for their participation in interviews, and sometimes the raw economic exchange of the transaction evoked a kind of exploitation. I often wanted to give some children more than others, figuring after a while that a particularly painful testimony merited a measure more than a less moving one. At times, in the midst of poverty, enmeshed in violence, among dead and dying children, frightened and saddened, I would experience Port-au-Prince for what it seemed to be at those moments—brutal, despairing, and surreal. It requires little imagination to believe that the children shared these emotions at least some of the time as well. To situate myself as a moral agent, to give myself significance in that world, I sometimes indulged the fiction that I was somehow separate from all of this, maybe even in a position of control over it. I never really got over the compulsion to tell children that I had just paid for an interview to spend the money on food, for example. Eventually though, I localized even my paternalism; I would just caution them to stick the money down their pants so that older boys wouldn't beat them up for it. I think it is only by witnessing and immersing oneself in these kinds of circumstances that one can come to understand what Hecht (2000) means when he writes of the "violent indifference" of observing the daily existence of children who are dying right before your eyes.

An Ethnography of Street Childhood in Haiti

While this book takes as its primary subject "the street child" in Haiti, unless otherwise specified in the text, when I refer to "street children" (or "*timoun lari*" in Haitian Krèyol) I am generally referring to boys between the ages of four and twenty who are distinguishable from the larger community of Haitian children by the fact that they are "sleeping rough"—a British euphemism for homelessness that, in its emphasis on the callousness of exposure rather than the lack of a home, seems to me an apt term to describe those children whose lives are lived completely on the street and without recourse to the security that a domiciled life provides. The four-to-twenty age range is consistent with that employed by global organizations such as the World Health Organization, is reconcilable with local definitions of street childhood in Haiti, and avoids essentializing a Western legal definition of childhood as anyone under the age of eighteen years.

The street in Haiti is a rather gendered terrain, with boys outnumbering girls by a ratio of about four to one, a ratio that mirrors a worldwide trend. It is of note that each year that I return to Haiti, the number of girls on the street seems to have risen since the year before. Impoverished girls are sometimes able to avoid the street by being placed by their families into *restavèk* situations, whereby a child is sent into domestic service to middle-class families, ostensibly so that the child might be afforded an education by the host family. This is rarely the case. Frequently abused and almost never educated, most of Haiti's 250,000 *restavèk* children live amid poverty and violence not so far removed from that which obtains on the street; the only difference is that *restavèk* are domiciled—they have roofs over their heads.

While I have known and worked with street girls in Haiti (some of their life stories are included here), the overwhelming majority of street kids with whom I have worked are boys. There are several factors that have contributed to my limited work with girls. I first began working with street children in Haiti at an all-boys outreach facility in Port-au-Prince that only began accepting girls into the program later in my fieldwork. Even after the girls were admitted, they were segregated from the boys both residentially and programmatically for both cultural reasons and to reduce the likelihood of sexual assault. By the time I was able to begin according time to working with the girls, the facility was violently shuttered by the Haitian National Police following an uprising of the children against their squalid living conditions in 1999 (a history of this outreach program is detailed in chapter 5). After the closing of the facility, my project now decentered, I shifted much of my fieldwork to the public domain of the street. This brought new challenges to working with girls. Their low numbers at large on the street made groups of them hard to find; and among the few girls with whom I did work, many were reluctant to divulge certain intimate information (about sexual history, for example) to a male ethnographer that boys offered relatively freely. Moreover, many of the girls did not want to discuss even the most basic information about where they slept on the street and with whom, for fear that street boys in earshot might take advantage of this knowledge and the relative physical weaknesses of girls compared to boys and harm them. In short happenstance, culture, methodological limitations, and practical realities conspired to place limits on my ability to work more with street girls.

It is worth mentioning however that the girls that I have known in Haiti have offered intriguing glimpses into how the street is perceived and engaged by the female children who are outnumbered and who have their own set of unique concerns that boys do not have. Girls are almost constantly at risk of sexual violence (many engage in survival sex either as an alternative to being beaten or killed or simply to garner the physical protections that boys can afford), they often are culturally barred from doing the work of boys, they run the risk of pregnancy if sexually active, and they have to deal with the difficult monthly regimens of menstruating while living on the street. Some of these challenges and the fears that they elicit from girls are explored in the brief life history of Bèl Marie that precedes chapter 2. More on the social experience of girlhood on the streets is integrated throughout the chapters. By all accounts street girls are the most vulnerable of all on the boulevards. It is hoped that what this book does have to say about street girls in Haiti will both speak volumes about the uniqueness of their experience and offer a meaningful contribution to the task of prying the lid off the largely unseen politics of being a girl in a street world dominated by boys.

While the neighborhoods and slums in which I worked are populated by literally thousands of children who could be classified as abandoned, displaced, homeless or of the street, and while I passed hours with a great many of them, I restricted my in-depth interviews and life history conversations to about fifty children over the course of ten years working in Haiti (1994–2004). They were chosen for special research attention by no more sophisticated sampling technique than my own informed judgment of which children would offer the best collective perspective of street life in Port-au-Prince. The sheer numbers of them working, playing, or otherwise using the street, in addition to the frequent and irregular migrations of these children from one section of the city to another, made it impossible to define fixed population parameters. I therefore sought out cooperative children who were engaged in behaviors that both seemed and were deemed by the children themselves representative of the range of adolescent lifestyles on the streets of Port-au-Prince. As a result I have been fortunate to work with children involved in a diverse array of economic activities (both legal and illicit), social networks, personal relationships, and survival tactics.

Because of their irregular movements throughout the capital, the Port-au-Prince street children with whom I have worked constituted a large, fluid, and evasive community for sampling. Rarely would I have occasion to interview the same child on two consecutive days if ever again, and this (combined with the children's fleeting attention spans) left me with many unfinished surveys, limited interviews, and abbreviated life histories. Add to these limiting factors the constant threat of violence against myself, my research assistant, and my child informants and the simple act of speaking openly in the street with street kids became at times a dangerous and often hasty thing. Given the political instability of Port-au-Prince since the early 1990s, any ethnographic work done in the capital, especially with criminalized street youths, had to be conducted with a certain methodological flexibility, and though not clandestinely, at least inconspicuously. This project was no exception to that basic rule. On the positive side I perhaps learned as much from informal ethnographic interviews, observations, and guided conversations in everyday circumstances more familiar to the children as I did in "formal" semistructured interviews that were usually more uncomfortable for the children and therefore less productive in terms of data collection.

Despite considerable problems and obstacles, I managed to collect substantial amounts of diverse data (ethnographic, written, photographic, recorded, and internalized) from scores of children over the course of my fieldwork. My conclusions about the meaning of these data emerged over time from recorded and transcribed interviews, life histories, and participant-observation research. Questionnaires provided the basis for in-depth interviews with different sets of street children. Devised as guided conversations, these interviews sought a deeper understanding of the lived experience of poverty and overt political and civil violence in the street, an understanding that I believe can only be had through a dialectical approach that pursues the multivariate and ever-changing ways that children relate to one another, the civil society, and the state. To this end many questions addressed issues concerning the everyday political economy of life on the street in Port-au-Prince: poverty, scarcity, personal health, hygienic matters, sexual abuse, hunger, sources of income (formal and informal, legal and illicit), differential levels of political involvement and encounters with the state authorities or their proxies. Interviews with the children also explored the unanticipated ways that they met the challenges and seized the opportunities that the street economy presented to them. Throughout my conversations with them, I sought to grasp their abstract engagements with street life; how did the children think about the street, and how did they think about their unique deportment to it?

Since my research began in 1994, I have tried to involve the children with whom I worked as partners in the work in recognition of the potential for agency I knew them to have. In fact the kids often guided our interviews toward subjects they thought important, recommended whom I should speak with and about what, and even recommended photographs that should be taken that they felt best illustrated their world. This kind of participatory approach has been adopted by anthropologists before (Hecht 1998; Theis 2001) and is valued by those of us who have used it in the same way that UNICEF advocates, as both a perspective and a method for understanding the lot of children on their own terms: "Child participation involves encouraging and enabling children to make their views known on the issues that affect them. Put into practice, participation is adults listening to children—to all their multiple and varied ways of communicating. It ensures their freedom to express themselves and takes their views into account when coming to decisions that affect them. Engaging children in dialogue and exchange allows them to learn constructive ways of influencing the world around them" (UNICEF 2004b: 1).[3]

This book presents childhood as a vibrant site of cultural formation, reproduction, and agency and recognizes street children in Haiti as vital contributors to and interpreters of society. It presents the social world of these children as logical, substantive, and worthy of serious attention. This approach to understanding the life of street kids is one that permits us to acknowledge them as shapers not only of their own identities, but of the larger society, culture, nation, and state in Haiti as well. Nevertheless we must keep in mind that the perilous social world of the Haitian street often makes agency difficult to detect, and sometimes places severe constraints upon it. It is nonetheless ever present, even if it is reduced to the autonomous choice to give up the struggle and succumb to unwanted sex, disease, starvation, or even death. The challenge for the anthropologist here lies in the ability to locate child agency, sometimes by limited degrees, in the unenviable lives of the children whose stories are presented in this book.

There is of course a danger in fully recognizing such things as street child agency. For if we emphasize that, then we must also be prepared to accept the fact that the brutal violence in which street children occasionally engage is an expression of their agency as well, and not the by-product of a psychological deviation that results from an absence of exposure to adult norms of rearage. For example, while perhaps troubling (after all, part of our seemingly universal urge to protect children is our tendency to protect them from their own culpability), to regard street-child behaviors, even violent ones, as concrete expressions of their autonomy is to go a long way toward destabilizing the dominant image of street children as unsocialized, acultural caitiffs, bent to irrational acts of juvenile selfishness, opportunism, and menace.

The Organization of the Book

While anthropology perhaps offers the most holistic and thoroughgoing approach to the study of childhood, our knowledge of the experience of children living under extremely difficult circumstances will never be as consummate or intimate as that of the children themselves. It is for this reason that I have chosen to introduce each chapter of this book (except the concluding chapter) with a brief "interlude" that offers the reader a glance into the life of a single child on the street. Derived from life histories that I have collected of street children I have known over the past decade, these stories are my best effort to facilitate the participation of the quiet voices of street kids in the dialogue about their lot. While no one child's account of sleeping rough on the pavement could ever be representative of all who do so, the stories of the children I have chosen to include in these interludes fairly capture the diversity of experiences of living on the street at the same time that they illustrate the challenges, fears, and strategies for survival that all street kids share in common.

The first chapter is intended to introduce the reader to the origins of the social and cultural context of Port-au-Prince streets today. At issue in this chapter is the historical roots of street childhood, traceable to the country's steady economic decline since the 1980s, and the subsequent high rates of domestic migration, degraded urbanization, child displacement, and adolescent morbidity that has come with it. The microlevel effects of these larger national dynamics are explored through an examination of the material conditions of poor rural and urban households that lead to the displacement of children from the home and onto the street.

Because displaced children in Haiti are defined locally by their special relationship to "the street" as a factor that differentiates them from other, domiciled children, this chapter also explores the nature of the street in Haiti as contested social space. The apparent dichotomy between "the home" or "the family" and "the street" is cast as a differentiation containing hidden assumptions about kinship, childhood, and domestic life that are identified and explored. Traditional notions about the street as a transitory place or

as a channel for the circulation of commerce are shown to be incongruous in Port-au-Prince, where urban public space is customarily co-opted as
an extension of the household and the workplace. Nonetheless, the larger
Port-au-Prince community's commercial and domestic comportment to the
street is still in marked contrast to those uses of the street by the children
who live there and regard it as a place for work or for sleep or for leisurely
roaming about. This conflict over the use of public space has shaped the
relationships that street children have with the state and the civil society. It
has also framed street children's means of distinguishing themselves from
settled school children. It is with these matters that this chapter is also concerned.

Chapter 2 is an exploration of the acculturative power of the street, its
capacity to contribute to the formation of the identities of the children who
live upon it. This chapter argues that the movement of children from their
natal home onto the street and into adulthood mirrors the stages of separation, transition, and reaggregation characteristic of the *rites de passage* as
described by the anthropologist Arnold van Gennep in 1909. Critical to this
chapter is an explication of the primary influences that lead to the displacement of children from their homes and onto the pavement, and the identification of the street as a "site of passage" where the identities and public
perceptions of street children are molded and defined. Drawing on the work
of Victor Turner, I argue that the street is a liminal space, and as such is the
unstructured and interstructural sphere where street children are secluded,
marginalized, and maligned as social pollutants.

Chapter 3 examines the response of the Haitian state to current escala-
tions in violent civil strife, with a special focus on the state's identification of
street violence with displaced childhood. This chapter in turn addresses the
Haitian government's paramilitary response to violent disorder in the street,
and its transgression of the civil and human rights of street children through
the activities of the Anti-Gang Unit (AGU). The AGU is a paramilitary unit
of the Haitian National Police that is chiefly responsible for the resolution
of *zenglendinaj*, a strain of youth gangsterism characterized by brazen banditry and ruthless broad daylight assassinations. Comparative perspectives
on street life are given here, as stories are told from the vantage of National
Police officers, agents of the Anti-Gang Unit and other paramilitaries, the
warden of the juvenile prison in Port-au-Prince, and the street children detained there. What emerges is a picture of the Haitian state's ambitious program to remove street children, perceived as unsocialized and supernumerary threats to social order, from Haitian public space. As we shall see, this
"official" view is one at odds with that of the street children themselves. It is

also a view that gives support to a prevailing popular ideology that actually works to keep the children on the streets.

Chapter 4 outlines the range of child labors on the street, the social networks of support established by the children for the sharing of food, goods, and information, and the development of comrade relations that are the very foundation of child survival on the boulevards. As an in-depth account of the economic character of violence on the streets of Port-au-Prince, here the reader will find discussions of the fierce competition for cramped street space, child self-protections against the very real dangers posed by other street children, and the informal norms and strategies for conflict resolution, both peaceable and violent. Here I present detailed accounts of the *lagè domi* or "sleeping wars" that are waged between children; brutal, ritualized confrontations designed to put a conclusive and often fatal end to long-festering animosities between street kids.

Chapter 5 explores the social and cultural life of street children in residence at the Lafanmi Selavi orphanage facility in Port-au-Prince. Guided by an educational philosophy dedicated to the development of a radically politicized child identity, this social history of Lafanmi Selavi provides a unique vantage for the critical examination of relationships and ideologies fostered among street youth narrowly removed from the raw circumstances of the boulevards. Lafanmi was the locus of repeated political violence over the course of my fieldwork, and the physical, social, and political conditions there over time deteriorated to the near-unlivable levels that obtain on the street itself, permitting me a long-term analysis of this failed institutional alternative to child displacement. Ultimately the facility's hostile closure by a government paramilitary in 1999 ended my work there, and redirected my complete attention to the children "sleeping rough" or otherwise living, to varying degrees, in the street.

Chapter 6 provides an account of the rebel uprising that succeeded in overthrowing the president in February-March 2004, and how the ongoing conflict sparked by it has impacted the social character of street life in Port-au-Prince. Also explored are the ways in which ordinary Haitians—especially street children—have adapted to the violence and have gone about the arduous project of reconstituting their fractured social worlds while the war rages on around them.

The concluding chapter draws correlations between Haitian street children's experience of poverty and violence to international economic inequalities and political agendas that have attended the expansion of global capital in recent decades. These developments have produced a set of social and material circumstances that make life exceptionally difficult for children living in the least developed countries of the world, and create living conditions that ensure the suffering and misery of millions of people. Much is at stake in drawing connections between global economics and politics and such pervading ideologies. Many nongovernmental organizations, advocacy groups, child welfare organizations, religious missions, political parties, and state policies are either maintained or even gain (to greater or lesser extents) from the reproduction of poverty and violence and the attendant issues surrounding street children in the developing world. It may be that changing the way we think about the global political economy will in fact change the way we think about our poorest children. Thinking the reverse has surely not created a world that is universally hospitable to our children. It may even be said that by denying them their agency or by viewing their lot simply as a tragedy we have done them the greatest disservice of all.

Some Notes to the Reader

The time I have spent in Haiti has given me many joys, perhaps none greater than the opportunity to speak and imagine in the beautifully complex language of Haitian Krèyol. But due to the limited opportunities I have to use the language outside of Haiti, I find myself always working against the slippage of proficiency. As such it should be noted that all translated quotations are my own, and I accept responsibility for any mistakes of orthography; they are, to be sure, either absent or few.

It should also be noted that I have heeded the lead taken by anthropologist Tobias Hecht in my use of the word *kids* as interchangeable with the word *children*. Like Hecht, I do not find the word demeaning, but rather embrace its celebration of a certain sense of rebelliousness. When I use the word, I use it with endearment.

All of the names of the children identified in this work have been changed in the interest of their anonymity. As the reader will discover, street kids in Haiti are more than frequently the targets of state violence. While their names are therefore obscured in the text, it is my sincere hope that their lives and their autonomy are not.

Ti Amos

He wears a filthy, ripped, red T-shirt and a torn pair of dirty, oversized shorts that he has to continuously hitch up when he isn't sitting. His name is Ti Amos and he looks to be not one day over five years old. He wears no shoes, and when I ask him if he finds it difficult to walk about the city in his bare feet, he tells me that he used to have a pair of sandals but they were stolen from him by older street boys as he slept and he never bought a new pair. He said that when he has money, he does not want to spend it on shoes, but prefers to spend it on food.

Ti Amos keeps a plastic juice bottle full of *siment*–a vaporous cobbler's glue to which he is thoroughly addicted—tucked into the neck of his shirt and he sniffs from it every few minutes. He does this all day, every day. Though his eyes are red and bloodshot and his breath is heavy with the vapor of the glue, he is an exception to the general rule about the sniffer-*zombi*. He is thoughtful and lucid, and at times almost philosophical.

He left his natal home in Les Cayes when he was around three ("I could walk very good by then," he says), eventually making his way to Port-au-Prince where he has lived ever since. Like most street children he maintains contact with his kin throughout Haiti, including an aunt, a godfather, and cousins in Jacmel. He also has an aunt who lives in the La Saline slum in Port-au-Prince, but he tells me that he has never really known her. His mother and father live together in Les Cayes with his brother and two sisters. His older brother and eldest sister are both enrolled in school, while his youngest sister is too young for school. He said that this sister is a "*ti bebe*," an infant still at the breast.

He says he left his home because his father beat him and forced him to "*vi lavi mizè*," to live a life of misery. Since his brothers and sisters were already enrolled in school when he was born, he had to work in the street as soon as he was physically able to help feed the family and pay for his siblings' school supplies. He spent increasing amounts of time on the street until he finally moved from Les Cayes to Port-au-Prince, seeking better opportunities for work.

Not long ago Ti Amos had come down with a fever that would not subside, and he took a *tap-tap* [rattletrap public bus] back to his parent's home and stayed with them for a while. When he felt better a few days later they asked him to leave because there was not enough food for him. He returned to the streets of the capital. When I ask him why he doesn't live with his other family members, he tells me that he doesn't know any of them very well and that they could not afford to feed him or send him to school anyway.

He never went to school when he lived at home, but after he arrived in Port-au-Prince he was taken into Centre d'Action, a small outreach program near Carrefour-Feuilles that offers food, a bed, and schooling to less than a hundred street children in Port-au-Prince. While there, teachers taught him how to write his name. He liked it there, but one of the other children who was his friend reported to the director of the center, a woman named Margaret, that he was urinating blood. Margaret immediately contacted a physician who examined Ti Amos and told him that he was sick and needed to go with him to a clinic to receive care for his condition. The physician made the necessary arrangements with Margaret and planned to return the following day to escort Ti Amos to the clinic for treatment. But that evening, Ti Amos ran away from the center. He tells me that he is afraid of needles and did not want to go with the doctor. He has never returned to Centre d'Action. Eventually the blood in his urine disappeared.

Ti Amos sleeps in Portail Léogâne, near the entrance to the National Cemetery. He tells me that he lives there with his "sister," gesturing to a fifteen-year-old street girl named Bèl Marie who sits quietly beside him. She explains to me that she is not Ti Amos's real sister, but that they have been like brother and sister since they met on the street about two years earlier. Ti Amos says that he sleeps alongside Bèl Marie to protect her from being raped by other street boys. He has watched street girls raped before and he worries about Bèl Marie. He believes that he can protect her by sleeping with her, though Bèl Marie whispers in my ear that Ti Amos is afraid to sleep with the bigger street boys and sleeps with her for his own protection.

Before he settled at the National Cemetery, Ti Amos had been sleeping in Pacot near the Teleco building, the main office of the state-owned telephone company, with a another street boy around his age named Kado. Kado has since left the street to live with relatives in Delmas, one of Port-au-Prince's poorer residential neighborhoods. Ti Amos left Pacot for Portail Léogâne after being beaten and harassed by a group of older street boys who kept taking his money from him. That is when he met Bèl Marie, and he has slept at the cemetery alongside her ever since.

He likes to go to sleep earlier than the other children with whom he associates in Portail Léogâne, typically around dusk. He curls up beside Bèl Marie and dozes off while the others stay up eating and sniffing glue. He sometimes stays up later, at times until midnight, especially when he and the other children are telling *krik?-krak!* stories. *Krik?-krak!* is a favorite pastime of street children in Haiti, as it is among children in general. A child who has a tale to tell will call out to his comrades "*krik?*" to which his listeners will hopefully cry out, "*krak!*" indicating their willingness and eagerness to hear the tale told. The stories are usually well-known fables about anthropomorphized animals drawn from traditional Haitian folktales. The children gather around the storyteller to listen intently. Since all of the children know the general plot of the tales, the excitement of *krik?-krak!* lies not so much in the anticipation of hearing a new yarn spun, but rather in seeing a demonstration of the storyteller's talents. In fact the children shout out playful admonishments if the storyteller strays too far from the established plotline. While the storyteller is permitted some latitude in embellishing the tale, the sheer joy of *krik?-krak!* lies in the cleverness with which the speaker embellishes the story, imitating the voices and mimicking the ridiculous gestures of the animals in the tale.

Ti Amos often awakens in the middle of the night and is unable to return to sleep. At these times he is apt to *vakabonnde*—literally, to wander or to stray. While the term can imply a more sinister kind of prowling, Ti Amos uses it here in an innocent sense, meaning that he walks around the city at night looking for friends or opportunities to make money. Sometimes he awakens because he has nightmares. He says that he sometimes dreams that he is picking pockets, even though he claims never to have stolen from anyone. The dream frightens him because he does not want to be arrested and put into prison. When he has this nightmare, he imagines himself about to pick someone's pocket, wakes abruptly, and begins to run senselessly and without direction. He runs because he is afraid and wants to get away from the person in his dreams from whom he is about to steal. Running takes away his fear, and sometimes he wakes from the dream and practices his karate chops and kicks instead, to fight away the person from whom he is stealing.

He sniffs *siment* before he lies down at night, a habit he picked up from the other kids at the cemetery, because the glue makes him sleepy and sometimes keeps the nightmares away. Except for when he sniffs at night for the purpose of sleeping soundly, he sniffs to get *sou* [drunk, high]. Occasionally he drinks moonshine rum that he buys by the sip from older boys around the neighborhood, and sometimes he drinks it in the evenings to help him sleep, though he does not buy it often because it costs more than glue.

Ti Amos understands that his dreams are not real, but they scare him awake so easily because he always sleeps "with one eye open" and is never fully asleep, a defense against the real threats of other street children who might want to hurt him. He is always on his guard against children who want to drop a cinder block on his head or beat him with sticks while he is sleeping.

Ti Amos and his comrades at the cemetery all wear the same color clothes at night so that no one will mistake friend for enemy and "drop a rock on our heads while we are sleeping." He knows children who have been hurt at night by their own friends who mistook them for their enemies in the dark of night.

He makes a living on the street engaging in a diverse array of tasks: washing cars, wiping windshields, carrying groceries, begging. "*M'fè tout bagay,*" he tells me. "I do everything." With regard to stealing, he is almost overly emphatic. "*Non,*" he says, "I will not." Other boys with whom he sleeps at the cemetery try to persuade him to steal with them, but he is too afraid of getting caught by the police and going to prison to engage in that kind of work.

Ti Amos makes a lot of money begging, though he usually prefers to ask adults whom he knows from the neighborhood for money. He explains that while he does ask many different people for money, often strange adults will berate him and call him *vòlè* [thief]. He understands why many adults feel this way about him. He is aware of how dirty he looks and he knows that many people see him sniffing glue and think that his habit makes him *atoufè*—desperate, despairing, and capable of vicious violence.

Ti Amos has a difficult time keeping his personal possessions for long. He used to own a toothbrush, toothpaste, soap, and a comb. All but the toothbrush was stolen from him by other street children. Like many of the kids, Ti Amos buys his clothes from Mache Salamòn, a market that has stalls worked by women who sell unwanted, stained, or unmendable clothes to street children. He knows that the clothes are so cheap because they are dirty or ripped or otherwise not salable. He pulls at his filthy red T-shirt. "*Rad malere,*" he says. Pauper's clothing.

He shares what he makes at each day's end with his close friends at the cemetery, because they do the same for him. He also sends money to his aunt and his godfather in Jacmel through a market woman he knows who makes the trip there from Port-au-Prince several times a year. He says that they are saving the money he sends to them to buy a pig and keep it for him so that, when he dies, they will be able to sell the pig and have enough money to bury his body (it is too sad of a parable for me to ask him if he is sure that this is actually what they do with the money he sends).

If Ti Amos were given the opportunity, he would leave the street, though he does have many friends who live there with him whom he would miss, especially Bèl Marie. And there are things he likes about the street, like playing tag and hide-and-seek with his friends. He likes that he has time to play when he is living on the street. It is something that he didn't have much time for when he lived in his parent's home in Les Cayes.

Ti Amos knows that there is more to fear on the street than there is to like about it. His list of fears is long and includes older street boys who may want to drop cinder blocks on his head, thieves who might steal from him, and the weapons of the police and the paramilitaries. He has never been a victim of state violence, but he has witnessed enough police actions to fear them. He is terrified of the prospect of prison and knows how easy it would be for him to be taken away in a police sweep through his neighborhood—they often round up street kids in aggressive anticrime blitzkriegs through Portail Léogâne. The last time he was present when the police swept his neighborhood, Ti Amos scrambled beneath a parked car and watched as his friends were clobbered with batons and taken to prison. One was left bleeding from a head wound in the gutter, a few feet from where Ti Amos was lying.

He once surprised me by regaling me with the tale of a trip he had taken to the neighboring Dominican Republic. About a year ago, he says, he jumped into a street fight to help his friend James, a teenage street boy of whom he speaks very fondly. Ever since that fight, the two have been good friends. Not long after the scuffle, James invited Ti Amos to accompany him on a *vakans* [a vacation]. James had been to the Dominican Republic before and had told Ti Amos wonderful stories about his trip. The two hitched a ride on a public bus that runs a cross-island route directly across the border and on to Santo Domingo, avoiding border checkpoints. Though James adapted well to the Dominican Republic and decided to stay permanently, Ti Amos found life in Santo Domingo too much like his life in Port-au-Prince, only far more alien. He was hungry, couldn't understand Spanish, didn't have his friends to protect him while he slept (though he did meet many other Haitian children on the street there) and found that he was treated even more harshly by the adult community there than he was in his native Haiti.

But this is not why he returned to Port-au-Prince. "So what made you leave?" I ask him as we sit in the gutter in Portail Léogâne, sharing a tin of kippered fish. He pulls me in close by tugging on the sleeve of my shirt. "*Sann Domingo se pa peyi'm. M'te pa vle se trèt Ayiti cheri'm*," he says—"The Dominican Republic is not my country. I didn't want to be a traitor to my sweet Haiti."

Salon Pèp

Street Life and Society in Port-au-Prince

According to a study done in 1991, a full two-thirds of Haitians residing in the Morne-a-Tuf section of Port-au-Prince and its populous environs arrived there from the provinces, not the city (Manigat 1997). But one doesn't need a demographic study to recognize the fact that Port-au-Prince is a city of migrants. Most residents came to the capital when the great exodus from the countryside began in the mid-1980s, as the agricultural economy began its slide into depression and as disenfranchised farmers relocated to the cities in search of factory work. The very parlance of Port-au-Prince is inflected with the multitude of regional dialects representative of the citizens' diverse regions of origin. And not unlike first encounters in large North American cities, Haitians typically ask new acquaintances not "where do you live?" but "where are you from?" The answers offer a glance into the history of agricultural decline that started the exodus into the cities in the first place. Mountruis. Hinche. Perodin. Thomonde. Papaye. Bois Joli. Gonaïves. Dondon. Jérémie. Deschapelles. Duréze. Lhomond.

And because Haiti is a place where one's ties are to neighborhood and yard and not to the city writ large, even those who were born in Port-au-Prince identify much more strongly with their natal section of it rather than with the metropolis in its totality. Delmas. Poste Marchand. Brooklyn. La Saline. Pacot. Ti Cheri. St. Martin. Cité Soleil. In its neighborhood balkanization, Port-au-Prince is much like New York. Everyone is from elsewhere, even those who are from here.

The Rural Roots of Urban Decay

A 2000 report issued by Haiti's Ministry of Social Affairs identified a direct link between Haiti's rural-to-urban migration and street childhood: "The worsening of socioeconomic conditions, the increasing pauperization of the country, and the unremitting rural exodus are the main factors causing an increase in the number of street children" (Haitian Ministry of Social Affairs, 2000). In order to understand street childhood as an urban phenomenon in

Figure 1.1. A street boy stands beside nationalist graffiti in Port-au-Prince. The majority of street kids in Port-au-Prince range in age from three to eighteen.

Haiti, we first must look at it as rural in its roots. The origins of child displacement lay in a series of economic, historical, ecological, and agricultural crises that may be described in their sum as *rural decline*.

Of its total land area (Haiti is slightly smaller than the state of Maryland), less than 20 percent of Haitian soil is arable (capable of being farmed productively) and only three percent of that land is irrigated (essential in a relatively treeless environment where soil parching is rapid). Deforestation is at the root of these problems, though social history is more to blame. With the state in economic distress for decades, a hungry peasantry has stripped the land of its tree cover in order to plant rapid-growth (but soil-depleting) foodstuffs. Remaining trees are felled for their wood to provide housing for a burgeoning Port-au-Prince population and by the rural poor for charcoal production, the nation's primary fuel source. Once covered with dense forest, Haiti's trees were rapidly disappearing by the late 1800s. By 1954 the country's tree cover was less than 9 percent of total land area. Today Haiti is almost completely deforested (less than 5 percent has tree cover), an ecological travesty indeed, but a profound agricultural crisis as well. Without a network of arbor root support, the last of the country's fertile topsoil is rapidly eroding. In the rainy season, rivers flow in torrents making effective irrigation a practical impossibility. Subsequent disasters follow. The silt carried downstream in deluges is dumped into the coastal waters, giving the Bay of Port-au-Prince the look of a churned pond. Algae die, aquatic plants die, fish die, fishermen die. Or they too migrate to Port-au-Prince.

It wasn't always like this. In the mid-eighteenth century, Haiti (then the French colony of Saint Domingue) was France's wealthiest and most prosperous plantation colony, the "Pearl of the Antilles." By the late 1700s Saint Domingue was leading New World production in coffee, sugar, and rum and bankrolling Napoleon's conquest of the Old World. But Haiti's colonial affluence gives the lie to her contemporary status as the most destitute country in the Western Hemisphere. Today Haiti imports more food than almost any other country in the Western Hemisphere, in part because of low domestic crop yields that have historical roots in the very plantation agriculture system that made the island so profitable under French rule.

The essential feature of the plantation system was its dedication to specialized monocropping. Intensive and scientific, the plantation agriculture system adopted by the French colonials was rather unconcerned with the sustainability of the land, giving preference instead to exhaustive uses of the soil toward rapid yield over nutrient replenishment through crop rotation. The system was profit-driven, whereby planters were financially rewarded for short-term productivity through constant trade, not for their conscientiousness in allowing the soil to lie fallow periodically so that it might rejuvenate itself for long-term yields. As a result Haiti's soil grew progressively more sterile from colonial season to colonial season, as its wealth in the form of cash crops (coffee and sugar, primarily) was slowly extracted and exported to metropolitan France. The sugar and coffee that made Saint Domingue so rich also made Haiti desperately poor. Today you can fill your hand with a dozen Haitian onions, their small size the result of over three hundred years of increasingly exhausted Haitian soil sweetening French pastries.

After declaring independence from France in 1804, President Alexandre Pétion initiated a radical land reform policy by subdividing plantations for subsistence use by emancipated slaves. This fractionalization of farming plots intensified over the decades that followed. By the mid-1800s Haiti's present land tenure system was largely in place, characterized by a trend toward increased fragmentation of peasant lands, an expanding role of sharecropping and renting, and a growing concentration of the highest quality land. Today farm units in the agricultural sectors of Haiti average one to two acres in size. Given Haiti's high rural population density and deteriorating soil, competition for fragments of the best quality land is intensifying. As farmers lose out, they pack up and head for Port-au-Prince.

Structural adjustments encouraged by foreign development agencies have sought to ease the crisis in Haitian agricultural production. In the early 1980s the World Bank and the United States Agency for International Development (USAID) organized an agroindustrial development strategy for Haiti that was adopted by then-President Jean-Claude Duvalier. Identifying cheap labor as Haiti's "competitive advantage," the strategy was designed to rapidly convert Haiti's economy away from subsistence agriculture and toward assembly-export. In 1982, following the enactment of the Caribbean Basin Initiative, USAID introduced a plan for the conversion of thirty percent of all cultivated land in the country from the production of subsistence crops to that of export crops, mainly coffee. The United States Agency for International Development's "Country Development Strategy" for Haiti that year anticipated that such a drastic reorientation of land use would prompt a massive exodus of peasants from the rural sectors of the country, which would have the dual effect of creating an eager industrial workforce in Port-au-Prince while at the same time relieving the land of erosion pressures. That hypothesis was supported by a World Bank assessment of the plan, which argued that "if soil conservation and reforestation efforts are to succeed, rural emigration [to the urban centers] will be needed to alleviate pressure on the land (World Bank 1983: 16).

This export-led strategy for economic development in Haiti meant a greater dependence on imported goods, especially foodstuffs that were no longer produced by the country's new domestic economy. An increased reliance on imported food has resulted in shifts in domestic consumption patterns. Historically corn meal has been the staple food of Haiti, with rice reserved for special occasions. But a glut of surplus rice imports from the United States in the 1980s drove down local market rice prices and rice increasingly replaced corn as the basis of the Haitian diet. Moreover, Haitians came to prefer the higher quality imported rice over the domestic product, forcing a crisis in the grain market. In 1991 and 1992 rice production dropped 35 percent, while bean production dropped 20 percent, root and tuber production dropped 15 percent, and sorghum production dropped 10 percent (Toler 1998).

Soil depletion, intensification of competition for arable land, and a shift in development strategy to export agriculture and the assembly industry have combined to stimulate the mass exodus of rural migrants to the city centers, especially Port-au-Prince. That emigration has in turn caused a crisis of urban overpopulation, which has had a critical impact on people's access to basic needs for their survival and has determined a very particular construction of urban space amid economic and political instability. The chaotic nature of this urban terrain contributes significantly to civil perceptions of the city and its street life and the children who grow up there.

Two decades of streaming provincial migration into Port-au-Prince (the World Bank reports that thirteen thousand rural migrants arrive in the capital every year) has had a profound effect not only on the design and structure of the streets (or lack thereof), but on the character of the everyday social interactions that take place on them as well. As the population of the capital began its geometric rise in the late 1970s, the Haitian state was conspicuously absent in the management of the functioning, economy, maintenance, security, and settlement of its largest urban core, a tradition of governmental neglect that continues today. The result is that

> the entire city of Port-au-Prince has acquired the physiognomy of a slum. . . . Entire neighborhoods are constructed in the course of a month, as the pace of family-organized construction of makeshift dwellings accelerates. In no time at all, spaces where before construction was prohibited or that were scarcely populated, are covered by networks of houses completely lacking in basic services. . . . The marginalized people hurl themselves at the task of conquering any chink of available terrain. The city is the contested terrain of this struggle. (Manigat 1997: 90)

City of Mayhem, Streets of Inertia

Port-au-Prince challenges the conventional wisdom that the purpose of streets is first and foremost to ensure a fluid movement of people and commerce throughout the city. No one who lives in Port-au-Prince expects the streets to be used solely as transitory channels, and the very erratic design of the city infrastructure suggests as much. Laid out in a manner devoid of any linear aesthetic, most of the streets through the commercial and residential areas twist serpentine through the neighborhoods, mazelike and bewildering to the unaccustomed traveler. In the congested slums of Cité Soleil and La Saline, the streets taper off into narrow dirt pathways, pocked with septic puddles and embedded rock footfalls. Homes of cardboard and tin are flooded with the filth of sewer and street when the heavy rains come. Then come dysentery and diarrhea—serial killers of Haitian children; and the otherwise abstract relationship of the street as physical space to cultural life is made tangible in human suffering.

Few of Port-au-Prince's streets are maintained in any real sense, and the extent of deterioration characteristic of most thoroughfares is so great as to beg the question of whether the term *paved* can even be used to describe them. Canyonlike potholes rake across macadam and concrete, slowing vehicles and wreaking hell on the undercarriages of cars, while mountainous heaps of garbage and stalled or abandoned vehicles obstruct traffic flow. Intersections are congested at all hours of the day in the busy city center, partly because of the poor condition of the road surfaces and partly because of the almost complete lack of traffic regulation.

For those on foot, negotiating the streets is more than hazardous, it is often menacingly so. Most Port-au-Prince streets lack sidewalks, and nearly all homes that line the avenues are surrounded by high concrete walls. Pedestrians are compelled to walk in curbed gutters, sometimes through raw sewage and typically through garbage. Cars seeking to circumvent the street's many obstructions swerve violently between throngs of people on foot, more than occasionally hitting someone. An acquaintance of mine was struck hard on the shoulder by the side-view mirror of a bus that skirted us as we walked in the gutter of a downtown street in the market district, and I have had countless close calls with taxis and motorcycles over the course of my research in Haiti.

There is little formal regulation of traffic (pedestrian, motor, or otherwise) in the capital. It was not until 1997 that I began to notice the consistent placement of stoplights downtown and the designation of some streets as one-way thoroughfares. Despite these roadway controls and a new standardized system for driver licensing and registration, traffic law is ignored as often as it is observed. Compliance with the formal rules of the road is all but lacking unless a National Police officer is within eyesight and even that may not be a deterrence. Drivers are apt to drive as they wish—down any street, through any light, on either side of the road, or against the flow altogether. Taxi drivers bump on their horns almost constantly, but are apt to tap the brake only if a collision appears to be imminent. Add to this the problems associated with recruiting and training the still undisciplined National Police force (many of whom are charged specifically with traffic control), as well as getting them to those intersections where they are most needed and one begins to grasp the magnitude of the logistical chaos that is the street in Port-au-Prince. The danger implicit in negotiating the streets is suggested by local appeals to the supernatural for protection against harm while on them. At certain notorious intersections, one can find modest appeals to Legba, the Vodou spirit or *lwa* responsible for the regulation of crossroads. His *vèvè* [ritual symbol] inscribed onto the pavement guarantees at least a modicum of protection against fateful collisions of steel against steel, or worse, steel against bone.

Perhaps the most treacherous hazards to pedestrians in Port-au-Prince are the sewer inlets that are unpredictably spaced along the gutters through which people must walk. Though some are closed off with embedded iron rebar, these bars are sometimes cut and pulled out by local residents who use the sewers for the disposal of their household garbage. Once open, the inlets become dangerous pitfalls, offering inattentive passersby a six- to eight-foot drop through ragged concrete and jagged iron into raw sewage. I once looked on as an elderly woman was pulled dead from one such inlet, killed by the fall.

More marketing goes on outside of Port-au-Prince's roofed markets than in them and trade activity often extends into the streetscape. *Machann* [street vendors] splay their wares onto the curb if there is one and in the street in front of them if there is not. Such sellers are accustomed to picking up the mats or tarps onto which they arrange their goods so that an automobile might pass and some will do so dozens of times in a workday. Pedestrians must negotiate their way around the *machann* as well, always courteous to step around rather than over the merchandise.

Tradesmen occupy the street as a workplace and one commonly finds welders, woodworkers, sculptors, carpenters, mechanics, coffin makers, and other craftsmen setting up their workspace in the street, aware of but unconcerned with the volume of foot and motor traffic that must circumvent them. Labor in Port-au-Prince is spectacle and one can track fluctuations in the Haitian jobless rate by observing the ratio of welders who are at work in the street to those sitting idly beside their acetylene tanks against the street's edge. More dramatic dips in the Haitian economy are observable in the labor of the coffin makers, who get busier when food prices climb.

The street is a place for stored things as well. Café owners and small restaurant proprietors are apt to stack racks of empty soda and beer bottles in the street, blocking both pedestrian and auto routes, where they may stay for one or several days until they are picked up by the trucks from the bottlers. Where waste removal is inconsistent or nonexistent, enormous piles of trash and garbage are mounted in the street itself. Sometimes this custom is merely in accordance with the socially sanctioned method of trash consolidation for easy pickup by state trucks. Other times, however, it is an expression of the people's frustration with the lack of trash collection in their neighborhood, a tactic designed to coerce politicians to either take action on waste removal in that area or suffer the public image consequences of an urban thoroughfare blocked by the detritus of state inaction. As fixtures of the urban landscape, garbage heaps are enduring obstacles to fluid commerce through the capital streets. They also afford street children a pool of potential resources. Kids forage through the refuse scavenging for razor blades, wire, boxes of matches, batteries, rags, sheets, mirror shards, cans, bottles, rods, rope, plastic bags, pails, chains, rubber, eating utensils, and infinite other things to use or to sell.

Though the streets of Port-au-Prince are hectic, congested, obstructed and hazardous, rendering them an absolute menace to pedestrians, the entropy of the avenues means something more. Whether the cause is unregulated urban planning, reckless driving, lack of traffic control, or infrastructural limitations, the result is a system of causeways that represent anything but channels for swift negotiation throughout the city. Although the idea of the streets' purpose is at least to some extent the circulation of people and things in a predictable and regular fashion, Port-au-Prince presents a case in which no one regards the streets' utility as solely transitory even if they would prefer it to be. Its function as a means by which one travels to home or work is secondary to its adaptation to an end in and of itself. The streets are places for work, places to socialize, and for some, places to sleep, eat, and live. Taken together as a social and cultural space, *the street* is described in the local vernacular as *salon pèp* [the people's living room]. In Haiti to be sure, the street is for most an end in itself.

A Place for Everything and Nothing in Its Place

Sabine Manigat argues against adherence to classical logic concerning migrant acculturation and adaptation to urban space when examining the case of Haiti. Rather than adapting to the city, she writes that Port-au-Prince dwellers "appropriate, assault and transform it according to their particular needs and vision" (1997: 90). As a result the public spaces of the capital are regarded less as transitory passage routes and more as extensions of the household. To suppose that sleeping on the street is antithetical to the street's intended purpose is to indulge a classical, Eurocentric paradigm of what the street *is* that is irreconcilable with the local reality. A brief examination of the political economy of shelter and the markets in Port-au-Prince is in order and will help to illustrate the acceptable range of use of the street as an extension of the home.

In Haiti the home of the urban poor is not at all definable as a bounded, spatial *place*; nor is it rigidly considered as a walled shelter or a landscape of interiors. Haitian households customarily extend well beyond the threshold of their doors (should there even be one), subsuming the public sphere that surrounds it. While the idea of living completely in the public domain is a remote notion, the common perspective is that inhabitants live in and throughout their neighborhoods. So the household is not necessarily unbounded, but with frontiers rather than borders.

The vast majority of Port-au-Prince residents live in dwellings that are on average no larger than sixty square feet in area (the size of a typical middle-class American bathroom), with around fifteen square feet of net habitable space per adult (the size of a typical American bathtub). A study done in 1976 revealed that some Port-au-Prince slum dwellings were so small that individuals were obliged to sleep on their doorsteps in shifts throughout the night, because the houses (if that is what they could be called) simply could not accommodate all family members at once (Fass 1990: 190).

As a consequence of the tight quarters characteristic of Haitian lower-class urban housing, most Port-au-Prince residents extend the household into the street immediately surrounding the dwelling itself and in some cases establish their household (or certain members of it) entirely on the street. The idea of subsuming the immediate area around the dwelling as an aspect of the home is an ethos imported to the city from the rural *lakou*. The *lakou* refers to certain forms of kinship structure and domestic arrangement that are characteristic of the Haitian countryside and is itself a cultural import from West Africa, carried by slaves into the French colony as an abstract notion of how the households of kinfolk should be arranged in relation to one another. Central to the space of the *lakou* is a common courtyard, shared by a cluster of extended family households for the purpose of cooking, eating, working, and socializing. The courtyard is usually oriented toward an ancestral shrine and so is also the locus of ritual activity as well. The impact of this peasant's view of the household on urban life in Port-au-Prince is suggested by the use of the term *lakou foumi* [a courtyard of ants] to describe an urban shantytown. In the city the street immediately surrounding the urban household is appropriated for domestic life in true peasant fashion, becoming in effect an extension of the home, a social space for preparing meals, gossiping, washing clothes, selling things, or in the case of children, work and play. As an extension of the home, the street is not regarded as threatening space by most. It is to the contrary considered a generally safe and acceptable place to eat, to socialize, and if need be, to sleep. So while a child sleeping or living in the street may seem as lamentable to Haitians as it does to foreigners, it is also the case that the child is appropriating the street in a manner not wholly inconsistent with local custom.

Simon Fass has pointed out that two discernable groups comprise the poorest subpopulations of Port-au-Prince, having dispensed with shelter altogether (usually due to financial misfortune) and who now regard the street itself as their household: those utterly without possessions and those with rudimentary possessions that are regarded as far more productive in providing health than a dwelling—food, pots, buckets, and tools (1990: 200). For these groups the street is regarded with less domestic sentiment than a physical structure would inspire, but it does remain the only version of a home with which they may identify. As a point of fact, the distinction between the improvised cardboard rain-roofs of these homeless and the corrugated tin and tarp dwellings of the sedentary houses of average quality in Port-au-Prince is one of relative degrees. From the perspective of the capital's poor, the street is very much home, whether it comprises some, most, or all of the household.

Market activities can also dictate the use of the street as a genuine living space. Numbering in the thousands on peak market days, rural-to-urban porters and vendors, most of whom are women, arrive in town a day or two prior to the market's opening with agricultural commodities for sale or with cash with which to buy and then resell goods for a modest profit. These sellers may sleep in open air stalls they have rented for the sale of their wares, or for a small fee may rent overnight sleeping space in the warehouse with their goods. Most however opt to sleep on the street as a matter of fiscal prudence. The sight of these sellers lying in the streets near the markets after dark is commonplace. They too are an assumed feature of the urban landscape in Haiti.

The assumption of public space as a primary site of social exchange and as an extension of the home reinforces for most Haitians that the street is far more than a means for traversing the city. In a very literal sense, it is public property. As I would squat on the pavement in the downtown public plaza of Champ de Mars in order to conduct interviews with children, rare were the times when our small group would not become surrounded by throngs of onlookers, some of whom would linger for hours with us, some eavesdropping a polite distance away and others crowding in on us, listening intently to the exchanges of the interviews. I would often become uncomfortable with these audiences, fearing the consequences of the compromise of my informants' confidentiality. But on every occasion that I asked the children themselves if they minded the broader audience, they replied uniformly and without exception that they did not. Many of the kids playfully scolded me for pretending that it was in my power to decide who could and could not listen to our conversations on the street. "After all," they would say, "*n'ap chita nan salon pèp sa yo!*" [we're sitting in the living room of these people!].

The Street as Contested Space

It was Blak Lovli, a fifteen-year-old street boy from the Portail Léogâne section of Port-au-Prince, who first told me about the "sleeping wars," rather matter-of-factly, when I asked him when he found it most difficult to sleep on the street. He told me that he found sleep difficult when he was preoccupied with the worry that older boys might drop a cinder block on his head while he sleeps. I asked him why an older boy would want to do such a thing and that is when he explained the brutal, ritualized violence of the sleeping wars (this form of ritualized violence among street kids will be discussed in detail in chapter 4). He explained how the best protection from being hurt by an enemy was to hide oneself when sleeping. This was the same conversation in which Blak Lovli instructed me in how important it was to wash one's mouth before sleeping on the street, otherwise rats and roaches would come to eat from there at night. He pointed to a small scar on his upper lip that he said was a rat bite. That's when I came to understand Haitian streets as deeply contested spaces, where street children vie with vermin and each other, with the paramilitaries and the street assassins, in a violent struggle for security in both wakefulness and in sleep.

Whatever its multivariate uses—for sleeping, for labor, for socializing, for marketing—the street in Port-au-Prince is a space ill-fit for child survival. In spite of the best efforts of the children who live there to negotiate their fates, there are profound structural limitations placed on their ability to live fully self-determined lives. Hazards associated with contaminated water and food, traffic, vermin, crime, and civil violence combine to create a social milieu conducive to high rates of child morbidity and death. In Port-au-Prince, where perhaps as many as fifty thousand children are living and dying on the streets, the fierce competition for space grows vulgar and desperate in the hidden corners of public spaces, creating a violent and dangerous backdrop against which adolescence is being hashed out. It is an "everyday" kind of violence (Scheper-Hughes 1992), one that frames daily life in such a way that the prospect of dying of starvation or thirst or gunplay is normalized and fever and diarrhea are the deadly and familiar doppelgängers of Haitian childhood.

Much of the misery is reducible to a water problem. Sewage runs through most areas along open trenches or gutters that line the major thoroughfares and during times of flood—Haiti's rainy season runs from May to November and is marked by sudden, torrential thunderstorms—flows freely into the homes of the poor, the market stalls, and the low areas in the streets that many consider an extension of their homes. With the open sewage comes

Figure 1.2. A street girl in the Haitian capital. Among the many risks to the well being of children who live on the street is the very real threat of animal attack. Thousands of stray dogs and likely millions of rats roam the city. Haiti has one of the highest rates of rabies infection in the Western Hemisphere.

a host of biological hazards, from malaria to dengue carried by mosquitoes, to microbes and viruses transmitted among humans who bathe with, cook with, and drink the same water. Food sold on the sidewalks, a common source of food for street children, is often unclean as well, having been prepared (or in the case of fruits or vegetables, cleaned) with filthy water. Two *machann* who sold mangoes in the street near my residence in the Pacot section of Port-au-Prince washed their produce in grayish water gathered from the gutters in buckets and strained of solid matter. The staple of Port-au-Prince street cuisine, *fritay* (boiled then fried bits of plantain and meat, usually goat or chicken), can also be a menace to public health when it is left too long draining on newspapers spread on the sidewalk and exposed to the legions of flies that light with regularity on the pieces.

The near absence of traffic regulation and control leads to countless collisions between motor vehicles and the bodies of children. At night, roaches, rats, dogs, cats, mosquitoes, centipedes, and other parasitic or scavenger species vie for limited sheltered space amid boys and girls sleeping in huddles of twos and threes in dark crevices as security against rape, gunfire and the beatings of the police and other street children. Indeed broken bones, lost fingers and toes, open sores, rodent and insect bites, razor wounds, and gunshot scars are common marks on the frames of children who regard the street as home and who engage daily and nightly other children, things, and creatures competing for the same pieces of pavement.

Given the hazardous experience of street life in Haiti, where every chink of street space is a site of constant struggle, it is unsurprising that Port-au-Prince street children die at a greater rate than otherwise sheltered children. Though no reliable statistics exist on the subject, the local knowledge has it that hundreds of street children die undocumented deaths from illness or violence every year. Of the several hundred displaced children with whom I have worked since 1995, most were in various stages of morbidity and some were in close and certain proximity to death. Many of the children I began working with in 1995 are dead now, some having succumbed to diarrhea, some wasted by disease, some killed outright at the hands of their peers or the batons of the state. From time to time the lifeless body of a child will be found clogging a sewer culvert, because street children sometimes crawl into secret hiding places when they are not feeling well, like so many cramping, feverish dogs. The street is home, but it is often an indifferent, hostile, unsheltering, and unforgiving one.

Without Threshold or Lintel: The Street as Home

The social character of life in Port-au-Prince takes to task the notion that the street is dichotomously opposed to some landscape of interiors constructed as "household" or "home." Haitians will, out of both necessity and preference, appropriate, reject, transform, and adapt public space to fit private needs; some, as we have seen, appropriate public space surrounding the house for domestic uses including sleeping. Insofar as this is true, the notion of the street as antithetical to the home is operationally invalid in the Port-au-Prince context. For the children who live on them, Port-au-Prince streets are deeply personal and subjective spaces, as these children identify with the street as their home. So unlike the adult rural-to-urban migrant who engages the urban street in one-sided fashion, transforming the urban landscape to fit individual need upon arrival there, childhood carries with it a degree of cultural vulnerability and adaptability that transforms the street into a powerful acculturative force. The street, like the home defined in any other way, molds and transforms the child who lives on it at least as much as it is transformed by the child itself. For such children the street has the

What stored does to the children

capacity to compel certain behaviors, mandate a particular consciousness, reinforce certain beliefs, structure everyday life, and inform a unique version of reality. While the street obliges a spatially decentered world, it is nonetheless as real as any domestic structure and as normative as the family. Despite its acculturative power, the street-as-home and its structural influences pose no more of a challenge to the imperative of child agency than do the constraints of the baby gate, the timetable of the elementary school, or the strictures of the household code of discipline in other circumstances of adolescent development. Children maintain their autonomy and will to act whether the acculturative force under which they act is a physical barrier to movement, a bell signaling the end of recess, the threat of a "timeout," or the need to beg, steal, or kill on the boulevard. It should be intuitive, as any parent in any cross-cultural context will attest, that the force of any system of behavior modification pales in comparison to the power of the will—the agency—of the child. The street may influence, it may compel, it may mandate, it may reinforce, it may structure, it may inform; but at all times it affords as much space for the expression of will, autonomy, and resistance as does the classroom or the dining room.

The street is also a gendered space for the children who live on it, where, by virtue of the fact that the overwhelming majority of street youth are boys, it is viewed as standing in opposition to the matrifocal household that is so common to the homes from whence many of them have come. When I asked Niksyon (a street boy in the Delmas section of the capital) why he believed there were more boys than girls on the street, he replied that "*lari renmem tigason!*" [the street likes little boys!], a sentiment that served as something of a mantra for many street kids in Haiti. The implication of course is that the assumption of the street by boys is a natural expression of some predetermined, sex-linked, urban imperative. The use of the term *renmem* [to like, to love] is falsely suggestive of the street as a nurturing place, which by all accounts, it is not, and the kids themselves know this. I would hear a reverse sentiment expressed with bitter irony just as often—"*tigason renmem lari*"—especially in conversations about the bitter hardships and hostile lessons of sleeping rough in Port-au-Prince. Some Haitian street kids speak in similar terms of their abusive households of origin (their previous models of "home") as sheltering but violent places without care. Over time I came to understand that street boys do in a way love the street, for its independence, its freedom, its opportunities for work, and for what it has done to shape their identities as friends, comrades, and social actors. But they love the street only insofar as they hate the conditions that have led them there and that keep them there.

Figure 1.3. A street girl in Port-au-Prince. The street in Haiti is very gendered terrain, with boys outnumbering girls by a ratio of around four to one.

One of the goals of my research in Haiti has been to better understand how street children are understood by the civil society (Haitian adults and other children, popular organizations, religious and other social groups) and the state (the government, its laws and institutions, the police, its paramilitaries). But another goal, given the dialectical approach taken up by this study, was to understand how street children understand their own lot in life and how they manage to get by from day to day through varying, often contrary, social situations. Over the course of the past three decades, there have been several models for understanding street childhood proposed by anthropologists, sociologists, social workers, development agencies, nongovernmental organizations, and others (Kendall 1975; Ennew 1986; Aptekar 1988; Swart 1988; Glauser 1990; Rizzini and Rizzini 1991; Campos, et al. 1994; Scheper-Hughes and Hoffman 1997, 1998; Hecht 1998; Márquez 1999; Kilbride, Suda, and Njeru 2001; Panter-Brick 2001; Matthews 2003; Olwig 2003). But because I left for the field concerned primarily with local definitions of *the street* and *childhood*, I privileged the Haitian constructions of street childhood in my work, and opted for a theoretical model that privileged the instrumental aspects of street childhood. What I share with most of these researchers is a commitment to an ethnographic approach to the lives of street children; one grounded in fieldwork and participatory engagement rather than one couched in theoretical conjecture. I molded the research around a distinctly ethnographic approach informed by my interviews and conversations with scores of street children, domiciled children and school children (one must not assume that the two are one and the same, though most street children in fact do), ordinary residents, laborers, civil servants, doctors, teachers, social workers, merchants, politicians, businesspersons, state authorities, Vodouisaints, Christians, and others; in short, the most comprehensive cross section of the Haitian civil society as was possible given my resources and abilities over the course of ten years in Haiti. Such an approach made good ethnographic sense as I attempted to understand street childhood in Haiti, insofar as childhood itself is as central to the cultural life of the country writ large as the street is to its social, economic, and political character. The ethnographic approach has also allowed me to avoid the rhetorical pitfall of problematic nomenclature that often reduces the study of the lives of street children to little more than a semantic debate over whether the children are "of the street," "on the street," "in the street," "abandoned," "at high risk," or "homeless," a debate that stems from thinking about street children in terms of what public space they occupy and how they use it instead of in terms of the identities that such children form while occupying and using public space. This approach has also allowed me (as it has others) to avoid similarly semantic debates over the differences in meaning between *child*, *adolescent*, and *youth*, as these categories of classification tend to be based on Western models of legal age distinction and are therefore incongruous with Haitian social custom. Because of the discipline's customary preference for the adoption of local terminology and ethos in thinking about the field, such debates are typically, though not always, found outside of anthropological discussions of street childhood. For the purposes of my research, a child was defined in accordance with local intuition and nomenclature, and so most of my street-child informants ranged in age from three to eighteen. Any other young person who was identified by other kids or who self-identified as *timoun* [kid or child] was similarly noted as such in my field notes. Further, that child was considered a street child if he or others identified himself as such—*timoun lari* (a term that evokes a particular living relationship to the street)—and if his lifestyle conformed to the local model of street childhood, characterized by what might be described as an *intimate*, if not always preferred, relationship to the street, spending most if not all of his/her time working, eating, loving, fighting, sleeping, and dying there.

Local Perspectives on Haitian Street Childhood

Throughout this section I take up the construction and representation of street childhood in Haiti within three local paradigms: that of the child on the street, which I privilege throughout for the theoretical reasons concerning agency already described; that of the greater civil society; and that of the state. Also at issue is my own perspective, which is closest to that of the street children themselves and which is further informed by my ethnographic reckoning of the larger social and cultural community of which they are a part. I see as my primary task in this book the translation of the street children's paradigm into my own for the sake of accurately describing their world and their worldviews from a distinctly anthropological perspective.

Each of the local paradigms rely on different but occasionally overlapping sets of criteria in defining the social status of the filthy, battered, laboring child sleeping rough on the pavements of the capital. Defining street childhood as a social status in Haiti is first a matter of deciding on the appropriate use of urban space; do children belong there in the first place and if so, what ought they and what ought they not be doing while there? Street childhood is also a status dependent upon a given child's physical appearance and dress, the perceived and actual nature of the child's relations to civil and state institutions, the child's age, the child's activities in the public domain, and a host of other criteria that may vary from person to person and from place to place throughout the city. These multivariate parameters for defining the nature, status, and social worth of children in the street serve to shape the highly diverse and subjective local attitudes about them, as well as the relative threat or value that they present to the community.

Somewhere between the child in the street on the one hand and the larger civil society and the state on the other, there is a disjuncture of experience. Whether a common citizen, a Vodou priest, a police officer, or an anthropologist, adults experience the world in a way markedly different from that of children, with immeasurable experiential differences and overlap among the adults. Where the citizen sees the city as a place for work, the priest sees the city as place of spiritual danger; where the police officer sees the city as a locus of crime, the anthropologist sees the city as a locus of data. But all of these adults share a common perspective about the city that is deeply informed by their civil, legal, and political rights to occupy and appropriate it to the fullest extent; these are rights that are categorically denied street children because of their legal age, their diminutive size, their relative physical

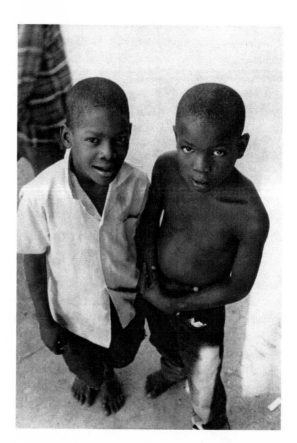

Figure 1.4. Street children in Port-au-Prince are easily distinguishable by their dress. Many go shirtless and very few wear shoes.

weakness, their lack of political power and economic resources, their limited educational backgrounds, and their absence of official representation. While one must bear in mind just how different the world looks from the knee-high perspective of the street child, we must also be aware that within both the adult and child spheres there are further subdivisions of perspective, varying and often competing ways of envisioning the social world of displaced youth.

Children who live on the pavement regard it both physically and phenomenologically different than how it is likewise regarded by a sheltered child who lives within the fold of the natal family and beneath the roof of an at least adequate sheltered space. Similarly, children living in the street comport themselves one way to the adult citizen-passerby and quite another way to an agent of one of the police quasi militaries. Convoluting these disparate perspectives is the fact that no individual represents a singular social identity, but rather occupies several statuses simultaneously—child, elder, girl, boy, sickly, well, criminal, mendicant—and passes dialectically through each or many at a time throughout the day and night. At any one given point in time, a person views the cultural milieu through a particular lens of judgment. The street child regarded one way on one day by an individual in one context, may be regarded quite another way on another day (or the same day) by that same individual in a different context, or by someone else in the same context. My own ethnographic perspectives on street and domiciled children, the police, the Vodou community, missionaries, and average citizens similarly shifted throughout the course of each day of my fieldwork, as I regarded others and was regarded by them in multiple, simultaneous, and ever-changing social relations. Identity politics are messy business and they defy universalizing definitions. Anthropologies of identity politics can often get even messier.

Sacrificing Selfhood: The Specter of *Siment*

Street kids do think in classificatory categories about the children with whom they share the pavement. The primary distinctions between groups of kids are age and sex—*ti timoun* [little kids] are distinguished from *gwo timoun* [older kids] and *tifi* [little girls] are distinguished from *tigason* [little boys]. There are also status distinctions that street children make between one another based on lifestyle. There are those children who are known to be sexually active and those who are not. There are those who participate regularly in minor criminal activity and those who do not. There are those that are politically attuned and those who are not. There are those who are literate and those who are not. And then there are those groups of *timoun lari* whose lifestyle is so divergent from the majority of street kids that they are conceptually segregated from that majority by other, more "typical" or "mainstream" street kids. Such groups may include prostitutes, gang affiliates, drug runners, or street kids who receive considerable and regular financial support from a wealthy benefactor with whom a given child may develop a special relationship. Perhaps no other group of street children better illustrates the street-child's notion of a "divergent subculture" than the hundreds of street kids in Port-au-Prince hopelessly addicted to sniffing glue.

The most observable distinction made between groups of street kids by street kids is between those children who are drug addicts and those who are not. While the variety of drugs available on the street is extensive, only a handful of drugs are effectively priced within the material means of street children. By far the most commonly abused drug among them is also the cheapest to acquire: *siment*, a cobbler's glue, the vapors of which are inhaled through the mouth and nose.[1] A day's dosage of *siment* can be purchased for as little as five gourdes (about eleven U.S. cents) from local shoemakers or other street kids.

Street children who sniff *siment* are readily distinguishable from those street children who do not use the drug. Invariably the breath of *siment* users smells strongly of vapors, and they tend to be absolutely filthy because the vapors bring on a lethargy that inhibits their motivation to clean their bodies and their clothes at nearby standpipes like most street children do. There are also physiological indicators. The eyes of long-term users are perpetually bloodshot and the mouths of many are surrounded by a ring of scabbing blisters caused by prolonged contact with the vapors. Their bodies tend to be much frailer and emaciated than nonusing street children, from a lack of interest in food. While most children do not cite it as their primary motivation for sniffing, the glue does seem to have the effect of hunger suppression that leads some users to go several days without eating at all. When I asked children who were abusing *siment* "Why do you sniff glue?" none of them said that it was because it alleviated hunger. Most simply said that it made them feel good. However, when I asked these same children "Does sniffing glue make you more or less hungry?" most said outright that it made them less hungry and one said that it makes him altogether *bliye manje* [forget food].

Once a street child becomes an addict to the glue (which can happen after only a few days of sniffing), he loses his motivation not only to eat but to work. Sniffers of *siment* are more likely to beg full time than nonsniffers, who generally prefer work to mendicancy.

Siment users tend to congregate in particular parts of the city, usually places where they will be left alone and where they are less likely to be chased away by the police or store owners. One group of kids I know sniff glue near the National Cemetery in the dangerous Portail Léogâne section of Port-au-Prince. Here there are both male and female users, ranging in age from about five or six to sixteen. Most of them here lie down on their sides to sniff the drug, but I have observed children all over the city walking about while they sniff. The *siment* is spread around the inside of a plastic juice bottle and stirred with a stick by the user while inhaling to agitate the release of vapor. Users carry the bottles lazily concealed beneath their shirts, with the mouth of the bottle protruding from the neckline just beneath the chin. When using, the child stirs the glue and places his or her entire mouth or nose into the opening of the bottle, breathing deeply and slowly. Users repeat this regimen—stirring, sniffing, stirring, sniffing—all day long or for as long as the glue lasts, with ten- to fifteen-minute intervals between inhalations. Some of the children engage in the rather dangerous habit of heating the highly flammable glue on steel can lids with matches when it begins to lose its va-porous quality, sniffing close to the glue and occasionally suffering flashes of ignited vapor. None of the sniffers with whom I have spoke said that they would continue sniffing if they were physically able to quit the habit, because long-time usage eventually brings an unpleasantness to the high. Some kids indicate that the glue gives them headaches and occasionally causes vomit-ing.

I inhaled the glue once in 1998 in order to get a better understanding of the immediate effects that the drug has on street children. I was interested in particular with how the effects of the drug might compromise a child's abil-ity to realistically perceive his/her surroundings. What I experienced after a few inhalations was a fleeting lightheadedness, coupled with a very unpleas-ant flush of heat in my cheeks and forehead (almost like a fever) and a rising pressure in my temples. It made me nauseous. I experienced no sense of euphoria, though the feeling could be described as temporarily intoxicating. The entire experience lasted about two-and-a-half minutes. The children who use the drug rarely report that they derive any sense of pleasure from usage, instead claiming variously that sniffing makes them "forget their hun-ger," "lose their misery," "feel drunk and easygoing," or they say that it brings on a drowsiness that allows them to sleep through the long days and nights on the street.

A child who sniffs glue is likely to be described in local parlance as *zombi*—an individual whose flesh is animated, but who lacks that aspect of the soul that otherwise determines individuality, character, willpower, and self-control. Even a cursory encounter with a child high on glue va-por is enough to convince one that such may be the case. Adult residents of Portail Léogâne have pointed out to me that like the living cadavers of Vodou folk belief, the children in the neighborhood who sniff *siment* live in and around the cemetery, wander the streets long after dark, and slur their words, mumbling incomprehensibly. Their eyes are glazed over, their breath smells unnatural (in this case, like vapor), and their speech is the mottled rasp of the corpse whose vocal chords have decayed. Glue vapor is caustic, causing not just damage to the vocal chords, but to the lips and mouth as well. Most sniffers have angry open sores and seeping burns around their mouths where, for years, they have held the plastic bottle of glue in order to inhale from it.

The effects of the drug at times makes talking with these kids very dif-ficult. Their attention spans are somewhat limited, though some of the chil-dren maintain a very high degree of focus while sniffing and being inter-viewed at the same time. The debilitating effects of *siment* seem to be highly variable and dependent upon how long the child has been an addict, how often the glue is sniffed, as well as the individual personality of the child who is using. Some kids grow aggressive and threatening while under the influence, but most become glassy-eyed, passive, and incoherent. Very few of these children made for good informants while sniffing, though a few can be remarkably articulate and thoughtful while in the throes of a *siment* high.

Other Drugs, Other Escapes

While *siment* by far is the most commonly (or at least the most visibly) abused narcotic among Port-au-Prince street children, other drugs are used by the kids as well. *Marijàn* [marijuana] is both relatively cheap and easily accessible. Because it is widely distributed and inexpensive, many children attest to having smoked it though few that I have known are regular users. It is most often purchased from older street boys who sell it to supplement their income, but rarely as a full-time occupation. It is sold in small quantities (as most things are in Haiti) and is typically wrapped in yellow parchment or leaves. A *sigarèt marijàn* [a marijuana cigarette or "joint"] can cost as little as twenty-five to thirty gourdes (less than US$1) and so is considered affordable. *Marijàn* is generally consumed as a social drug, and most children describe how the drug makes them *fè tenten* [act silly], which is probably why they prefer to smoke it in groups rather than in isolation. While most children report having enjoyed the experience, some have indicated that they found it rather unpleasant, with one boy telling me unequivocally and morosely that "*marijàn se pa zanmi'm*" [marijuana is no friend of mine]. Nearly all of the children who have smoked marijuana have indicated that the experience leaves them *ampil grangou* [very hungry], which is why some prefer not to smoke it at all. One boy suggested that he prefers to drink *kleren* when he smokes marijuana, because then he does not feel hungry.

Kleren, a raw sugarcane moonshine rum that is very high in alcohol content, is consumed occasionally by some of the children when they can get it, and it is used in a manner similar to that of marijuana. It is generally drunk as a recreational indulgence rather than as a vehicle for escapism or intoxication and few drink it with any regularly. When street children did discuss alcohol consumption, the alcohol in question was invariably *kleren*, and it almost always was said to have been consumed during *Kanaval* [Carnival] by the sip or gulp, passed on to them by revelers. Few of the kids have the material means to cultivate a full-blown alcoholic addiction to *kleren* year-round, and none of the children with whom I spoke ever suggested that they craved it the way that sniffers reported craving *siment* once they were addicted to it.

The use of harder narcotics that are widely available on the streets of Port-au-Prince—*woch* [crack cocaine], *kòken poud* [powder cocaine], and a rainbow of prescription pills—is not common among street children in Haiti, though some do use any or all of the above. Only one child ever reported to me that he had smoked crack, but upon hearing him say so, his comrades laughed and emphatically discounted his admission as a boastful ruse. In any event these harder drugs are relatively high in price—as much as 250 gourdes (around $5.75) for a rock of crack cocaine containing about one-quarter of a gram of cocaine and as much as 2,050 gourdes (around $47) for a gram of powder cocaine, rendering both of these drugs well beyond the material means of most street youth.

The vast majority of Haitian street children are a thrifty lot and few of them believe that narcotics are worth their weight in food. Many street children smoke cigarettes, but those that do consider even tobacco to be a luxury. By and large the day-to-day activities of most street children are wholly consumed with work and their economic well being is far too tied up in social obligations to their peers for most to participate in addictive self-indulgence.

School Children

For all of the distinctions that street children make among groups of themselves, the sharpest distinction that they make are between *timoun lari* in general and the settled children who have homes and families that care for them. Interestingly, in their argot, *timoun lari* do not distinguish themselves from these settled children by assigning a linguistically opposed signifier to them. That is, nonstreet children are not identified as *timoun lakay* [house children] or *timoun fouaye* [home children] by their street-child counterparts. One reason for this is the fact that many street children in Haiti are not in fact orphans and some children maintain relations with some households to which they might turn for a night or two of sleep in the kitchen or yard before being turned back out onto the street. As such, street children do not necessarily envision themselves as unique because they lack hearth or kin. Street children certainly consider their circumstances much deeper than just the superficial absence of material shelter. They examine their lot well beyond the present state of their existence on the street and in fact look to the causes, both domestic and civil, which resulted in the effect of their displacement. And the civil cause that most street children in Port-au-Prince point to, either directly or suggestively, is indicated by the term that they use among themselves in identifying other children who are not of the street—*timoun lekol* [school children].

According to Articles 32.1 to 32.3 of Haiti's most recent, 1987 Constitution, public primary school education is free and compulsory for children between the ages of seven and thirteen. Despite this constitutional provision however, there are simply too few public schools to make this aspiration a reality for settled children, let alone for street children. Public schools are not obligated to admit "illegitimate" children and few in fact do, effectively barring any child without the proper documents (that is, nearly all street children) from matriculating into the school system. Access to primary education through the parochial schools is sharply limited by tuition (more than 90 percent of the best schools are private and expensive, what Haitians call *lekol tèt neg* [big-shot schools]), the cost of school uniforms (mandatory for most students in both public and private institutions), and the cost of other supplies (texts, notebooks, and pencils are not provided by the state), which can average over 10 percent of household income for most poor families (de Regt 1984). Perhaps most prohibitively expensive are textbooks. At an average of 280 gourdes (around $6.42) per text, the cost of books alone per student per grade level can be as high as 1,400 gourdes (around $32.10). Given that the per capita income among the poorest classes, which comprise over 60 percent of the total population, is around 10,500 gourdes (around $240), as much as 13 percent of the total household income must be allotted *per child* per year for textbooks alone. With an average of almost five children per household, 65 percent of household income would be expended on just the required textbooks for all five matriculated students. It becomes fiscally impossible for all children in most poor households to attend school. The upshot is that the ancillary costs of primary education in Haiti (primarily books, but also uniforms, paper, pencils, and a lunch) are sufficiently prohibitive for the overwhelming majority of Haitians who compose the poorest sectors of the population. Demographic indicators of education in Haiti reveal as much: less than half of all eligible children actually attend primary school, well over one million of Haiti's primary-school-age children have no access to education at all, and almost 60 percent of all Haitian children abandon primary school before completing the six-year course (UNICEF 2004b). The irony of a free education whose subsidiary costs are prohibitively expensive is certainly not lost on the greater Port-au-Prince street-child community. The legend *"aba lekol tèt neg!"* [down with expensive schools!] is scrawled in graffiti and signed by street children on walls throughout the capital.

A recent UNICEF report (1999) argued that the rising cost of education in Haiti is driving poor families to divert their children into domestic servitude, illicit child labor, or directly onto the street and that is exactly what is

Figure 1.5. School girls carry the flag of Haiti in a procession marking International Women's Day, 2000.

happening. Over 250,000 children are working as unpaid domestic servants in Haiti, and the number of children on the street in Haiti is on the rise each year.

The cost of education is paramount among the primary causes for child displacement in Haiti. Of street children that I interviewed in Port-au-Prince over the course of my fieldwork, most had siblings still in the natal home who were attending primary or secondary school. The number of children in the continuous care of impoverished households appears to correlate to the maximum number of children a family can afford to keep enrolled in school. This is not to imply that poor families turn children outright onto the street because of the costs of education (though some in fact do); but it is to argue that families, often mothers, are forced to work a bitter calculus to determine which children are to go to school and which are to be sent into the streets to labor or beg and ultimately to fend for their own welfare in support of the household and their educated siblings. Once on the street, the children find it rather easy to stay. As will be seen in chapter 4, the money that street children make working or begging on the pavement in Port-au-Prince is substantially higher than that paid by a minimum wage job in Port-au-Prince—as much as 300 percent more. The decision to stay on the street is made even easier when the child's natal home is physically abusive, which is somewhat common.

School children are readily identifiable by their school uniforms, by the books they carry under their arms, by the kettles they carry filled with their lunch (for some the only real meal they will have that day), and by their relative cleanliness in comparison to their counterparts on the street. There is little if any observable animosity harbored by one group of children against the other. At worst, street children are envious of school children, but they inevitably come to the resigned understanding that, regardless of constitutional mandates to the contrary, not all children are extended the right to an education in Haiti. Many school children are friendly with street children, nearly always against the proscriptions of their parents who fear street children as criminal menaces and as threats to their own children's well being. It is not at all uncommon to see school children and street children squatting together in the street or on the steps of the plazas, playing jacks, exchanging jokes, or engaging in a game of *kay* (a game that can be played on the pavement using small stones as playing pieces). One of my favorite pastimes when in Port-au-Prince is to sit in the open amphitheater in the Place de Héros de l'Independence across from the National Palace (a favorite spot for children to play) and watch integrated groups of young children—*timoun lari* and *timoun lekol* alike—take turns riding in long, slow circles on the

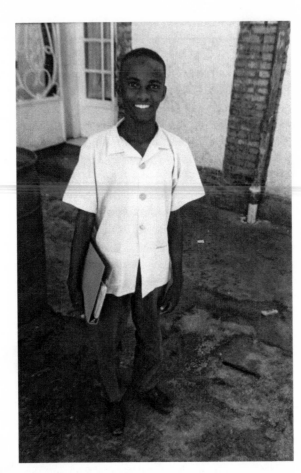

Figure 1.6. The dress and possessions of *timoun lekol*—school children—are coveted by street children in Haiti. Many express a strong desire to wear a school uniform and own books.

bicycles of teenage boys who allow them to do so while they talk with girls or play dominoes beneath the few sparse trees that have made it up through the concrete and gravel. Despite the lack of any substantive animosity between them, school children do tend to stay away from street children, who tend to avoid school children. The separation is not so much born of dislike as it is of incompatible approaches to the street—school children ultimately pass through it, street children ultimately live on it.

Identity and Invisibility

There is a sort of transcendent quality to the street that *timoun lari* regard as inseparable from their identity, irrespective of their actual occupation of place. It is as if the street were as much a fundamental aspect of their personal identity as it is of their personhood, unshakably attached to how they are perceived, how they perceive themselves to be and therefore inseparable from what they may ever become. Institutional affiliation—with a shelter or an outreach, or even a school—is not sufficient for *timoun lari* to transubstantiate into *timoun lekol*, even if they are no longer sleeping on the street and even if they are attending classes at an institution that has extended some degree of care to them. The children who had come to Lafanmi Selavi, a Port-au-Prince orphanage where I did research in the mid-1990s, illustrate this point exactly. Many of the kids at Lafanmi slept at the facility full time, some never leaving the gates of the facility once inside its sanctuary. Primary schooling was provided truly free of any costs to Lafanmi's children, and many of them were children from poor (but at least domiciled) families who had arrived at Lafanmi with only two real options before them: try to get their child an education through Lafanmi, or send the child onto the street to work. Yet without exception, the kids at the facility continued to describe themselves in interviews with me and in conversations among themselves as *timoun lari*, some long after they had processed through the program at the age of seventeen. By superficial standards, these children (and eventually teenagers) would be considered *timoun lekol*; but from the perspective of the child whose formative years were spent exposed on the pavement, they will always be *nan lari* [from the street]. This attribute of their identity remains with them forever, regardless of their age or subsequent institutional affiliations.

Most adults in Port-au-Prince, whether they live sheltered or themselves are sharing the pavement with street children, agree that life on the street is detrimental to the physical and psychic welfare of children. Sickness, scarcity, sexual abuse, hunger, thirst, and violence all contribute to a set of conditions that routinize greater rates of child morbidity and child death on the street. The persistence of these conditions has been compounded by both the Haitian public and private sectors, which have come to normalize child morbidity and death as the expected outcome for children who live and work on the street. The very fact that such an attitude has become veritable Haitian custom further amplifies the problem as it contributes to the social invisibility of street children. As their suffering has become routine and then normal, it has slipped into the urban field unnoticed, a regularized feature of the urban milieu.

Just as the child on the street has over time become a cultural fixture in Haiti, so too has the labor that they perform. Street children carry groceries, wash cars, wipe windshields, shine shoes, and perform other small but essential tasks that have made them indispensable to the informal economy and invisible features of the urban landscape. I once climbed into the back-seat of a rattletrap taxi and discovered a few fifty-centime coins wedged into the seat. I handed them over to the driver, who laughed and told me that *"ti monnen sa-a se pou Gèdè"* [This change belongs to Gèdè]. In one of his many manifestations Gèdè is the contrary Vodou spirit of the cemetery and the protector of children. The driver's remark is at once illustrative of the normalization of street-child labor in Port-au-Prince and indicative of one way that street childhood is embedded in Vodouisaint terms in the everyday parlance of the people. The driver explained that he often finds spare change in the back seat of his taxi and that he saves it on his dashboard in a small tin cup to give to street children, as payment for wiping his windshield when he stops to buy petrol. The cabbie was suggesting that it was Gèdè who jarred the coins loose from the pockets of his passengers and between the cushions of the backseat of his car, so that they would eventually find their way into the hands of street children. By saving such change specifically for the services of street children—and he is not the only driver who does this; most reserve some coins for tipping street kids—this driver illustrates the general normalization of child labor in the street. The services of street children are not anomalous; rather, they are expected and assumed facets of daily life in Port-au-Prince, as will be seen in greater detail in chapter 4. In this and in other ways, street children are rendered socially invisible, obscured into the cityscape as indeterminate features of street life and subsumed as fixtures of the urban economy.

The Stigma of the Street

If street children have not slipped into social invisibility, then they are maligned as a social menace by Port-au-Prince citizens who are both frustrated and panicked by a recent spectacular rise in political gunplay and criminal terror in the streets. Since the late 1990s, an intensification of civil crime in the capital—much of it gun and drug violence perpetrated by youth gangs, though some is political in nature—has been paralleled by the popular perception that street children are in some measure responsible for it. The recruitment of street children by gang lieutenants for the commission of violent crimes, though hardly the norm, is not unheard of given the desperate poverty of the kids and the coercive intimidation of noncooperatives by some of the gangs. But the oversimplified and erroneous association of *all* street children with the crisis has elicited the social ire of a greater Port-au-Prince community that has isolated displaced youth as dangerous criminal agents, who are the primary causes of the escalation in social ills. This powerful sentiment is amplified by the fact that most adults in Port-au-Prince generally regard street children as noncitizens, living outside the bounds of social mores and civil law and beyond the normative acculturating control of adult society. Since they are reared by the street and not by a family in a home, street children are perceived as unsocialized and noncultural and certainly without a civil identity. They are in effect nonpersons, whether they have been rendered invisible through their routinized street labors or criminalized by the civil society. It becomes easy under these circumstances to see them as undeserving of their civil and human rights.

The impression that street children are functionaries of disorder and malevolence is especially pervasive in the Port-au-Prince merchant community. Sensitive to the preservation of my informants' privacy while interviewing, I routinely sought out secluded and comfortable spaces for my discussions with street kids. I discovered very early on in the fieldwork, however, that those spaces that would have otherwise proven ideal for interviews, such as restaurants and cafés, were off-limits to street children. Proprietors made it clear to me that we were not welcome in their establishments. When asked why, the reply was variable in tone and delivery, but consistent in the underlying message—street children are not to be trusted, are prone to thievery, are dirty and (as such) are better left outside and far from the premises. On one occasion, after eating lunch in the Plaza Hotel in downtown Port-au-Prince, I had asked my waiter for something with which to package my uneaten portion so that I might take it with me to give to the street children who congregated outside the hotel and wiped the tires of taxis for tips. He quietly but firmly refused to do so, explaining to me that the owner of the hotel does not allow such things, because street children are *zòdis* [wicked] and feeding them close to the premises invites trouble. After assuring him that I would not give the food to street children, he packaged the portion in aluminum foil for me. I gave it to a street boy, several blocks from the hotel.

The perceived malevolence of street children is not the only reason why I was forced to do interviews in the street. The obvious place for seclusion and privacy for interviews would have been my residence, but this was imprudent for two reasons. First, it would have made the children uncomfortable to be in such foreign surroundings and I wanted them to be as much at ease for interviews as possible. Secondly, it is well known that some foreigners in Haiti take advantage of child prostitution while in Port-au-Prince and I would stand to cultivate an unsavory reputation if locals in my neighborhood were to observe me regularly bringing street children into my home. Given the fact that my quarters and most cafés were off-limits for interviews with the kids, downtown and in the street itself ended up being the necessary setting. One would think that the street would at least be free from local contempt; it is, after all, *salon pèp*. But the street as an interview space is not without its problems.

There is a genuinely palpable social desire to negate street childhood from the public sphere and this is made apparent by the aggressive civil stance taken toward street youth, particularly in the ongoing construction around the plazas of Champ de Mars since the mid-1990s. For generations Champ de Mars has served as a hub of street-child activity. Alive with pedestrian traffic and colorful street life and abundant with work opportunities for the child who can muscle some space for himself, the open thoroughfares serve as a safe place for street kids to interact with each other and often with school children. Since 1994 Port-au-Prince public works initiatives have centered on the rehabilitation of Champ de Mars's monuments and public squares as a matter of civic pride and ultimately in preparation for the country's bicentennial celebrations to take place in 2004. A large billboard was erected in 1995 at the main intersection of Rue Capois and Avenue Lamartiniére proclaiming that *"Chanmas se paske'w!"* [Champ de Mars is for you!]. Statues of national heroes have been scrubbed free of political graffiti against the former Cedras regime (it has since been replaced with anti-Aristide graffiti), park benches have been sanded and painted, and colorful flowers have been planted in beds long before abandoned to weeds.

In a grassy park lined with pretty concrete walkways near the Musée d'Art, a playground has been built, replete with swings, slides, and jungle gyms. It is clear for whom these new facilities are intended—settled school children. Street children are kept from congregating for long in the parks and plazas of Champ de Mars by National Police officers who are ever-vigilant to the presence of the scrappy loiterers. On the first day that I tried to speak with a handful of street children in the Place de Héroes de l'Independence on Champ de Mars, we were chased away by a National Policeman with a bull-horn barking out an order for us to vacate the area—*"W'ap pa chita toupre laflè!"* [You can't be sitting near the flowers!]. Pervasive is the idea that street children are contaminants who threaten the growth of things by their proximity to them; a similar notion is behind the general belief that street kids carry diseases and parasites that threaten the public health. We are again reminded by these examples of the polluting nature of street children, a trait that they seem to have acquired as permanent residents of liminal space.

Finding a quiet and inconspicuous space to conduct interviews downtown without being chased away by wary merchants was also problematic, especially at night. Street lamps are hardly pervasive throughout the capital and they tend to be clustered around walled government compounds, certain market areas, and major thoroughfares. Many small shops that are open after dark have installed flood lamps that project intense light in a bright arc around the entrance to the store. Because most of the children with whom I have worked congregate after hours far from the market districts and because the larger lighted boulevards and government building sections are notoriously dangerous places after daylight hours, I frequently sought out the lighted facades of convenience markets for interviews with children at night. More than occasionally, our conversations were interrupted by the armed guards of the shops. Security men with combat shotguns and machine pistols have been fixtures in banks and even small stores since the recent rise in gun violence has given Port-au-Prince the feel of a latter-day tropical Dodge City. To rouse us, these security men would ask, politely at first and then more sternly, for us to move on because the presence of the children outside the store was intimidating to customers. While I was conducting a nighttime interview with three street boys outside the Big Star Market on Rue Capois, a guard emerged from the store and asked that we leave. I explained to him that I needed the light that was only available in front of the market in order to see what I was writing. He told me that while he sympathized, he was told by the market owner that the children were dangerous and threatening to his patrons. After some negotiation with the guard and the store's owner, I was permitted to stay under the light of the lamp, provided that the children concealed themselves in the shadows. The irony of this encounter is that the store owner knew two of the children and in fact welcomed their labor (carrying groceries for customers) during daylight hours as a convenience for his patrons. But as general nuisances, street children who make themselves visible are maligned as persistent reminders of Haitian society's inability or unwillingness to protect its children, so they are best tolerated when unseen.

I have occasionally received words of caution from passersby when I am socializing with street children in Port-au-Prince. Almost always the comments are sincere and blunt, spoken within earshot of the children themselves and without regard for their sensitivities. *"Timoun yo la se trè danjere!"* [Those children are very dangerous!]. *"Fètatansyon! Y'ap vòlè lajan ou!"* [Be careful! They will steal your money!]. Though well-intentioned—they are after all intended to safeguard my well being—these words of caution are suggestive of the general attitude of wariness and contempt that most self-respecting Haitians direct toward street children. Occasionally the civic goodwill extended to me by passersby contrasts sharply against the public's unsavory visceral reaction to the street children. Often after an interview with a child, I would go into a nearby shop to buy a soda or juice for my informant and discreetly slip some money into the bag with the bottle, a method that I typically used for paying the children for their time. My discretion in concealing the money in the bag was preferred by the children, who do not usually want other street youths to know that they have money. It was not uncommon for the child for whom the bag was intended to snatch it from my hands when I offered it and run away laughing out of exuberance, but never disrespect or malice. On one occasion a young businessman walking toward me saw this happen and wasn't so sure. He chased the boy down to retrieve what he thought was my stolen bag. I thanked the man for his concern, but explained that I was a friend of the boy's and that I had actually given him the bag. The man looked at me incredulously and asked, "*Eske ou sèten?*" [Are you certain?].

While on the street in Port-au-Prince, I have been confronted by Haitians concerned about what I was discussing with the children. Most are interested only insofar as some Haitians dislike foreigners propagating stories about poverty and destitution in Haiti, which they assumed I must be doing if I was talking with street children. I suspect that this sentiment is only aggravated by the sporadic tours of journalists and photographers whose particularly extractive industries come to bear on the Haitian citizenry only when disaster, coup d'etat, or famine become of interest to their Western audiences. While I sympathize with this attitude (which I really only experienced a handful of times), I can't help but think that if I were not talking to the children, these concerned individuals would never even have noticed them in the first place. Experience and observation have taught me that the habitus of Port-au-Prince society has conditioned most people to walk over, around, and past street children without even recognizing that they are there. They are routinely ignored when not begging, casually avoided whenever possible, and often tread upon while sleeping. After some time in Haiti, I had so acculturated my street behaviors to that of the children with whom I spend most of my time when in Haiti—squatting against walls while talking, speaking in hushed voices, avoiding areas of high pedestrian traffic—that I have at times slipped past the observation of many adult passersby. I once inadvertently startled a gaggle of young women when I stood up to stretch my legs, reentering the altitude of the socially visible. My considerable height (I stand several inches over six feet tall) and my light complexion make it very difficult for me to be physically inconspicuous in Haiti, so my ability to occasionally fuse with the cityscape by adopting the manners and comportment of street children is especially noteworthy. Like the overhead telephone lines in my neighborhood, one generally doesn't see street children unless one looks for them.

The fact that the sight of street children gathered in a circle in the plazas talking excitedly or dejectedly or passionately with me was so inapposite as to draw attention in the first place is evidence enough to say that for most people these kids do not otherwise exist in the social reality. For some adults listening in, the interview segments that they overheard were the first time that they had ever heard displaced children speak on their own behalf about their lives on the street, although some of these conversations were curbed by the fact that some children preferred not to speak with me about certain subjects (sex and crime victimization mostly) in mixed company. As our relationships with one another were cemented through mutual trust over time, the children and I learned to read each other's unspoken cues, indicating when to avoid certain subject material, when to conceal the tape recorder from the view of outsiders, and sometimes when to terminate the conversation altogether and leave the area because of the presence of certain parties that threatened to stifle disclosure—other street children, adversaries, adults, police officers, even children of the opposite sex.

It would be wrong to argue that all Port-au-Prince residents have negative impressions of street kids; but the pitiful lived experience of street children has led the public sector to normalize their hardships and to regard them in one of two ways: with indifference or with contempt. As children beyond the normative control of adult society, they are associated with the urban blight and unmediated violence that is also outside the normative control of the larger society and that has plagued Port-au-Prince for more than a decade. This social composite of street-child identity—as alternatively invisible and then conspicuous as unsocialized threats to civil order—perpetuates the image of street children in Port-au-Prince as supernumerary nuisances and criminals, at the same time that it provides justification for the establishment of a negative conception of civil and human rights that denies children on the street as nonpersons.

While little mention of street children is made in the Haiti literature before the 1990s, as early as 1959 Alfred Métraux had detailed a trial by ordeal to which a street youth was subjected after having been accused of theft, and the example helps to illustrate that social preconceptions of street youths as guilty of crime by default of their apparent "wildness" is not a new phenomenon in Haiti. Though not dangerous in any real sense, the trial by *balai* is traditionally believed to be effective in determining the guilt or innocence of the accused by mimicking strangulation around the neck of a suspect. The *balai* plant is a species common in Haiti that is believed to have the power to clench the neck of a culprit who resists truthful confession. When bunched together, *balai* stalks have the peculiar property of tangling in such a way

as to make them difficult to disentwine once interlaced. Métraux explains
that all one need do to manipulate the outcome of the ordeal is to bring the
stalks together around the neck of the accused, enmeshing them and form-
ing a clench. The foregone conclusion of the street-child's guilt by virtue of
his status as displaced is evident:

> A theft having been committed at a house at Marbial near which chil-
> dren were playing, the owners decided to have recourse to this ordeal.
> The principal suspect was an orphan [street child] whose unruly be-
> haviour had awakened the deepest misgivings among the peasants.
>
> A woman who was something of a magician asked for a sheaf of
> the *balai* (*Corchorus siliquosush*) plant, which was duly brought. She
> sprinkled it with ash and uttered some spells over it and then squirted
> water over it from her mouth. She put the children in a long line. Then
> with a bunch of the *balai* in each hand she went up behind each child
> in turn, moved the branches three times round before his eyes and
> then put them caressingly against the nape of his neck. When it was
> the turn of the suspected orphan the two sheaves interlocked round his
> neck like a garrot. Terrified, the poor wretch let out piercing screams;
> but when pressed to admit his guilt, he refused. . . . It was later discov-
> ered the children were completely innocent and that the money had
> been taken by a servant. This ordeal is much feared and many young
> culprits prefer to admit their guilt rather than be unmasked by the
> plant. (Métraux 1972: 319–20)

Whereas Métraux's account of the ordeal of the *balai* helps us to frame
the marginalization and criminalization of street children in rural Haiti in
the 1950s, times and circumstances have changed, as has the geographic
locus of the crisis. Rural concerns about property theft have been replaced
with urban fears of unbridled gunplay in the streets and the stress of the *balai*
has been replaced with the terror of the pistol. In Port-au-Prince today, as in
Marbial, street children's perceived "unruly behaviour" has again "awakened
the deepest misgivings among the peasants," now urban dwellers. Today as
then, the guilt of the street child is presumed, the *balai* has clenched and
street children have become acceptable targets for civil and state reproach.

There are two primary ways in which the Haitian state's perspective toward street children is made manifest: Haitian national policy (including
constitutional law and international treaty agreements) and the "on the
ground" civil-state relations between government agents (including the
police and the paramilitaries) and street children. Careful examination of
both of these sites of government-child interaction reveals little consistency

between the state's claims for the rights and protections of children (as expressed through legislative instruments) and its actual relations toward street children through its police forces.

The Haitian Constitution of 1987 makes limited provisions for the protection of children and in fact only two articles of Haitian law provide explicitly for children. Article 260 makes limited reference to the state's obligation to "endeavor to aid and assist mothers, children and the aged," and Article 261 "ensures protection for all children" and emphasizes that "any child is entitled to love, affection, understanding and moral and physical care." A more explicit statement on children's rights was made in 1995, when the Haitian parliament ratified the United Nations Convention on the Rights of the Child (UNICEF 1989). The Convention laid out for the first time universal standards for the international establishment and recognition of the rights of children. Setting aside the considerable debates concerning the universalization of childhood, the Convention does address (albeit in broad generalities) some of the major social and political problems that children face in Haiti. But in part because of Haiti's desperate poverty and persistent instability since the Convention's ratification, the government has been slow to comply with its mandates.

A fundamental guarantee of the Convention is its acknowledgment of a child's inherent right to identity, established in part by that child's right to be registered immediately after birth. Birth certificates in Haiti (Acte de Naissance) are rarely issued outside of the urban centers and most children in the countryside do not have them. Even in the cities, the vast majority of children born in the sprawling slums are completely undocumented, making it impossible to account reliably for the identity, age, and paternity of most poor children. This is part of the reason why census data on Haiti is notoriously unreliable, especially data related to urban population estimates. Most poor mothers are vague when asked the ages of their children, so it is of little surprise that nearly all of the street children with whom I have worked gave rough (and oftentimes clearly inaccurate) estimates of their year of birth. Most ascertained their ages the way their mothers would—by relating the child's birth to some local or national event, usually the reign of a given president or dictatorship. Even in those cases where birth certificates are issued, the documents are registered and stored in the poorly maintained National Archives in Port-au-Prince, where the likelihood that any one is actually locatable on demand is close to nil. The lack of sufficient birth registration and other personal identification proving a child's age further aggravates violations of child rights when they are confronted by the police, a common instance among street children. At the time of arrest, the police arbitrarily evaluate whether or not a suspect is a minor. Medical examinations or background checks with neighbors or family are rarely used to determine the child suspect's age more precisely, despite the fact that such a determination is essential to deciding if and how a minor is to be tried. Admittedly this appears to be of relatively small consequence, given that the Haitian judiciary rarely makes substantive distinctions between the proceedings for minors and adults.

The Convention also stipulates the responsibility of state parties to safeguard a child's right to be protected from economic exploitation and work that interferes with education or jeopardizes the child's physical, mental, moral, or social development. One major source of concern with regard to the implementation of this provision in Haiti is the persistence of the *restavèk* system. From the French *rester avec* [to stay with], *restavèk* refers to a system in which poor (usually rural) families send their children to work as household domestics with better-off families in the cities, in exchange for safe housing and education for the children. Eighty percent of the estimated 250,000 *restavèk* in Haiti are girls under the age of fourteen years, which helps to explain the gender imbalance on the street. Whereas the public domain—of the field or the street—is traditionally the site of a boy's socialization into Haitian manhood, the domestic sphere is where a girl learns to be a woman. The gender division intrinsic to traditional Haitian child rearing is mirrored in the gender divisions of child displacement: four-fifths of *restavèk* are girls, three-fourths of *timoun lari* are boys.

While viewed by the poor as a way for their children to escape poverty, *restavèk* are often neglected and physically or sexually abused in their host homes and are typically denied the promised access to schooling. The *restavèk* system is widely accepted in Haiti and its persistence is frequently rationalized as necessary given the deep poverty of the country. The practice is so entrenched in Haitian custom that Haiti's Ministry of Social Affairs has assigned monitors to oversee the welfare of *restavèk* children and a law has been adopted specifically concerning this form of child labor. Under this legislation, *restavèk* fifteen years of age and older are to be paid not less than one-half the amount payable to a hired servant to perform similar work, in addition to room and board. Most host families avoid this legal provision by sending many if not most *restavèk* away from the home before the children reach the age of fifteen. The consequences are manifest in the demographics on the street. Port-au-Prince's burgeoning population of street children includes an increasing number of *restavèk* who have either been sent out of their host homes in their early teens, or are runaways from those host homes.

Figure 1.7. A *restavèk* in Port-au-Prince. There are over 250,000 children, most of them girls, living in a form of institutionalized domestic servitude in Haiti. Poor families struggling to provide for their children are frequently enticed into "giving" their children to better-off families to work in exchange for schooling. Rarely do these children ever receive the promised education, and they frequently are physically or sexually abused in their adoptive homes.

In Haiti there is ongoing concern and debate over the degree to which and under what circumstances children (be they *restavèk* or *timoun lari*) should contribute to household economy. Some argue that restricting children's domestic or street labor completely would increase the economic deprivation of extremely poor families who often depend on money brought in by these children for their basic needs. Others say that removing children from *restavèk* situations and street industries will only force more of them either onto the streets or, if already there, into more dangerous, exploitative, and illicit forms of work, such as prostitution or drug peddling. The necessary legislative and regulatory steps to alleviate the ill effects of the child labor system do not at present appear to be forthcoming.

Unlike *restavèk*, who have received at least some measure of legislative attention in the past few years, no such attention has been paid by the state to street children in Haiti. Though street-child issues do fall under the jurisdiction of the Ministry of Social Affairs's Institut du Bien Etre Social et de Recherches (Institute for Social Well Being and Research, IBESR), there exist no substantive state outreach programs that provide for displaced youth. The government does offer some economic assistance to a few overcrowded private orphanages, though this support is quite limited and pales in comparison to the private financial contributions made to street-child outreach centers and shelters run by the various foreign Christian missions throughout the country.

In the absence of any significant government programs or policies concerning street children, the Haitian National Police (PNH) and the Anti-Gang Unit (AGU)—a paramilitary subdivision of the PNH—have become the state's primary interlocutors in dealing with street-child issues. Though official National Police policy regarding street youth is one of paternalistic protection and intervention, individual child encounters with officers of the PNH and the far more militaristic AGU frequently prove to be marked by verbal abuse, physical violence, and arbitrary detention. As the civil and human rights of street children are compromised by these state agents, the Haitian civil sector has been slow to react, largely because of the attribution of youth gangsterism to the rising levels of street violence in Haiti, especially in the capital city of Port-au-Prince. As urban citizens grow increasingly fearful of the explosive urban landscape, a quiet acquiescence to police violence against street children has permeated the public conscience. A malign civil distrust of street youth coupled with an ambivalent state position concerning their lot has led to the criminalization of displaced children, who are erroneously designated as the primary causes for the recent escalation of drug violence and gun terror on the streets of Port-au-Prince. Perhaps nothing is more contributory to the civil mistrust and state ambivalence with regard to street children than the liminal space that displaced kids occupy and use as their home—the street—and the marginal, polluting, and dangerous status accorded to them as a result. In the following chapter, I will explore how the cultural identities that they assume and the public perception of them are informed by the unstructured public spaces that they occupy, and how their identification with the street as home contributes to their identification in the public mind with blight, crime, violence, and danger.

Bèl Marie

Her body is riddled with scars. The worst of these are concentrated on her legs and arms, but she has some nasty ones on her face as well. Freshly scabbed scratches rake down the curve of her right shoulder toward her back, the result of a recent fight with another street girl over money that was given to her by a passerby. A massive, corrugated scar spreads across the entire inside of her left upper thigh, an indelible souvenir of the abuse that marked the beginning of her life on the pavement. She has scores of small pockmarks up and down her legs and arms from a bacterial infection that has come and gone over the years. She wears very little—a flowered cotton sundress and sandals that, if they were clean and mended, would be rather pretty. But like this they are not; her sandals show the miles of wear she has put on them, and her faded, stained, and frayed dress hangs from her slight frame, poorly concealing the plastic juice bottle of *siment*, a cobblers' glue, that she has tucked down the neck of the dress and sniffs from as we talk. Her name is Bèl Marie, a name that means "Beautiful Marie." She was born around fifteen years ago in Coteaux, a small village near Port-á-Piment in the south. Now she sleeps rough in Port-au-Prince.

Her mother drowned in a fast moving sewage canal when the floodwaters of Hurricane Gordon hit the southern peninsula in November 1994. Bèl Marie was six years old at the time. Her father, a security guard at a local grocery, was struck by a car and killed as he walked home from work a month later. Frightened to sleep in her empty home and with no one nearby who could care for her, she began to sleep on the streets of Coteaux with other homeless victims of the floods and mud slides that followed Gordon. She later moved into the home of her aunt and mentally ill cousin in nearby Les Cayes, but began to spend more and more time on the streets to get away from the abuse of her new home. What pushed her into street life once and for all happened one evening in late December 1994. As Bèl Marie slept on her mat in a corner of her aunt's house, her cousin inexplicably pinned her down, held her mouth closed, and injected her left inner thigh with a scavenged syringe full of what Bèl Marie called "*dlo malad*" [sick water]—stagnant water drawn from a fetid puddle left by Gordon's rains. The wound grew infected and festered and she was taken by her aunt to the hospital. After she was treated and released with the wound dressed but still seeping, she left her aunt's house for the capital and has lived near the National Cemetery in Port-au-Prince with the glue-sniffers ever since. She tells me that even now, years later, she weeps when she looks at the scar on her leg, a bitter reminder of why she is here. She can offer no explanation as to why her cousin did this to her beyond the fact that he is mentally ill. I don't push the point.

Like most children sleeping rough in Haiti, Bèl Marie has other living kin with whom she could ostensibly live. She has a brother who drives a taxi in Petionville just outside of Port-au-Prince, and he has taken her into his home on several occasions in the past. But she says that her brother's wife is a *"gèp panyòl"* [mean wasp] who treated her badly and told her that she was too poor and too dirty to live in the house, so Bèl Marie left. This brother still tries to bring her to his home from time to time, but when he finds her she tells him that she would rather live on the street than sleep under the same roof with a woman who does not respect her. She has a grandmother who lives in Gonaïves, but she cannot go to live with her because she is already caring for other grandchildren who live with her in her tiny house. She also tells me that because her parents died so incredibly, so fatefully, she fears that she would bring a *maldjòk* [evil curse] into the home of her grandmother whom she loves so much. Bèl Marie is certain that she carries some preternatural responsibility for her parents' deaths.

She has two other relatives who live in Port-au-Prince—an uncle in Carrefour-Feuilles and a cousin in Delmas—but neither of them know her very well and both live in households too poor to take her in anyway. She has a second brother who lives in New York, but she has only seen him once and I sense that she is estranged from him. This brother returned to Haiti briefly in 1994 and visited her when she was in the hospital with the injection wound, but said then that he was unable to take her back to the United States or to otherwise care for her. He used to send her money she tells me, before the wound when she lived with her aunt. Her aunt would often take the money from the letters, reading them to Bèl Marie, who says that her aunt would even read her the passages of the letters that refer to the money that was intended for her.

She spends most days working on the street alongside the women vendors who sell fried bits of goat, chicken, and plantain called *fritay*. Bèl Marie washes their utensils and cleans their pots out for them. In exchange for this, she makes a fair amount of money—around seventy gourdes each day—and is permitted to eat as well. She sometimes begs for money when the opportunity presents itself, and she knows that she can make more than boys doing so. She says that people know how hard it is for girls who must live on the street and will give her a little bit of money and sometimes something to eat because they are *tris* [sad, melancholy] for her. She has never been to school and cannot read or write, nor can she spell her name;

but she understands basic number systems and counts money by identifying their value according to the color and size of the bills, which vary in these ways by necessity given the high illiteracy rate in the country. She tells me that she can make as much as fifty gourdes a day when she begs, but begging makes her feel *malpróp* and *dego* ["dirty" and "disgusted"]. She would rather work for the vendors.

Bèl Marie never steals for money, but she knows many other street girls who do. Girls who have been on the street for a long time try to persuade younger girls like herself to accompany them when they go out to do *de dwèt* [two fingers]—pickpocketing—but she refuses whenever she is asked because she is fearful of being caught and beaten by the National Police.

Bèl Marie shares what she has generously with other children on the street, especially five-year-old Ti Amos who has adopted her as a surrogate older sister. She is always sure to give him a little bit of her money each day so that he can get *piti bagay espesyal* [little special things] for himself like candy and a particular kind of juice that he prefers. She also uses her money to buy the sorts of things that she needs to take care of herself—water, food, clothes. Sometimes cigarettes. Sometimes *siment*. When she suffers a fever, which occurs frequently, she buys aspirin and a cupful of *tizàn*, a medicinal herbal broth.

Bèl Marie is unique among street children in her conscious efforts to save her money, hiding a few gourdes each week in a *kachèt* [secret place] so that she can make enough to buy a few guinea hens that she will someday send to her grandmother in Gonaïves to raise for her. She says that guinea hens are *tankou labank* [like a bank] and can be sold later on so that she can have enough money to buy a little house in the countryside far from the city and its streets. Looking forward to a life beyond this one on the pavement is a rare ambition for a street child in Haiti. Most concede that they will be on the street their entire lives. So as Bèl Marie saves to buy guinea hens to buy a house, Ti Amos sends money to his extended kin to buy a pig so that they can someday sell it to pay for his body to be properly buried when he dies, likely on the street.

Each night, Ti Amos follows Bèl Marie and the other girls with whom she sleeps to their meeting place at the entrance to the cemetery. There they gather together the day's take of food and money so that it may be shared. She tells me they often sniff glue after eating to help them *bliye lamizè-nou* [forget their misery] and go to sleep. Bèl Marie and Ti Amos then go with the other girls to a weedy piece of earth nearby and curl up to go to sleep. Sometimes she and the other children sleep in the cemetery between the crypts, especially if they need to hide themselves from older street boys who are looking to have sex with them. She tells me that she got her first period last year, which frightened her because she didn't understand what was happening. Other street girls explained that it meant that she was a woman now, and taught her to tuck scavenged squares of cloth or paper in her underwear to keep her clothes as clean as possible, and to periodically remove her underpants altogether and squat to let the flow drain onto the pavement. This initiation into womanhood has intensified her fears of rape and pregnancy. She hasn't been raped yet, but she is fearful of the prospect and is certain that it will happen to her in the future. Though she worries about the violence of the assault itself, she worries more about getting pregnant. She knows several older girls who have gotten pregnant as a result of a rape. While some of these girls are able to send their babies to relatives, many of them have no family to take the child. I have seen some of these young women nursing their babies on the street like tragic boulevard Madonnas.

Bèl Marie's past conflicts with other street girls stokes her everyday fear that they will someday come in the night to kill her. Although she doesn't fight with street boys ("*Y'ap osi potorik*" she tells me. "They're too strong"), she worries about them because she knows of many girls who have been brutalized by boys under the cover of night, sexually and otherwise. She also worries about the Haitian National Police Anti-Gang troopers, some of whom harbor a special dislike for street children who sniff *siment*. The most notorious troopers are known by name in the neighborhood as they have a regular habit of kicking and beating street children, or worse, when they catch them sleeping unawares at night.

Though her fears are many, they are not in themselves what make Bèl Marie's life as hard as it is. It is *petit bagay*, she says; the little things. She has some trouble sleeping under normal circumstances for example, but finds it most difficult when it rains. Rainwater can be an insidious harassment to street children who cannot always find overhead shelter from it, especially at night. She has a sweater to keep the damp chill from shivering her body, but most children don't invest their money in such warm clothing, and Bèl Marie shares this garment throughout the rainy evenings with the girls with whom she is sleeping. She also shares a cotton bed sheet that she found last year, but it is difficult to keep it dry let alone clean.

For Bèl Marie there is nothing of redeeming value about the street. Unlike most of the street boys I know, there is nothing at all that she likes about her life on the pavement. "*Tout bagay lari se ap mechan*" [Everything about the street is bad], she tells me. Contrary to the perspective held by many street boys, Bèl Marie sees herself as having fewer freedoms now than she did when she was a young girl living under the roof of her natal home a lifetime ago when she could rely on the certainty of a mother and a father who loved and cared for her. On the street, she says, she cannot freely sleep, she cannot freely eat, she cannot freely live. She tells me that if she could find a safer place to live she would go. She is afraid of the shelters in Port-au-Prince because there are so many boys in those places, and she can often eat better food by working with the vendors and sharing with other street girls. She tells me that no children who live on the street sleep well, few eat well, and most are treated harshly by other street kids, policemen, and ordinary passersby. Some like herself have family that they can go to but do not. "This is not a life," she says wearily.

Toward the end of our conversation, Bèl Marie grows tired and dazed from the glue she has been sniffing, but she still speaks lucidly. As she rises dozily to leave, she claps the street dust from her dress and smoothes the wrinkled pleats across her lap. *"M'ta ap vle mouri pase pou vi lari-a. Konsa m'pa konne poukisa m'vi jodi-a,"* she says. "I would rather die than live on the street. So I don't know why I am alive today."

Is the author helping these children?

Ritus Ruptus

The Street as a Site of Passage

In 1909 Arnold van Gennep described the basic features of the ritual process by which an individual moves from one social identity to another, defining such *rites de passage* as those "which accompany a passage from one situation to another or from one cosmic or social world to another"(1960: 10). Victor Turner summarizes the three stages through which an initiate passes during the course of the ritual:

> The first phase of separation comprises symbolic behavior signifying the detachment of the individual or group either from an earlier fixed point in the social structure or a set of cultural conditions (a "state"); during the intervening liminal period, the state of the ritual subject (the "passenger") is ambiguous; he passes through a realm that has few or none of the past or coming state; in the third phase the passage is consummated. The ritual subject, individual or corporate, is in a stable state once more and, by virtue of this, has rights and obligations of a clearly defined and "structural" type, and is expected to behave in accordance with certain customary norms and ethical standards. (1967: 94)

These respective phases are identified by van Gennep as *separation, transition* (or *limen*), and *reaggregation*. Rituals that mark the transformation from childhood to adulthood are classic anthropological examples of the kinds of rites that van Gennep is describing. Among the Nandi of Kenya, boys are ushered into adulthood through pubescent circumcision rituals. At sunset on the evening of the circumcision, the boy-initiates are led out of the village and into the bush by initiated men (separation). They remain sequestered from the community until they are circumcised in the predawn hours of the following day. They remain in the bush until their wounds have healed. While there the initiates receive formal instruction in traditional lore. Throughout this period of seclusion, the initiates are considered neither boys (as uncircumcised boys are not permitted to attend this phase of the ritual), nor are they considered men until the completion of their instruction and triumphal return to the village. This phase of the ritual constitutes the *transition* or *limen*. The reintroduction of the now-circumcised and thus newly minted men to the village constitutes their *reaggregation* into the village as members of one of seven age-sets and bearers of a new identity and all of the rights and privileges that come with being a man (Oboler 1996).

In the sections that follow I will demonstrate how the identity of *timoun lari* is the result of an interrupted rite of passage whereby domiciled children are transformed into a liminal state where they remain and are generally vilified variously as aberrations, monstrosities, or social threats, and in all cases as *nonpersons*. Insofar as all rites, initiatory or otherwise, must take place in some form of ritual space, I will discuss the street as the transitional "site of passage" for street-child identity formation in Haiti—an unstructured space of seclusion and marginalization where liminal identities have been assumed after old ones have been shed, without any promise of a full reaggregation back into structured society with the status, rights, and privileges that come with being a full Haitian "person." Is the street then the site of a *ritus ruptus*, a ritual of passage interrupted at the limen? Are Haitian street children separated from their domiciled identity and simply abandoned in the limen where they remain stalled, devoid of structural identity, lost in the transition to full adult personhood? Or is there some resolution to their liminality, some eventual reaggregation of these children into the social structure and the cultural community?

To get to the answers to such questions, we will need to follow the course that children take as they move from their homes and onto the pavement and beyond. I begin with a discussion of the factors that contribute to the displacement (separation) of children from their homes and into the liminal space of the street.

Separation: Some Observations on the General Features of Child Displacement

In spite of the variable and relative contexts within which each street child lives and is perceived, some observations can be made about the lot of street children generally, especially with regard to the means by which they end up on the street in the first place. Despite a devastated economy and some of the most ominous indicators for child welfare, it is not the case that all children in Haiti have the same likelihood of ending up on the street. While it is both unreasonable and impossible to construct a predictive profile of a child bound for street life in all cases and under every circumstance in Haiti (no model in the sciences, natural or social, can claim that degree of certainty), a profile can certainly be constructed of a Haitian child who runs a very high likelihood of ending up on the street, given certain conditions that seem to be common to the stories of many of the street children in Port-au-Prince with whom I have worked.

As has been seen, certain demographic factors over the past twenty-five years of Haitian history have created the economic preconditions for child displacement in Port-au-Prince. Specifically the collapse of the Haitian rural economy, the consequent decline in agricultural production, the mass exodus of disenfranchised rural peasant families to larger villages and urban centers, a coincidental rise in urban population and a depression of employment rates, and a steady decline in public health complemented by a rise in child mortality and morbidity have all been instrumental in Haiti's dramatic rise in child displacement since the 1980s. Several social and cultural factors, in part or in sum, dramatically increase the chances that a child will become displaced from his/her natal household onto the street, when considered along with the larger national demographic pressures that have made Haitian youths more vulnerable to displacement than youths in other developing nations in general.

1. *A domestic arrangement marked by a fractured kin group, broadly defined, which disrupts or otherwise prevents the stable and reliable exchange of goods and services (such as child care) among its members.* Haitian kin groups are like extended support networks. Families survive by taking advantage of systems of exchange and distribution among and between relatives. When that social support system fractures and members of the family leave the home permanently or die, the likelihood that the children will end up on the street increases.

2. *A domestic arrangement marked by an unstable household economy, where no member is employed in the formal or informal economy or where too few household members are employed to reliably support all members of the household in their sum.* In such cases children's labor, often street labor, becomes essential for household economic stability. Working in the street is a first step toward sleeping there.

3. *A domestic arrangement composed of a kin unit with a high number of dependent children (especially nursing infants) relative to the house-*

hold economy. Child rearing is generally considered to be the primary obligation of motherhood, and the greater the number of dependent children the greater the likelihood that some children will need to be displaced onto the street to work and to free up household resources.

4. *A domestic arrangement characterized by an "instability of place," with significant intraregional migration of the kin group over recent time.* Most of the children with whom I have worked in Port-au-Prince have ended up there after a complicated history of family movement throughout the country, usually from rural village to rural village, ending up in the capital. From there children spend increasing amounts of time on the street, until some of them move themselves permanently there.

5. *A domestic arrangement characterized by abuse or neglect.* While not all street children come from abusive or neglectful households, many do. Domestic abuse is common and most of my child informants reported having sustained beatings from relatives before they left for the street. The severity of child abuse in Haitian households must be tempered against the fact that child rearing practices in Haiti customarily involve a measure of corporal punishment. Haitian parents often administer harsh beatings to their children, sometimes with a stick or a leather strap called a *fwèt* that is made for the purpose. Many of the children who reported to me that they had left their family home for the street because of domestic abuse cited examples of corporal punishment that frankly are rather typical of household discipline and in that respect are not usually cases of what most Haitians would call "excessive." Nonetheless I have recorded incidents of child abuse against children in their homes that were clearly brutalizations.

Add to these major factors enumerated above the incalculable number of case-specific circumstances that also increase the likelihood of child displacement, such as drug abuse or alcoholism on the part of a caregiver (which not only places an added drain on domestic resources but also statistically heightens the odds of abuse or neglect); a motivation on the part of the child to alleviate strain on the household economy by working, eating, or living part-time on the street; a desire on the part of the child for greater social or economic independence from adult norms that is promised by street life; the belief on the part of the child that she or he has no other viable option for self-preservation other than displacement onto the street. While street children's individual stories of displacement are as varied as are the children who tell them, these domestic circumstances emerge repeatedly in children's accounting of reasons for their displacement onto the street. It is critical to point out at this juncture that the considerable agency of street children is always mediated by the kinds of structural impediments outlined here. From the outset of their displacement, factors ranging from migration history, to familial relations, to domestic abuse, to limited household resources place severe constraints on the autonomous decision-making capabilities of the child who is about to become *timoun lari*. Even the child's deliberate decision to leave the house for the street never to return is one that is shaped and at least partially determined by factors beyond her or his will. While this is surely the case for children (and for many adults) generally, for the children who become displaced specifically, life decisions are even more constrained by the strictures of the deeply impoverished and profoundly unstable household from whence they come. In a way, as will be seen, many street children experience a sense of unbounded freedom once they have made the decision to leave the house for the street—freedom to go where they please, freedom to dispose of their money as they see fit, freedom to sleep and to work and to play whenever and with whomever they wish. They may also experience a flush of freedom from abuse, from poverty, and from the often restrictive rules and harsh discipline of the adult-dominated household. With their exodus from the gerontocratic home comes a liberation from the structural factors that make the deeply impoverished household so deterministic. With displacement then comes a notable increase in agency that has been previously unexpressed or unbeknownst to the child; but it comes as the child is entering the street, a new and foreign terrain that exerts its own powerfully acculturative influence at the expense of the child's newfound agency.

While most *timoun lari* are disconnected from the everyday life of family following their displacement onto the street, in Haiti the term *street child* does not necessarily presuppose orphanage or kin abandonment and many of the street children with whom I have worked have locatable kin who have not necessarily divested care of them. In fact many street kids maintain some economic relationship to the homes of their families. Some send money or other gifts of support back to their natal homes. The primary distinction of *timoun lari* in Haiti is not based upon the idea that street childhood is counterdistinctive to or separate from sheltered life, family, or home. Rather street life is a free alternative to the settled household, which is sometimes sufficiently abusive as to be regarded as anything but nurturing. For street children the pavement is a site of uneasy sanctuary from domestic violence, a place to work undirected, to live beyond the normative control of adult society, and to engage in what may be considered a "household at large." They do not regard the street as a space to live that is in opposition to home; for them the street *is* home. Milen, a street boy of around ten, explained it to me this way:

> You see, I sometimes go to my aunt's house. She raised me, you know? But when I am there, she always yelling orders to me and beating me when I don't jump to it *tout swit* [quickly]. She do this even when I bring her little things like flour or sweets. She yell to me, "TiMi! Go to get water! Get to sweeping the yard!" When I am on the street, I don't have to work for anybody but my own self. I can smoke, I can sniff [glue], I can be with my girlfriends. Man, when I get out of there back to here? I am in my *own* house, you see?

Among street children who have spent time in outreach programs that seek to "rehabilitate" them, only to return to the street, there are those who explain that the failures of the programs lie in the mistaken belief that given the opportunity, most children would eagerly leave the street for a shelter or an orphanage. Duchenel, a fifteen-year-old boy who had been in and out of at least two different outreach facilities organized and supported by European-based nongovernmental organizations, explained that the reason he left the first facility was because "there were too many rules" about when to sleep, eat, wash and work; he left the second because, he said, the over-crowded conditions of the place made it feel "too much like my mother's house," which he left when he was around ten for a life on the street. "I don't have a house, but I have this street," he tells me. "And these guys here [he gestures to two other boys with whom he works and sleeps], they are like my brothers. We take care of each other." The larger problem of "rehabilitating" street children is the availability of the opportunity for work in the formal sector when rehabilitation is completed. Chapter 5 will explore this problem in greater detail.

The Intimacy and Liminality of the Street

However they end up there, for the children who sleep on the street in Port-au-Prince the term *timoun lari*—street child—is one that first relates to a given child's relationship to the street, not necessarily to their legal age or whether they actually sleep on the street full time. *Timoun lari* comport themselves to the street on an ontological level that is dramatically different from that of other children who have co-opted the public spaces of the capital on somewhat less intimate terms—as merely a place to play or to pass through for example. This relational intimacy between *timoun lari* and the street, characterized by the street's status as the primary site of acculturation, is one that extends well beyond a child's use of it merely for work, sleep, or socializing. Indeed nearly all poor Port-au-Prince dwellers use the pavement in such ways for greater or lesser periods of time throughout the day and evening. Street children relate to the street as the site of their individual physical development (through puberty and adolescence) as well as an acculturative institution central to their social and cultural development, as it shapes how they conceive of themselves in relation to the larger political economy of urban life. Whereas vendors, market women and craftsmen might use the street in ways not unlike those of street children (for work, for sleep, for socializing), the street remains only a field for social interaction to them insofar as their cultural identity is largely developed elsewhere—in a home, within the context of a family, as part of the construction of a larger, settled, community identity. For street children the city is not so much a thing to be molded and transformed to suit their needs as adult migrants from the countryside mold and transform it; rather it is the street that is the social and symbolic force that molds and transforms their identity and agency.

In this sense Port-au-Prince streets are liminal spaces, sites of passage that are akin to otherwise rites of passage that shape and transform child identity. A similar approach to conceiving "the street" has been taken up before. The geographer Hugh Matthews describes it as "a liminal setting or a site of passage, a place that both makes possible and signifies a means of transition through which some young people move away from the restrictions of their childhood roots towards the independence of adulthood"; he goes on to argue that "the street is infused with cultural identity," and is a place where young people frequently collide with adults and with other groups of young people. Confrontations of this sort are the rituals of transition within the socially *barbed spaces* of the street" (Matthews 2003: 101, emphasis in original). While Matthew's study area is a blighted, low-income public housing estate in an East Midlands town in England, none of his child informants were street children and as such their relationship to the street was limited to its utility as a place to play or meet friends but not as a place to work or sleep. Moreover, given that his informants all enjoyed the security of being domiciled and sheltered by adults after leaving the street at the end of the day, they surely engaged the street as a liminal space in a far less intimate way than do street kids. In writing about Paraguayan street children in Asunción, Benno Glauser has also described "the street" as a site of transition and socialization for some children. He describes it as a "realm of change and transition," and a site of socialization for the children who grow up there (1990: 158–59).

Victor Turner (1967) has pointed out in his classic essay "Betwixt and Between: The Liminal Period in *Rites de Passage*" that the transitional states between social statuses in rites of passage are "essentially unstructured" and marked by the isolation of initiates from the larger community of which they are a part for the duration of the transition. Here the streets inhabited by *timoun lari* fit that description as similarly unstructured sites where some—in this case, street children—are isolated or at the least marginalized in the urban community. As has been seen the streets of Port-au-Prince are essentially disorderly and disorganized spaces in marked contrast to the at least nominal structure of the social institutions (like the markets, families, the police and the law) that pervade and surround it. Turner goes on to point out that "the symbolism attached to and surrounding the liminal *personae* is complex and bizarre. . . . They give an outward and visible form to an inward and conceptual process. . . . Insofar as they are no longer classified, the symbols that represent them are, in many societies, drawn from the biology of death, decomposition, catabolism and other physical processes that have a negative tinge" (1967: 96). Moreover, since the social status of such liminal *personae* are at once "structurally 'invisible' (though physically visible) and ritually polluting, they are commonly secluded, partially or completely, from the realm of culturally defined and ordered states and statuses. . . . They have a physical but not social 'reality,' hence they have to be hidden, since it is a paradox, a scandal, to see what ought not to be there" (1967: 98).

Seen as an uncannily consistent analogy to Turner's notion of the liminal state and the polluting attributes accorded to those who inhabit it, the street as a liminal space in Port-au-Prince and the generally negative regard with which most of the city's denizens hold for the children who inhabit it is illustrative when sorting out the ideas of personhood (or the lack thereof) that are accorded to *timoun lari* as a social group. I was routinely admonished by passersby who would see me at work with kids on the street. Some would see me speaking with street children who are known glue-sniffing addicts and would shout to me things on the order of "Stay away from them, *blanc*! They are filthy!" and "Those kids will make you ill!" and "What could you want with them, *blanc*? They are *zombi*!" The association of street children (especially glue-sniffers) with the *zombi*—a body without a soul, without will, without autonomy, without agency—is a common theme among the citizens of Port-au-Prince, especially those who live or work in the closest proximity to street children in the worst of the capital's slum districts where they typically congregate. In these neighborhoods such street children exist all at once in the spatial, social, and cultural margins of the urban community: haunting the gutters of the most destitute slums, stripped of any social or civil rights, and tabooed as *zombi*, which itself exists in a perpetual limen (it is an animated dead body, welcome neither in the world of living "persons" nor in *Ginen*, the realm of the souls of the deceased and the spirits). Street children, like the *zombi*, continue to maintain their physical visibility, but their agency has been rendered invisible. They are the walking dead.

Where they are not constructed as *zombi*, they are virtually ignored or subsumed by the streetscape they occupy—they are structurally "invisible"—or they are maligned as the primary causes for the escalation of urban ills. In this manner it is marginalization of street children as liminal polluting entities that is underscored. As will be seen, it is this community tendency to coidentify *timoun lari* with street violence, urban blight and decay, community contamination, and other social decompositions, or to ignore them utterly (as was glimpsed in the previous chapter), that is not only most commonly found in the public rhetoric but in the actions of the state against street kids as well. As street children are subjected to the malign and marginalization of the Port-au-Prince citizenry and the state, so emerges among groups of them a sense of "unstructured or rudimentarily structured and relatively undifferentiated *comitatus*, community or even communion of equal individuals who submit together to the general authority" (Turner 1969: 96); in this case, the citizenry that derides them and the state that targets them. Turner uses the term *communitas* to describe this unique sense of liminal collectivity in the face of authority. Expressions of communitas among street kids in Haiti are most readily observed in the camaraderie of their friendship groups, the commonality of their sleeping arrangements, their socialized sense of wealth, and the generalized reciprocal nature of their economic exchanges. All of these will be explored in detail in the coming chapters.

None of this is to argue that *timoun lari* constitute a homogenous subculture of Haitian urban society, all of whom would chose to sleep rough even if they had viable alternatives; *viable* of course meaning that such alternatives would meet their needs both physically and in terms of their desires for some degree of self-determination. The Lafanmi Selavi program, discussed in chapter 5, may have been an example of one such alternative. Unfortunately and as will be seen in that chapter, the program failed in spectacularly violent fashion before its vision could be realized, in the midst of a confrontation of politics that had little to do with the intrinsic value of its philosophy and approach to street-child outreach.

Reaggregation in the Limen: The Transformation of Identity in the Site of Passage

I have argued that street childhood is an identity forged through an intimate experience of the liminal space of the street. There are parallels that can be identified between a child's movement from the home to the street and the phenomenon of separation and transition characteristic of rites of passage. We have seen how following a child's departure from his home and onto the boulevards, the child exists in a liminal world in which his identity is ever-transformed from what it was; furthermore, that existence may be characterized as a form of isolation, seclusion, and marginalization not unlike that experienced by an initiate in a rite of passage. And like that initiate, the child who occupies the liminal space of the street is often regarded as every bit polluting, dangerous, and taboo. As Turner has pointed out, though liminal individuals have a physical reality, they lack a cultural one in that they are socially invisible until reaggregated into their community with their new identities acquired with their passage through the transition.

So what of the street child in Haiti? Does our analogy of his plight to that of the initiate end here, in the limen? In a sense yes, it does. Insofar as few *timoun lari* ever make it out of the site of passage that is the street, their physical occupation of that unstructured and transitional space often is a lifelong one. It would be easy to say that such children end up forever stalled in a liminal state without any further actualization of personhood, never to reaggregate into society with an identity other than that of their liminal one. This is not in fact the case. While most *timoun lari* end up spending their entire lives in the limen of the street, some manage to successfully leave the pavement to reunite with family or to enter an orphanage or shelter. Some of these children eventually find their way into school. Others succeed in securing a job and occasionally an independent home for themselves, enabling them to shed their street-child identity and integrate themselves into the mainstream Haitian economy. There are also children who leave the street in less encouraging ways, by entering a brothel or ending up in prison, thereby trading the mark of the street child for that of the prostitute or the prisoner. For the vast majority of street kids, however, the street remains their home for the duration of their lives. While these children may never escape the spatial liminality of the street, they inevitably will as they grow older acquire new identities: *travayè lari* [an adult who works and lives on the street], *epav* [beggar], *vakabon* [vagabond], *diyè* [drug dealer], *kriminèl* [common criminal]. Tragically, many street children leave the boulevard by dying or being killed on it. In all of these cases, street kids complete their rite of passage from childhood to adulthood or from childhood to death, without ever leaving the site of that passage—the street.

Blak Louli

Blak Lovli doesn't have a birthday. He thinks he is around sixteen, but he is unsure of his exact age because he doesn't know the month let alone the year of his birth. He's a very likable boy—polite, attentive, and eager to tell every detail of his hard life on the street. That life has clearly taken a physical toll on his body. A large curving scar extends along his scalp and ends halfway down his forehead, the result of a razor fight in which he was involved. Several mottled burn scars cover the tops of his feet and a number of his teeth have been lost to decay.

He has been on the street since the late 1980s, and he recalls his arrival in Port-au-Prince coinciding with "*letan apre Jean-Claude*," the period right after Jean-Claude Duvalier left power in 1986. Though both his mother and his father live in Port-au-Prince, Blak Lovli is quite clear on his reasons for preferring the street to that of his natal household. He says that he was often locked in the house and beaten for what he considered to be small infractions, such as not returning with water in a timely fashion when he was sent to fetch some. He has two sisters and three brothers, all of whom live with extended family in the countryside and all of whom attend school. I ask him why he does not go to live with them. He tells me that there is not enough money for him to be taken care of and that there is certainly not enough money for him to go to school.

Blak Lovli's own educational history is so brief as to be inconsequential. He never attended school prior to ending up on the street and spent only three months in classes at a street-child outreach center before voluntarily leaving because he found the lessons discouraging. He can neither read nor write even the most rudimentary words and he cannot verbally spell his own name. His illiteracy is the source of all of his frustrations with school.

Given the absence of opportunity afforded him for a viable education, Blak Lovli has opted to stay in Port-au-Prince where he says that he makes a little bit of money, "enough to survive," he says. His labor is typical of street children in Port-au-Prince. He washes cars and wipes windshields with friends and carries groceries for patrons of the small convenience market where he congregates with his comrades. He sometimes begs as well, though he customarily resorts to this only when he is not feeling well enough to work.

Blak Lovli smokes cigarettes almost constantly, a habit he picked up years ago when he used to hang out with older street boys who would send him to buy cigarettes and then make him light them for them. On special occasions like Carnival, he might indulge in a small cup of moonshine rum, but not often. He is a casual glue-sniffer, though he never buys the stuff with his own money and in fact only uses it when he is with some habitual sniffers he knows who offer it to him. Though he sees these friends infrequently (they work in another section of the city), when he does he might ask for *"de souf osnon twa"* [two sniffs or three] from the bottles of the other children. He points out that he prefers to save his money for food and cigarettes rather than *"gaspiye sa"* [waste it] on *siment*.

By far most of Blak Lovli's money goes to food and as is the case with most of the street children that I have known, he manages to eat with greater frequency than many poor but domiciled Haitian children. On average he eats three small meals a day. At night he eats his largest meal, usually bread, hard boiled eggs, and a bottle of Juna (a sweet, viscous fruit juice) or a can of sweetened condensed milk.

He suffers fevers rather frequently—his forehead is almost always warm to the touch—and he often suffers long and painful bouts of diarrhea. He goes weeks at a time drinking unclean water that he purchases from vendors who sell it by the cupful from buckets that they fill from filtered, but not treated, sources.

Blak Lovli owns very little beyond the clothes on his back. His T-shirt, trousers, and sandals are the garden variety tattered rags of Haiti's young and displaced poor, purchased for a few gourdes in the markets that sell such clothes to street children on the cheap. He knows that his clothes are priced very inexpensively compared to the clothes that school children wear. He says with some shame that the clothes that he buys are "not very good" and are usually ripped and somewhat dirty when purchased. The fact that garments that are too stained or are unmendable are earmarked by sellers in the market for sale to street kids offers evidence of the normalization of their lot in Port-au-Prince. Blak Lovli sees little reason to invest much money in nice things, especially clothes, because possession of attractive goods invites cruel attention from older street boys. He once saved his money for weeks to buy a brand new pair of tennis shoes, only to have them stolen from his feet by another street boy as he slept mere days after he had purchased them.

Blak Lovli shares the common street-child perspective that both food and money should be shared among peers, including older homeless folk who either beg or work alongside him. His exchange of money and goods with his friends is reciprocal and contributes to the maintenance of protective friendships among a handful of street kids in his neighborhood.

He sleeps in front of the brightly lit Commerce Building on Boulevard Jean-Jacques Dessalines, in a neighborhood on the rough frontier of Portail Léogâne, though he doesn't sleep in the same place all of the time. He tries to avoid developing a pattern to where he settles at night as a defense against the police who he fears will arrest him for vagabondism. On occasion Blak Lovli forgoes sleep altogether, particularly if nighttime activities can offer the chance of making more money after dark. This is usually the case during Carnival, when the celebrations provide street kids ample opportunities to make money, drink moonshine rum, and temporarily negate their lives of scarcity.

Blak Lovli has had several encounters with the National Police and is routinely searched for drugs and weapons by the paramilitary Anti-Gang Unit, but he has never been arrested, and he recalls only one occasion when policemen beat him. At that time he was sleeping in a vacant market stall in Portail Léogâne when three Anti-Gang officers kicked him awake and ordered him to his feet. As he rose the troopers beat him with batons about his head and torso. He says of that incident, *"yo te frap'm fasil"* [they beat me easily, but not so badly] and told him to sleep somewhere else. Aside from this instance and in spite of it, Blak Lovli believes that the police afford him a modicum of protection. He tells me stories of individual officers who have intervened in street fights on his behalf, who have given him food or money, or who have arrested older boys who have stolen from or beaten him.

Like many street kids, Blak Lovli regards sleep as a fearful and dangerous necessity. He considers harassment by state officers to be little more than an occasional inconvenience, his greatest anxieties stemming from molestation by animals and malicious youths. He explains that there are times when he is awakened by swarms of roaches that had come to eat crumbs from his lips and cheeks. He points to a small scar on his lip; it is, he explains, a rat bite. But his fear of these pests is secondary to his dread of the *lagè domi*—the sleeping wars of which he is a hardened veteran.

Sometime in the late 1990s, Blak Lovli got embroiled in a fistfight with another street boy named Franzi who had taken money from him. Beaten roughly by his foe, Blak Lovli solicited the assistance of older youths that he knew who sought and delivered retribution on his behalf. When Blak Lovli encountered Franzi later that day, he was informed that their differences would now be settled with a sleeping war. Several evenings had passed before Blak Lovli was jarred awake by Franzi, who was burning an empty juice bottle over him and allowing the molten plastic to drip onto his bare feet. Days later Blak Lovli took vengeance. After finding Franzi asleep in a secluded alleyway, he dropped a large chunk of concrete onto the head of his foe, nearly killing him. Franzi was found by a merchant early the next morning and taken to the state hospital where he made a moderate recovery. Their *lagè domi* is over now.

On another occasion Blak Lovli was severely beaten by a group of older boys after he refused to turn over his day's earnings. This was not the first time that he had been assaulted by older boys, but it was the worst. His ribs were bruised, he lost some teeth, and his head was banged hard enough against the pavement to cause him to lose consciousness. He couldn't work for several days thereafter. Though no street child grows accustomed to beatings, Blak Lovli was familiar with them prior to ending up on the street. When living in his parent's home, he was routinely beaten by his mother and father and occasionally by his sisters and brothers as well.

The jagged scar along his scalp and forehead is the result of yet another violent clash with another street boy. In 1998, too sick with fever to work, he was begging alongside another boy on the street. A foreign tourist gave Blak Lovli a U.S. dollar bill, but gave the other boy nothing. The other boy asked Blak Lovli to share the money, but he refused. Angered, the other boy wrestled Blak Lovli to the ground, pulled a razor blade from the cuff of his pants and slashed him across the scalp. After taking the dollar bill the boy ran off, leaving Blak Lovli bleeding on the sidewalk.

Blak Lovli has a brief history of political involvement, which begins and ends with the Cedras coup d'etat from 1991 to 1994. During that time he participated actively in several demonstrations against the regime. His role was limited to throwing rocks at soldiers from afar and breaking the windows of army vehicles during prodemocratic marches. Though never arrested for political crimes, he has been beaten by army *attachés* for sleeping in the street after dark during the coup, his homelessness a violation of the de facto government's urban curfew.

Despite a long history of violent victimization by the police, the paramilitaries, the *attachés*, and other street boys, Blak Lovli carries no weapon himself. He tells me that at one time he carried a razor for protection, but lost it and never bothered to replace it. When pressed, he admits to throwing rocks at old enemies from a distance when he sees them, but it is clear that experience has left him fearful of instigating new clashes. He understands that violent encounters with other street children are not isolated instances, but rather have a temporal depth that allows any affront or confrontation to extend well into the future. His sentiments concerning fighting are best expressed in his own words: "*M'grangou. M'pa vle mouri.*" It means, "I'm simply hungry. I don't want to die."

Zenglendinaj e Arimaj

The Street-Child "Problem" and the Paramilitary Solution

It would be incredibly difficult to overstate the suffusion and intensity of violence in Haiti. This country is overarmed and heavily militarized. A 2005 assessment conducted by the Small Arms Survey found that there are in the neighborhood of 209,000 small arms and light weapons in the country, distributed among a bewildering array of armed groups: civilians, the police and its paramilitary wings, the coast guard, popular organizations, youth gangs, organized criminal gangs, resistance fronts, pro-opposition groups, former military, death squads, government security units, petty criminals, prison escapees, "zero tolerance" political groups, self-defense militias, private security companies, and children (Small Arms Survey 2005: 29). Fire, sticks, rocks, knives, machetes, and explosives are just as likely to kill or maim in Haiti as firearms. Dozens of Haitians are killed and scores are wounded each month in political, protopolitical, and criminal attacks. Arson, torture, rape, dismemberment, necklacing, and summary street execution have long been a part of the tradition of civil conflict in the country, and more recently kidnapping and beheadings have been added to the lexicon of political difference. Armed gangs roam the most destitute of slums and kill, steal, beat, and pillage with impunity. Entire units of demobilized soldiers control whole towns and villages with the authority of their machine guns alone. Bystanders are routinely ripped apart in the crossfire between competing factions gunning out their differences in the street at midday. To simply live in Haiti is to run a greater risk of violent death than anywhere else in the Caribbean.

Since the Duvalier dictatorships, which stretched across two generations from 1957 to 1986, the use of state violence has routinely violated the "cultural code" that traditionally excepted certain individuals from attack: children, the elderly, entire families, women, high-level civil servants, members of ideological institutions (such as schools and churches), "notables" (such as judges, clergymen, physicians, literary authors, artists, and village elders), and even individuals and groups that could not be defined in explicitly political terms—entire towns, soccer teams, social clubs, or persons who simply shared a personal, not a political, relationship with a state target (Trouillot 1990: 167–68). Indeed today no one is exempted as a possible victim of violent assault or death. The violence in the country has grown to such a frighteningly feverish pitch that there are whole slum neighborhoods in Port-au-Prince that Kevlar-clad, heavily panoplied, armored Humvee-driving U.N. peacekeeping units simply will not enter because the threat of massive attack by gunfire is too great. The situation has grown so chronic that the violence is now threatening to topple the country utterly. A microcosm of the current crisis can be found in the violent stance that the Haitian state has taken against street children in some of the deadliest slums in Port-au-Prince.

Working the Street: Portail Léogâne

State-sponsored violence against street children in Haiti is concentrated in Port-au-Prince, especially in the crowded pedestrian districts like Portail Léogâne, one of the city sectors where I conducted the bulk of my field research. Situated near the southern entrance to Boulevard Jean-Jacques Dessalines in the neighborhood of the National Cemetery, Portail Léogâne is a crowded and congested place, the boarding area for the *tap-taps* [rattletrap public buses] to Léogâne, a town about twenty miles west of the capital. It is a destitute and loathsome place, where sewage runs raw and uncontained through street gutters and into homes, where rats and roaches abound, and where the air fairly vibrates in anticipation of the next unleashing of gunfire. In the late 1990s the sector became a maelstrom of civil and political gun violence, which continues to bark out in sputters at unpredictable times, prompting locals to refer to the neighborhood uneasily as "Kosovo." For the past five years urban gangsterism, gunplay, and drug terrorism have intensified, leading to violent, chaotic sweeps by tactical units of the Haitian National Police (PNH). Portail Léogâne is also home to over a hundred or so street children who range in age from four to eighteen years.

Most of the kids in Portail Léogâne (they are mostly boys, but there are quite a few girls here as well) are *siment* sniffers and many tote razors called *jilet* [from the disposable razor manufacturer "Gillette"] that they have scavenged from trash piles. Some of the kids have vicious scars from fights with them. Though they keep the things primarily for grooming (shaving their heads, trimming their fingernails), the children who sniff *siment* have a tendency to brandish them with little provocation. These children are difficult and frequently dangerous to approach, but the perspective that they offer the anthropologist is invaluable insofar as these kids are clearly comported

to the street in a manner profoundly different than that of other street children.   *dangerous – why do it ?*

My strategy for working with these kids was to enter Portail Léogâne
touni [naked]—no camera, no recorder, no bags, and often no notebook or
pen. I was careful to scan the field discreetly for poorly concealed pistols,
unsheathed machetes, paramilitary agents, and other potential dangers. I
wore my shirt untucked at all times, in order to give the impression that I
could be armed, not only because my lack of a weapon seemed to put me
in the minority in Portail Léogâne, but vulnerable to attack as well. Field
techniques like this were informed by a minute-to-minute reassessment of
what was going on around the neighborhood and adjusted accordingly. One
moment I could speak freely with street children and perhaps take notes. But
the next moment, suddenly under the scrutiny of police agents, we would
have to *pa dan nou* [shut our mouths], hide the notes, and let the anxious,
sweaty silence that now prevailed bespeak the volumes of data that hours
of testimony could never provide. Because silence can operate as a survival
strategy (Green 1995), it is not simply a symptom of fear but is an aspect of
cultural reality and as such is a valuable piece of datum.

Because older street boys in Portail Léogâne had a tendency to tightly,
and at times menacingly, surround me as an expression of their authority, I
made every attempt to keep my back to the wall, with the boys and the street
in front of me. I occasionally had to abort an interview with a street kid in
Portail Léogâne after he or others would grow impatient for money and
threaten me. Other times, if the interview environment was growing palpa-
bly dangerous with the threat of gunplay or rock-throwing in the surrounding neighborhood, I would retreat with a few children by taxi to Champ de
Mars, the large, open, and mostly safe plaza just outside of Portail Léogâne
near the National Palace. There we would continue our conversations.

These kinds of hostile circumstances and the desperation with which they
come have contributed to the Haitian state's hard-line position on fighting
a war against a young, displaced, and poor populace among whom street
children are its most numerous casualties. It is not the petty crime and violence of street children per se that has prompted the current crackdowns by
the PNH and its paramilitary Anti-Gang Unit (AGU). It is rather a recent
escalation of the more severe forms of street terror for which street children
are typically (though mistakenly) held responsible. As opposed to the strictly
junior-grade criminal activity of some street youths—petty theft, pickpocketing, cutpursing—the problematic violence that is prevalent in places like
Portail Léogâne is quasi political in nature and is perpetrated by brazen,

broad-daylight assassins and violent stick-up artists. Some are organized, and have formed urban terror syndicates. *Lamè Rouj* [The Red Army]. *Lamè San Manman* [The Army of the Motherless]. *Lafanmi Kanno* [The Family of the Gun]. Some work independently or in smaller cartels, and a few have achieved individual notoriety for their neighborhood terrors and are known by their street moniker. Ti Loulou. Pouchon. Patatou. Labanyè. Colibri. Whether they are gangsters or privateers, they are collectively known in local parlance as the *zenglendo*.

Shapeshifters: The Changing Character of Violence in Port-au-Prince

Zenglendo is a compound of *zenglen* [shards of broken glass] and *do* [back] and was originally used in an old folktale told to children about the *djab*, a demon. In the story the *djab* is described as the malicious trickster, bent to the torment of children. Always seeking ways to lure youngsters into despair, the *djab* takes the form of an older person who appeals to a child to massage the tired muscles of his back. When the child obliges and begins to rub the back of the elder, the *djab* transforms himself into *zenglendo*, the "glass-back." The muscles of the creature's back ripple into a twisted mess of broken glass, horribly cutting the hands of the child. The moral of the tale is clear—sometimes those that we trust can turn on us with malice.

Though *zenglendo* is used as a general signifier for various forms of gangsterism prevalent throughout Haiti today, the origins of *zenglendo* violence can be traced to the now-defunct Forces Armées d'Haïti (FADH), the Haitian army. In 1988, amid a rapid succession of coups d'etat following the fall of Jean-Claude Duvalier's dictatorship, army colonel Prosper Avril assumed control of the government by overthrowing General Henri Namphy. With Avril's ascension to power, large blocks of international aid monies to Haiti were suspended, leaving the Haitian army with little capital to pay its *ti sòlda*—the "little soldiers" of the rank and file. In response to this crisis, the *ti sòlda* began to use their weapons against the Haitian citizenry for their own enrichment, mostly through armed robbery and home invasions and with unofficial state sanction. Avril did nothing to stop this rash of violent army crimes against the civil society, as it served as an effective means for quelling what might have otherwise been a mutinous situation within the unpaid Haitian military. By the end of the 1980s the problem had worsened. In 1989 a popular radio host in Port-au-Prince coined the folkloric term *zenglendo* in describing the military offenders, implying that with their involvement in armed crimes at a time the Haitian people needed to trust state authority the most, the army had transgressed the public confidence (to say nothing of its constitutional mandate) and had turned on the populace in new and treacherous fashion.

The lucrative local drug trafficking trade has also contributed significantly to the proliferation of *zenglendinaj*. The use of Haiti as a primary transshipment point for cocaine by the Colombian Cali cartel dates to Avril's zenglendist regime of the mid 1980s. Profits from the estimated $250 million a year in contraband drug traffic through Haiti's ports has long been considered a perquisite of high rank in the army. Those profits were exploited even more by the regime of Raoul Cedras, who turned to cocaine transshipment as a means of maintaining his 1991–94 military government in the midst of an international embargo against the country. In early 1994, during the waning days of the Cedras coup, Patrick Elie (then the coordinator of Haiti's antidrug campaign) delivered a press briefing at the Haitian Embassy in Washington, D.C., at which he referred to drug trafficking as the "engine" that drove the Haitian army and overwhelmed the island's commerce with numbers-running, smuggling, and money-laundering operations. He went on to point out that the Cedras coup guaranteed a "quantum leap" in the trade, involving government agencies of public service and state-controlled institutions such as the Port Authority, which regulates not only imports and exports, but access to the civilian and military airports as well (Elie 1994: 163–64).

With the movement of several former officers of FADH into the higher ranks of the National Police, cocaine profiteering has passed from the disbanded army and into the PNH. In June 2001 the Haitian government announced that a high-ranking officer from the PNH's Anti-Drug Trafficking Brigade (ADTB) was detained on suspicion of corruption and accused of embezzling over $700 thousand from a drug seizure operation at the National Airport. In February 2003 Evans Brillant (then Haiti's drug czar and the director of the ADTB) and five other National Police officers were arrested on narco-trafficking charges. Brillant allegedly ordered his officers to block off a stretch of Route 9 on the outskirts of Port-au-Prince and to allow a Colombian light aircraft carrying 1,760 to 2,200 pounds of cocaine to land on the highway. The arrests came shortly after U.S. drug enforcement officials urged President Aristide to remove several officers from the PNH ranks after they were conclusively linked to the regional cocaine trade. The Haitian government responded by canceling visas for nearly a dozen senior police administrators (one a high-ranking officer of the Presidential Guard) and lawmakers.

During the Cedras regime, *zenglendo* functioned as a loose paramilitary, most of them off-duty soldiers of FADH. They were encouraged and protected by the Haitian army and often worked in complicity with neighborhood vigilance brigades and death squads for personal profit. Their close relationship to FADH is exemplified by the term used to describe those *zenglendo* in particular who cooperated with military agendas and who were outfitted and protected by FADH—*attaché*, meaning, "attached to" the Haitian army. While the exact relationship between *attachés* and FADH during the Cedras coup are yet unclear, there was a notable coincidence of targets between the two groups. Both singled out prodemocracy activists and supporters of the Lavalas party of then-exiled president Jean-Bertrand Aristide for violence. Eventually paramilitary *zenglendo* began to recruit poor civilians to assist them in the commission of their crimes, allowing the phenomenon of *zenglendinaj* to pass into the civil sector.

With the restoration of a tentative democratic order following the U.S.-led U.N. invasion in September 1994, the Haitian army was officially disbanded, decentralizing control of cocaine interchange. The result was a fragmentation of the local trade, with former army officers colluding with civilian lieutenants in the formation of autonomous criminal gangs that have since diversified themselves into other areas of criminal activity that use zenglendist tactics of home invasion, car-jacking, armed robbery, and conspiratorial execution.

Occasionally *zenglendo* are complicit in political violence as well. Animosities between Aristide's Fanmi Lavalas party and the Democratic Convergence (Haiti's sixteen-party opposition front) are being hashed out in neighborhood firefights in the urban slums. Haitian politics has been reduced to a kind of handgun democracy, and *zenglendo* operatives are the parties' foot soldiers. Fanmi Lavalas has a history of farming out violence and intimidation of opposition members to *zenglendo*, including summary executions of opposition members and their sympathizers. In December 2001 Brignol Lindor, the news director for Radio Eco 2000, was stoned and hacked to death by a mob of pro-Fanmi Lavalas *zenglendo* near the town of Petit-Goave. Lindor had received death threats the week before his assassination, after he invited members of the Democratic Convergence to speak on his radio show. *Zenglendo* proxies of Fanmi Lavalas have since used gunfire and barricades to shut down the capital a half-dozen times in the past two years as displays of progovernment power. The opposition party has responded in kind. In May 2003 five Fanmi Lavalas supporters were shot and killed in Cité Soleil and Fort-Liberté by members of *Lamè Sans Manman*, a *zenglendo* gang that claims ties to the Democratic Convergence.

That same month, twenty individuals were killed in street battles between *zenglendo* gangs in the Boston and Bois-Neuf neighborhoods of Cité Soleil, who are fighting for control of the slum on behalf of Fanmi Lavalas and the Democratic Convergence.

The dramatic rise in street violence over the past ten years has been due in part to the failure of state authorities to disarm and prosecute human rights violators in the aftermath of the Cedras coup d'etat. After the arrival of the U.S.-led United Nations Multinational Force in September 1994, scores of FADH soldiers deserted their barracks, taking with them thousands of automatic weapons and handguns. A 1995 report of the U.N. Commission on Human Rights suggested an interrelationship among these stolen firearms, the failure of U.N. forces to locate and confiscate these weapons, and the dramatic postinvasion rise in both criminal and political street violence that is still ongoing (U.N. Commission on Human Rights 1995). In 1995 the local police chief of Cité Soleil (a sprawling slum in Port-au-Prince) estimated the membership of *Lamè Rouj*, the dominant *zenglendo* gang in that area, to number over two hundred individuals, all of them armed with FADH weapons. Residents of Cité Soleil have suggested that the large majority of armed civilians in their neighborhoods, including some from *Lamè Rouj*, are former secret police and paramilitary who have seized upon civil distrust of the PNH—the force has been scandalized since its founding with civil and human rights violations—as an opportunity to stir up trouble and to blacken further the already dirty image of the PNH, which is widely believed to be in the pocket of Fanmi Lavalas.

Though some *zenglendo* today are former death squad operatives, soldiers and *attachés* left over from the coup regime, the term is almost completely divorced from its army and paramilitary origins and has become emblematic of a new kind of youth violence in Haiti. While the motivations have changed somewhat, the crimes are sufficiently violent as to retain the zenglendist moniker. Today's *zenglendo* are typically young, autonomous, bold, brazen, and well-armed assassins whose prime (but not always exclusive) motivation for killing is banditry and profit. They usually work alone or in pairs, frequently off the backs of motorcycles, though they have been known to push into crowded buses in order to assassinate targets on foot. They tend to operate at night but have been known to kill in broad daylight as well. Though they are known in the countryside, they pose the greatest threat to civil security in the slums and working-class districts of Port-au-Prince. In their October 1993 "Report on the Situation of Democracy and Human Rights in Haiti," The U.N./OAS International Civilian Mission detailed the activities of the *zenglendo* at the time, anticipated their relationship to corrupt elements of the PNH, and described the political ambiguity that sometimes characterize their crimes:

> The term *zenglendo* is used to refer to members of armed criminal groups, usually operating at night and particularly in the slums and working-class districts of Port-au-Prince. Some of this violence may be assumed to be purely criminal, without political motivation. However, it is widely believed in Haiti that even *zenglendo* operate under the cover or with the express tacit consent of the police and that their operation, while involving armed robberies, may also be intended to intimidate the population of localities most opposed to the post-coup authorities. (U.N./OAS International Civilian Mission in Haiti 1993)

Zenglendist violence has escalated dramatically since the end of the Cedras coup and has intensified in its brutality since 2000. Though nearly all of the violence continues to target Haitians, some *zenglendo* have singled out foreigners for assassination and kidnapping. On the night of January 11, 2000, a French businessman and his eighteen-year old daughter were killed with a Haitian companion by *zenglendo* in Jacmel, a quiet resort area in the south of Haiti. Four days later an American tourist was assassinated by a gunshot to the face when she refused to surrender her car to *zenglendo* on the outskirts of Port-au-Prince. Also that month two of the country's largest newspapers, *Le Matin* and *Le Nouvelliste*, referred to the increase in zenglendist violence against foreigners as "a new precedent." The foreign casualties were in addition to several Haitians shot to death during pre-Lenten festivities in the capital in the same month, some in broad daylight. Two months later, scores of Haitians were shot or stabbed by zenglendist assassins taking advantage of the large crowds in the streets after dark to settle old scores, some personal, some political. In three weeks in 2001 alone, two Americans were killed in *zenglendo* violence. Maureen Neilson, an acquaintance of mine and an American missionary who worked at an orphanage in Port-au-Prince, was shot to death by a *zenglendo* as she was leaving a bank in the Delmas section of the capital in March. One week later five *zenglendo* opened fire on a vehicle driven by American Alejandro Morales in a carjacking attempt. Morales was killed and his passenger wounded in the attack, when a bullet pierced his shoulder blade and lodged in his lung. These killings accounted for half the number of Americans killed in Haiti by *zenglendo* in 2001. In 2002 zenglendist murders of Americans doubled to eight. What is truly astonishing about these killings is that prior to 2000, Americans had generally been protected from violence in Haiti by their citizenship. Today, amid rising antiforeigner sentiments that are occasionally endorsed by the

Fanmi Lavalas government, Haiti is becoming a very dangerous place for Americans indeed.

Kidnappings of wealthy Haitians and foreigners by *zenglendo* have also increased in recent years, with ransoms demanded in the hundreds of thousands of dollars. In April 2001 (the same month that Morales was killed), Marc Ashton, a prominent American businessman and longtime resident of Haiti, was abducted by five *zenglendo* lying in wait for him. He managed to escape several hours later.

In some areas *zenglendinaj* has become regularized to the point that the law conforms to the dynamic of its practice instead of limiting it. Through the first two weeks of February 2000, the diaspora weekly *Haïti Progrès* reported on *zenglendo* attacks and holdups of hundreds of people on buses making the 170-mile run between Cap Haïtien and Port-au-Prince. There are several points along National Route 1 north of Port-au-Prince that are favored by *zenglendo* as points of ambush. One is at a sharp curve in the road near Gros Morne Saint Marc, a scrubby mountain about halfway down a desolate seven-mile stretch of highway between Pont Sondé and Saint Marc. Another is amid the curves just below the mountain pass of Puilboro between Plaisance and Gonaïves. In response to these holdups, the PNH has directed bus drivers to wait until three A.M. before leaving Cap Haïtien, the buses' common point of origin, for the four-hour drive into Port-au-Prince so as to arrive at Gros Morne Saint Marc (by far the most problematic of the two points of ambush) closer to the six A.M. sunrise, when the threat of holdup is diminished. Many drivers ignore the warning and leave Cap Haïtien closer to one A.M. so as to squeeze more runs into the day. Leaving at this time, the buses arrive in the ambush zones at the hours of peak risk for holdup, between three A.M. and four A.M. Though the police periodically set up weapons checkpoints in the Artibonite town of l'Estére, they are unwilling to patrol areas of substantial *zenglendo* activity along National Route 1, instead arresting bus drivers who leave Cap Haïtien before the recommended three A.M. departure time. Justifying this practice, police inspector Sénat Félix claimed that "it is the stubbornness of the drivers who leave Cap [Haïtien] before the designated hour which is the cause of the *zenglendo* being able to do whatever they want on the road."

While a great deal of *zenglendinaj* is perpetrated for criminal profit and without political motivation (most gun down citizens not over politics but simply to facilitate banditry), it is widely believed throughout Haiti that some of them are working under the protection or tacit consent of some precincts of the PNH and that their criminal activities may also be intended to intimidate those localities most opposed to the postcoup authorities.

Such accusations began in 1994, when the U.N. Commission for Human Rights suggested the complicity of the Haitian police forces with *zenglendo* attached to the FADH, who operated out of uniform but with service weapons. The report goes on to point out that *zenglendo* violence was

> aimed, in some cases at least, at intimidating sections of the democratic opposition and goes hand in hand with the upsurge in arbitrary executions for political reasons. In the working-class districts, *zenglendo* are creating a climate of general fear, for their victims are not necessarily political militants or sympathizers. . . .
>
> The [U.N. International Civilian] Mission has further reported that their investigations into [zenglendist] human rights violations have indicated that they were armed with automatic weapons (Uzis and M16s) and operated in red and white pickup vehicles, sometimes with government plates. In several cases there was information regarding a direct link between the perpetrators and the Haitian Armed Forces (FADH) and the impunity and logistical support of their operation is strongly indicative of FADH involvement. (1994: 6)

Suspicion of police collusion with the *zenglendo* is becoming increasingly apparent. Between May 19 and 21, 1999, *zenglendo* in the Poste Marchand district of Port-au-Prince went on a violent crime spree, robbing stores, houses, pedestrians, and motorists indiscriminately. Six days later in the same neighborhood, eighteen armed men sealed off two streets for two hours and, working systematically in two groups, robbed over twenty homes, frisked residents and passersby for money, stole over $300 from a small boutique, raped a woman, and shot a man in the foot. Many of the *zenglendo* involved were known to area residents, who identified the weapons used in the attacks—9mm semiautomatic handguns and .38 caliber revolvers—as identical to those issued by the PNH as service weapons. Some residents of Poste Marchand identified several of the *zenglendo* as current or former PNH officers. On June 15, 1999, seven *zenglendo* occupied Poste Marchand again, firing their weapons in the air, robbing merchants, and stealing rice, beans, and plantains from market women. It was four hours before the PNH arrived to quell the violence, by which time all of the perpetrators had fled the area (*Haïti Progrès*, June 24, 1999).

On December 21, 1999, three armed *zenglendo* invaded the medical clinic of former Social Affairs Minister Dr. Pierre Denis Amédée in Pétionville, a suburb of Port-au-Prince, making off with U.S.$400 from the clinic coffers and anything of value that could be seized from the patients in the waiting room. The following day, thirty-two-year-old Eladrès Jean François was shot

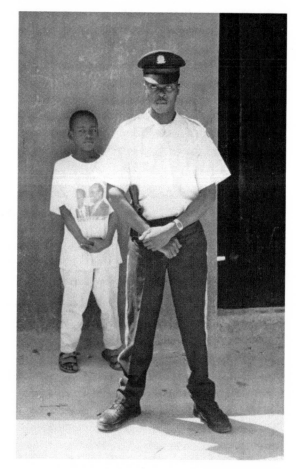

Figure 3.1. A street boy poses behind an officer of the Haitian National Police (PNH). The reputation of the PNH in Haiti has steadily deteriorated since its establishment in 1995, in part because of their alleged collusion with *zenglendo* and other criminal elements. Street children are unanimous in their fear of PNH officers, who frequently beat or arrest them for little more than sleeping on the pavement.

to death by *zenglendo* in the Avenue Fouchard area of Port-au-Prince as he was opening his bakery. At noon on the same day, two men dressed entirely in black opened fire in a crowded downtown market near Croix de Bossales in the capital, wounding seven. Later that evening, in the Linthaud section of the Cité Soleil slum district, fifty houses were burned by *zenglendo*, leaving over 270 families homeless (*Haïti Progrès*, January 4, 2000).

In late July 2001 *zenglendo* wearing the uniforms of the disbanded Haitian army launched simultaneous attacks on several National Police precincts around Haiti. Five PNH officers were killed in the attacks, fourteen were wounded, and arms and documents were stolen. The news agency Reuters reported that four former PNH officers suspected of participating in the assaults had requested political asylum in the Dominican Republic a few weeks after the attacks. The Dominican newspaper *El Listen Diario* identified these policemen as former soldiers of the Haitian army (*Haïti Progrès*, August 7, 2001).

Civil pressure on the government to eliminate the violence from the streets has prompted a violent, martial crackdown on street crime. In June 2001, during a public visit with the Inspector General of the PNH, Aristide reiterated his "zero tolerance" policy toward street violence—first announced in his February 2000 inauguration—in a speech to the National Police that appeared to endorse the summary executions of *zenglendo*:

> If it's a *zenglendo*, zero tolerance. If a *zenglendo* stops a car in the street, puts his hand on the key to make the driver get out so he can take the car, he is guilty, because the car is not his. You do not need to lead him to the court to have him judged because if the car is not his he is guilty. If a criminal grabs someone in the street by the collar and puts him on the ground to beat him or shoot him, [the police] do not need to wait to go to court with him to prevent him from doing that. (Presidential address, Port-au-Prince, June 20, 2001)

In the aftermath of his remarks, Haitian and international human rights organizations condemned the president for what they saw as an explicit presidential sanction of police extremism, brutality, arbitrary arrest, and vigilantism. Less than three months after Aristide made the "zero tolerance" speech to the PNH, Ronal Francais, a member of Mouvman Revandikatif Ayisyen pou Devlopman ak Demokrasi (MOPRADD) was ruthlessly beaten by Haitian National Police officer Jean-Marie Dominique. In an article printed in the Haitian daily newspaper *Le Nouvelliste* in late September 2001, a witness reported that officers of the Port-au-Prince district of the PNH delivered a suspected *zenglendo* into the hands of an angry mob. Within eyesight and earshot of the National Palace and the Port-au-Prince headquarters of the PNH, the suspect was stoned by the crowd, pushed to the ground, and killed with a bullet to his head (*Le Nouvelliste*, September 17, 2001).

Aristide's "zero tolerance" policy for dealing with suspected *zenglendo* and the PNH violations of human rights that it has engendered, still stands as government policy and police protocol. Amnesty International's 2003 Annual Report cited numerous cases of intimidations, extrajudicial killings, and disappearances of suspects throughout 2002. In February of that year, a PNH officer fired his service weapon indiscriminately into a crowded marketplace as he was pursuing a *zenglendo* in Port-au-Prince. One woman was killed and a pregnant woman and a child were wounded in the shooting. On June 24, 2002, Fleury Lysias of Haiti's Justice and Peace Commission was arrested without a warrant by PNH officers accompanied by three other armed men in civilian clothes. He was taken to the Bon Repos police station where he was systematically kicked and beaten with clubs (breaking one of his arms) and struck repeatedly on the ears (damaging his eardrums). Lysias was released without charges being filed the following day. On November 13, 2002, former police commissioner Jean-Louis Bourgouin was reportedly taken into custody by men in black police uniforms on a street in Pétionville. The men forced him into a vehicle with official PNH tags. He has not been seen since. On December 7, 2002, three brothers—Andy Philippe, Angélo Philippe, and Vladimir Sanon—were reportedly taken from their home in the Carrefour section of Port-au-Prince by PNH officers. Their bodies were discovered in the city morgue the next day with bullet wounds to their heads. After the parents of the boys filed a formal complaint with the public prosecutor, an internal investigation was conducted, resulting in the firing of the police commissioner and three PNH officers. One officer implicated in the incident went into hiding during the investigation to avoid arrest. Amnesty International also reported that a potential witness to the assassinations was killed by hooded men on December 17, 2002 in Carrefour (Amnesty International 2003).

Guilty by Suspicion: Street Children and *Zenglendo*

The fact that most *zenglendo* are young, poor men has contributed significantly to the popular association of street children with the rise in street violence that is at the core of Haiti's urban woes. One well-publicized incident that took place in June 1999 solidified the identification of street children with *zenglendinaj* in the Haitian public mind. An uprising of street youths at the Lafanmi Selavi orphanage in Port-au-Prince began when around forty teenagers from the facility staged a demonstration over decrepit living conditions and unfulfilled promises by the orphanage directorate that they would be assisted in getting jobs now that they had processed out of the orphanage's educational program. The demonstration escalated when the youths barred the orphanage staff from entering the compound and began throwing rocks and bottles at National Police officers sent to quell the disturbance. News reports of the incident indicated that the teenage provocateurs were armed with pistols, machetes, hand grenades, and Molotov cocktails, despite the fact that no one saw such weapons and none were recovered by police after the incident. Later in the day a tactical riot control unit of the PNH was dispatched to the orphanage, lobbed tear-gas canisters over the compound wall, and stormed the compound. Thirty youths were arrested and four were wounded in the siege.

Following the incident Dany Toussaint, a leading member of the ruling Fanmi Lavalas party and the former head of the Interim Police Force that preceded the PNH, arrived at the scene on behalf of Jean-Bertrand Aristide (the founder of the orphanage) and declared to the press that the youths were "manipulated to create disorder since we are only some days from an election," implying that the youths were put up to the occupation of the facility by partisans of the Democratic Convergence. Toussaint went on to identify several of the arrested street youths as known *zenglendo*.

Links between street childhood and innate psychological impulses to engage in acts of extreme violence have even been proposed to further indict street children of *zenglendinaj*. Dr. Legrand Bijoux, a Haitian neuropsychiatrist, argues that "it is no coincidence that we find so many armed teenagers, who have become '*zenglendo*.' He [the street child] tells himself that he has nothing to lose" (Siméon 2002). Employing a limited psychological model of analysis rather than an ethnographic one that takes anthropological factors into consideration, Bijoux explains that street children proceed through a mental state of despair to pathological zenglendist violence. He argues that, "violence calls up more violence; it is not surprising that street children turn out violent . . . violence is a pathology characterized by the conscious or unconscious wish to make others suffer what one suffered oneself. A second variant of this violence is the complex of identifying with the attacker: the person who suffered the attack nourishes hope for taking vengeance one day and it is not important whoever is the victim" (Siméon 2002).

A Haitian reporter covering street children in Port-au-Prince for the Panos Institute, a Washington-based international organization that supports journalists throughout the developing world, agrees with Dr. Bijoux's psychological association of street children with *zenglendinaj*. "The street child is more exposed to delinquency than anybody else. His moral consciousness little by little crumbles. . . . These children have no models. Delinquency expresses itself little by little; in the beginning it is only thefts, then they start to sniff thinner until this is no more sufficient. The moment for hard drugs can come and for armed attacks" (Siméon 2002).

The recruitment of street children by local gang chiefs in the commission of zenglendist violence does occur, but it is hardly common practice. Despite the fact that there is absolutely no evidence in either police reports or social experience to support the claim that street children are categorically involved in zenglendist crimes, a quiet civil sanctioning of the use of all necessary state force to quell the *zenglendo* crisis at the expense of street children (the perceived sources of the problem) has emerged. Enter the Anti-Gang Unit and the *arimaj*.

Under the Monkey's Gun

The AGU is technically a subunit of the PNH, though it has always operated in Haiti with a certain degree of autonomy from them. In fact the AGU precedes the National Police in origin by at least seven decades. It is a descendant of the Bureau de Recherche et d'Identification des Criminel (BRIC), formed in 1921 in order to institutionalize the state's domestic intelligence efforts. Largely responsible for the investigation of criminal as well as political and "social" crimes, BRIC was complemented in 1958 by the Police des Moeurs, the Morality Police, which used strong-arm tactics against the poorest classes of Haiti in a bid to eliminate pimping, prostitution, and street begging. A subunit of the Police Militaire [the Military Police] and therefore under the direction of the Haitian army, BRIC gained a measurable degree of autonomy under Jean-Claude Duvalier, remaining a military detachment but functioning independently. Duvalier formally changed the unit's name to Service d'Investigation et de Recherche Anti-Gang [Anti-Gang Investigation and Intelligence Service], SAG, in the mid 1980s. In 1986 Anti-Gang was divested of some of its intelligence responsibilities when the Ministry of the Interior created the Service d'Intelligence Nationale (SIN) in order to take jurisdiction over domestic intelligence. The reconstituted Anti-Gang Unit (AGU) continued to be housed in the headquarters of the military police until the army's dissolution in 1995, when it became a demilitarized state paramilitary force, with its offices and detention center relocated to its present headquarters in the Port-au-Prince central police station known as the *Cafétéria.*

The paramilitary jackboot tactics characteristic of Anti-Gang today are best understood when one considers the unit's historical foundations in the Haitian army, as well as the personnel dynamics that have taken place within the unit since 1994. In November 1994 the Haitian legislature passed a law creating the Haitian National Police (PNH). In early 1995, along with the establishment of a Code of Conduct and an Office of Inspector-General, an Interim Public Security Force (IPSF) was formed and composed largely of former soldiers and refugees from rapid-training camps at the U.S. naval base on Guantanamo Bay. Its raison d'être was to ensure civil security and order until the first contingent of PNH officers could be trained and deployed. As PNH officers successively graduated the four-month training at the Académie Nationale de Police in Petionville, the IPSF was steadily demobilized until the PNH's ranks were sufficient for the complete dissolution of the interim force by presidential decree in December 1995. Over the course of their demobilization, IPSF officers were absorbed into a range of

Figure 3.2. Members of the Interim Public Security Force (IPSF) in Port-au-Prince in 1995. Members of the force were recruited from the ranks of the former army and from refugee camps at Guantanamo Bay in Cuba.

newly created security units, including the Unité de Sécurité Générale du Palais Nationale [the Palace Guard], which together with the Presidential Guard is composed of over 460 former soldiers, and the Corps de Sécurité Ministérielle [the Ministerial Security Corps], whose commanding officers until fairly recently were all former military personnel. The remaining 1,598 IPSF officers were incorporated into the PNH, over 600 of whom are former soldiers of FADH (OAS 1997).

From its inception the PNH has been fraught with civil and human rights violations, a tendency from which it (and its various descendant subunits) has never truly been divorced. The force is indicted yearly by international human rights groups, the U.S. State Department and the U.N. High Commission on Human Rights for a broad spectrum of abuses ranging from the beating, torturing, and killing of suspects to the blind discharging of weapons into peaceful crowds (U.N. Commission on Human Rights 1996;

Drummond 1997; U.S. Department of State 1995, 1999, 2005; Amnesty International 2000, 2002; OAS 2002; Human Rights Watch 2003).

Since 1994 paramilitary subunits of the PNH have increasingly divested themselves of police authority and today operate as almost completely autonomous agencies. Among them are the Compagnie d'Intervention et de Maintien de l'Ordre or CIMO (a tactical riot-control unit), the Groupe d'Intervention de la Police Nationale d'Haïti or GIPNH (a rapid-response intervention group, similar to American SWAT units), and the Bureau de Lutte contre le Trafic des Stupéfiants or BLTS (the counter-narcotics bureau). But the unit with the clearest paramilitary tendencies and repressive proclivities is the Anti-Gang Unit.

Today's AGU functions as the principal state weapon against civil violence in general and as its name suggests its primary targets are the *zenglendo* gangs engaged in a diverse array of violent criminal activities such as home invasions, neighborhood occupations, bank robberies, and street assassinations. But few of the arrests that AGU agents make are clearly related to collective criminal activity. Most of their arrests are of solitary armed bandits and frequently street children who are picked up on neighborhood sweeps for *zenglendo.*

While street children do not account for even an insignificant portion of Port-au-Prince's *zenglendo* problem, one Anti-Gang commander characterized street children as at the core of the street violence problem. He told me that street children are a "preoccupation" of the AGU primarily because of the lack of parental control over malign child behaviors that "lead to" *zenglendinaj*, a theory that resonates with the psychosocial model of street-child deviance presented by Dr. Bijoux.

Foot soldiers with the AGU have explained to me that few of the children that they arrest are ever armed (and almost never with a firearm when they are) and most are not arrested while in the act of committing any crime at all. As justification for the arrests, the AGU hierarchy describes Port-au-Prince as a city in the midst of a crisis, defines crimes committed by street children as a major part of that crisis, and underscores the difficulties intrinsic to its urgent task of *ap toufe sibit* [suddenly suffocating] *zenglendinaj, youth crime,* and the disorder that they are cited as causing. He indicated that the AGU's profile of the average street child is one of a regular participant in zenglendist violence and is the result not of specific evidence but of the current climate of fear, panic, rampant gunplay, and heightening desperation that has become a pervasive part of Port-au-Prince life. In Port-au-Prince they say that it is like living under the constant threat of gunfire from an armed monkey: wild, erratic, unpredictable.

Figure 3.3. Street girls pose in front of a wall etched with graffiti depicting the violence of Anti-Gang *arimaj.*

Specifically targeting hyperviolent slum areas like those of Cité Soleil and Portail Léogâne, Anti-Gang agents employ rapid-intervention street sweeps to combat the rising criminal violence. Given the civil sector's collective fear of the randomness of the violence and the state's frustration with the brazen lawlessness of the *zenglendo,* the cleanups have been swift and aggressive. The method is the *arimaj,* and the targets are primarily street children.

One doesn't often see *arimaj* coming until the last minute and that is exactly the point. Rapid and violent in execution, *arimaj* is a blitzkrieg sweep into a targeted neighborhood, a surprise tactic designed to catch the *zenglendo* off their guard. Firing tear gas in advance, Anti-Gang screams into the targeted district in unmarked, black pickup trucks and armored sport utility vehicles, sealing off the neighborhood's main traffic arteries. AGU troopers, clad in riot gear and gas masks, pile out of the vehicles and beat and arrest any youths idle on the street, especially those whom troopers suspect of zenglendist activity. One Anti-Gang officer that I spoke with explained that a likely suspect is anyone "not doing anything" at the time of the *arimaj,* suggesting that idleness is probable cause for arrest and detention. If this criterion for suspicion were a standard for Anti-Gang method, then one might expect to find a high number of street children arrested in *arimaj* sweeps. One in fact does.

Justice Denied

Nowhere is the Haitian state in greater disharmony with the U.N. Convention on the Rights of the Child (to which it is a signatory) and its own constitutional mandates than in its dealings with children in the national criminal justice system. With regard to the treatment of child detainees by state parties, the U.N. Convention is quite clear: children are to be (1) presumed innocent until proven guilty; (2) informed promptly and directly of the charges for which s/he is being detained; (3) separated from adults while incarcerated; and (4) provided without delay a trial by competent, independent, and impartial authority. But in Haiti, once a suspect is arrested and incarcerated, Western notions of civil rights, presumed innocence, and due process dissolve completely, especially when the suspect is a child. Children who are arrested by the Anti-Gang Unit, especially street kids, are extended few civil or human rights. Officers need no explicit evidence in order to make an arrest, nor do they need to inform the courts of the arrest or pending charges. Anti-Gang brings street children directly from the street to the juvenile prison. In practice neither a lawyer nor any other adult need be present for the questioning of adolescents and no evidence of a committed crime need be presented at any time to the courts for the continued incarceration and questioning of juveniles. Once detained, adolescents are not even necessarily entitled to a trial. One street boy described the martial situation on the street to me in this way:

> Anti-Gang are like monkeys who have guns. The monkey without one, he is funny, you see. He throws his arms about, this way and that way. He screams loudly. He throws his shit! But give the monkey a gun, and he is not funny. He is *mafubè* [crazy-thinking]. He waves the gun about and shoots everything. That is what Anti-Gang is.

Street children arrested during *arimaj* sweeps have no right to be informed of the charges associated with their arrest, no right to see a judge, and no right to a fixed and finite sentence if they are in fact found guilty of a crime. Guilty until proven innocent, all that is necessary for the indefinite incarceration of a street child in Haiti is an arrest report from an PNH unit such as the AGU, which considers the living circumstances of street children —unsupervised and idle—as probable cause for the assumption of their association with criminal elements.

Located in Port-au-Prince, Fort National is Haiti's main correctional facility for women, but it also houses the Prison Juvénile-Sous-Fort, the prison for youthful offenders. While Fort National is the only prison in the Republic where boys are incarcerated separately from adult men, here women and girls (some as young as thirteen) are still housed together. Although Haitian law proscribes that children under the age of sixteen years are not to be incarcerated in prison cells at all, the complete lack of alternative judicial disciplines results in children as young as ten detained in the Fort National system. Here children are locked into a single dormitory that (depending upon the youth population in the prison at any given time) permits each child anywhere from six to twelve square feet of living space. Most of the children are from the street, few understand the judicial procedure, and rarely can any of them recall precisely when they had last seen a judge. Most have never spoken with a lawyer about their case.

The boys' confusion over the law is understandable, given the fact that even the Haitian state is unsure of what to do with youth offenders. There currently exists no juvenile criminal code in Haiti, though the Haitian Parliament was considering the framework for one when their deliberations were stalled in 1998 as a result of political in-squabbling over the confirmation of Haiti's prime minister. Their deliberations over a juvenile code has yet to resume. As a result nearly all youths arrested in Haiti today are tried in the adult criminal court system and are sent to adult prisons. Fort National holds less than 10 percent of Haiti's total youthful offender population. The rest are incarcerated throughout the country in adult detention facilities.

In 1999 Haiti did inaugurate the Tribunal pour Mineurs, a court for minors in Port-au-Prince. While this tribunal exclusively hears cases involving juvenile offenders, it still applies an adult code to those offenders in its deliberations and sentencing. Moreover its efficacy has been significantly hindered by a lack of resources and a consequent inability to reliably transport defendants to the tribunal for their hearings. There is currently a single judge in all of Haiti who is responsible for presiding over this court, but his time is divided between the tribunal and the civil court where he also serves as a senior justice, so juvenile cases are not adjudicated very quickly.

When I visited the juvenile prison in January 2000, fifty-seven boys between the ages of thirteen and seventeen were being detained at the juvenile prison, and all but five of them were street kids. Though three of the boys were being held on homicide charges, the overwhelming majority of them were being detained on Anti-Gang charges of *"association avec malfaituer"* [associating with criminal elements]. The warden of the prison explained to me (with what seemed to be genuine compassion) that none of the children incarcerated in her facility had been formally charged with a crime, nor had any been handed an indictment of any kind. She explained that most of the youths had been held without trial for several months and some for as long as a half-year.

On visits to the prison since that time, I have found among the incarcerated youths street children with whom I had worked on the outside. I had known Gregoire for six years when I found him in the prison in 2000. He told me that he was on the street in September of 1999 when Anti-Gang came in "*tankou loraj*" [like thunder] on an *arimaj* sweep through the neighborhood he was working in near Champ des Mars in downtown Port-au-Prince. Gregoire said that as he was backing away from an officer who was beating another street boy nearby, he was hit from behind by an AGU trooper who then bound his wrists with plastic ties and forced him into an armored AGU sport utility vehicle. He was taken to the *Cafétéria* where he was held (with no sense of irony) in *ferme nwi* [overnight lockup] for sixty days. He was then moved to Fort National. Since that time, he had not seen a lawyer, nor had he been formally charged with a crime, nor had he been given a reason for his continued internment. By the time I had spoken with him, he had been incarcerated under these circumstances for four months. Gregoire's case is typical of most street children held in the prison and is indicative of the ambivalent stance that the Haitian state has taken toward street children, especially those it holds in its custody.

This examination of the Haitian state's relation to displaced youths reveals a social project of constructing street children as a punishable category of youths, pushed to the margins of state and private responsibility. It is difficult for either the government or the citizenry to recognize any culpability in the general societal failure to extend civil and often human rights to these children. The tactics of *arimaj* are more than just police excess. The Anti-Gang Unit is a paramilitary extension of the tacit and fearful will of the people, who see few alternatives for the termination of zenglendist violence in Port-au-Prince and who are therefore willing to acquiesce to explosive and brutal police tactics to provide some semblance of civil order. Tragically the chaotic violence of the street in Port-au-Prince today is evidence that what the AGU has accomplished (and then only partially) is just that—*a semblance of order*. The reality is that Haiti is burning. The *zenglendo* kill and rob at will, the AGU fights back without prejudice or restraint, and the poor and the dispossessed fill the morgue and the prisons as the chief causalities in what is amounting to a full-blown urban war. But the real danger lies in Haiti's failure to divorce itself from the paramilitary solution to its social ills. The *zenglendo* are a deadly menace to social stability, but the police forces are as well. Worse yet, prejudiced and unsubstantiated profiles of street children as prone to *zenglendinaj* are fanning the flames of the crisis.

The popular but poorly founded association of street children with zenglendist violence and gang activity has elicited the social ire of a Port-au-Prince community that has isolated displaced youths as supernumerary nuisances at best, criminal elements in the *zenglendo* wars at worst. The criminalization of street children leads logically to the social denial of both civil and human rights that would otherwise be extended to them. This negative conception of human rights denies street children who are perceived as noncitizens, living outside of social norms or civil law. A culture of violence persists reflexively here, combining the everyday violence of social scorn, poverty, and scarcity in the street with legitimated and routinized police violence against the children who live there. The stubborn persistence of arbitrary AGU arrest and brutality in Haiti is prototypical of cultural trends evident in many struggling postcolonial, democratizing states in which government violence continues to be reproduced and sanctioned for the preservation of a socially constructed perception of civil stability. The civil society's assent to the abuses of paramilitary power might be seen as part of what Nancy Scheper-Hughes has called in a Brazilian context a "discourse on criminality / deviance / marginality and on the 'appropriateness' of police and state violence in which all segments of the population participate and to which they acquiesce, often contrary to their own class or race interests" (1992: 225).

While state-child relations in Haiti have contributed to the violent backdrop against which street children are hashing out their identities, the threat of being beaten or killed or incarcerated at the hands of the AGU is secondary to the daily preoccupation of street kids who are struggling to earn a living on the boulevards. In the next chapter I will examine the subsistence strategies, economic activities, and political arrangements that are the day-to-day preoccupations of street children in Haiti. The reader will discover that the political economy of the street brings with it a different kind of violence, one which pits child against child in a competition for space that is as ritualized as it is ruthless.

Michel

It is 2000 and I am back in Port-au-Prince for another field season. While the violence in the streets has gotten worse, Haiti is otherwise exactly as I left it the year before. The poverty is still here, as it has always been, but so is the vitality and beauty of everyday life in this country. The mangoes in the baskets of the market women are all greens and reds and yellows. The smells of cooking and coffee and the sea imbue the air; I can pick them out distinctly from the other odors of the city. Schoolboys grin pleasantly at me as I greet them on their way to classes. I pass a young man and woman sitting and speaking softly to one another in the shade of the bougainvillea. Nearby a young girl is squatting over a plastic basin of wash water, scrubbing clothes and humming to herself. She looks up and giggles at me. Somewhere in the neighborhood, a radio is playing a Sweet Mickey song that has overtaken a pair of mechanics working under the hood of a truck halfway up the street. They stop their work to dance and to sing along. An old woman walks by me and delivers a very formal greeting in elegant French: "Bon jour, Monsieur," she says. I reply to her in Krèyol, "Bonjou, Madanm," and she turns to me and smiles. I then notice that she is wearing a black T-shirt certainly donated from somewhere in the United States; the back of it is emblazoned with the legend, "What the fuck are you looking at?" Such is Haiti: warm and genteel, absurd and risible, alive and recalcitrant, and always unpredictable.

I am making my way to Portail Léogâne, specifically the area around the National Cemetery where I know a handful of street boys who congregate there to sniff glue throughout the day. As I approach that section of the neighborhood, a few passersby who have seen me with the boys there before hiss well-intentioned admonitions at me: "Stay away from them, *blanc*!" "They are dangerous!" "Those boys are *zombi*. What could you want with them?"

The city is at its worst in Portail Léogâne. The smell of garbage and charcoal smoke and diesel exhaust is overwhelming here, so much different from the air a few streets over from whence I came. I am walking through raw sewage. I watch as a boy in his teens, naked to his waist, splashes the grayish water from the gutter across his chest. He is bathing.

I walk in the broad daylight of the morning but there are rats nonetheless foraging a massive pile of garbage heaped in the intersection of two major thorough-fares that run through the district. They screech and fight over rotting mango peels, chewed stalks of sugar cane, and chicken bones.

I walk past the entrance to the National Cemetery. Men sit around the gate, smoking cigarettes and joking. One of them, the cemetery watchman, holds an old bolt-action rifle. They stare at me blankly and nod in my direction as I pass by. I return their nod. Now I am moving between squatter huts set up messily in the squalid, tree-shaded area against the cemetery wall. There are old women and dusty young girls crouching here and there, cooking and washing clothes. There are men and boys here too, leaning or lying against the wall in dirty and ripped clothing, some drinking, others dozing in the heat. Flies and puddles of cloudy gray water are everywhere.

I continue along the cemetery wall and come to a corner. As I turn it, I can hear the familiar voices of some of the street boys I have come here to see. There is a gaggle of seven of them here, ranging in age from ten to about seventeen. They are as they were days ago when I last met with them: lying about here and there, some in the sun, some in the shade, on the broken concrete steps that ascend a rise along the cemetery wall. They are sniffing cobbler's glue from plastic juice bottles that they stir with sticks to agitate the vapor. All of them are hopeless addicts. Two of the boys show the physical signs of a long-term habit. Pussing scabs form a halo around their mouths and noses where the skin has been blistered by the caustic glue vapor. They are emaciated and filthy because the glue takes away their ambi-tion to work and to feed themselves, as well as their motivation to keep their bodies clean. One of the boys is defecating in a nearby corner as I approach.

I sit down beside a shirtless boy of sixteen named Michel whom I have come to know somewhat well. I know from past conversations with Michel and other younger street boys in the neighborhood that he is generally regarded as a menace to street-kid society. He is one of the many older street boys who roam the streets, sometimes alone and sometimes in groups, and harass, intimidate, and more than frequently beat children brutally in order to take away their money. Many such boys, and Michel is one of them, regard this as their "work." He boasts openly and often to me about his history of street violence. He routinely regales me with stories about how he beat this little one for his money, or how he forced this street girl to perform oral sex on him at razor point, or how he slashed the chest of this street boy in a fight over either a transistor radio or a canister of glue (he can't remember which). Sometime before now, Michel confided in me that he had once killed a street boy by beating him with a wooden board as the boy slept, and I believe him. Michel habitually uses force and violence to get what he wants: sex, respect, glue, money, a reputation. But mostly money.

On this day Michel is glassy-eyed from the glue and his speech is slurred, but he is lucid enough to recognize me and make small conversation. As we talk I am wondering why I have come here to speak with these kids at all. While they do have a relationship to the street that is unlike that of many other kids sleeping rough in Port-au-Prince, it is very difficult to carry on a cogent conversation with them while they are in the throes of a glue-high. I also know from bitter experience that many glue-sniffers are prone to explosive acts of violence. In the past I have been menaced out of other areas of Portail Léogâne by glue-drunk boys. But this particular group is somehow, strangely, different. We all get along well. Perhaps its because there are fewer of them here. Perhaps its because they know that I am a better source of money as a friend and a researcher who pays them to talk with me about their lives, than I am as a one-time target for mugging.

Despite his propensity for brutality and the distasteful fact that he goes about beating younger children for a living, I would have to confess that I like Michel. There are times when his natural and vivid sense of humor shines through when he turns a clever phrase or holds forth on a description of how he can tell what a street kid has eaten from the smell of his shit. He also laughs at his own jokes, which I find endearing. And there are other times, usually when he is high and always when we are alone, that Michel grows melancholy and sometimes weeps as he talks about how much he hates his life and the horrible things he does on the street in order to survive.

I do like Michel, and so I sit with him for a while and chat. He tells me that he is hungry. I reach into my pocket and give him a handful of gourde notes, enough for him to eat a few modest meals, though I am sure that at least some of the money will be used to buy more glue. Michel asks me for a cigarette and I give him several. He thanks me and lights one, and I do the same. We smoke in silence.

Michel asks me if I want to interview him again today and I tell him no, that I just stopped by to see how he was doing. We chat for awhile about nothing of any significance. After about a half-hour, Michel hops down from the concrete ledge that we are sitting on and gathers up his T-shirt and the cigarettes I have given him. He is getting ready to leave. I ask him, "So where are you going now?"

"*Fè travay,*" he says. "To work."

4

Violenz Lari

The Violence of the Street Economy from Below

Few of the children working on the street in Port-au-Prince were actually born there. Most have made their way to the capital from the countryside for the same reason that nearly all adult migrants come to the city—they are seeking better opportunities for work. Once displaced from the home, children customarily attempt to make a living in their natal town—Les Cayes, Jacmel, Petit-Goâve, Saint Marc, Montruis, Mirebalais, Jérémie, Limonade, Cap Haïtien, Thomonde—eventually making their way into the city, frustrated and hungry and hopeful for the chance at a better livelihood.

Few street children in Port-au-Prince are orphans. Most have living kin, often in the capital, and some even maintain a certain degree of contact with those relatives. Orphanage is rarely the reason for child abandonment to the street. I have found that the economic pressures of the impoverished household are the greatest contributory factor in child displacement from the natal home. Most of my street-child informants have siblings who continue to live at home, and these siblings are almost always enrolled in school. Ancillary school fees (for books, uniforms, and other supplies) are sufficiently high as to prohibit most poor households from sending all of the family's children to school, despite the fact that primary education is free and compulsory for all children in Haiti. As a result poor families are compelled to make painful decisions about which children will attend school and which will be turned out onto the street to work and thus contribute to the household income.

As will be seen, a child's labor on the street, both legal and illegal, can be very lucrative by local standards. Customarily making over three times the national daily minimum wage through street labor, children who are displaced from the household are relied upon by kin to act not only as their own breadwinners but as breadwinners for the rest of the family as well. Once on the street, children experience a sense of freedom that they do not enjoy in the home and increasingly spend less and less time within the fold of the family. This observation lends qualitative support to the analysis of street children drawn by Benno Glauser (1990), who worked with street youth in Asunción, Paraguay. As in the case of Paraguayan street youth, Haiti's street children loose vital ties to their homes through a multitude of circumstances that prompt the family to give up on educational and other support efforts. Street children over time have a tendency to move away from their natal home both physically and psychically, until they cross a conceptual threshold that marks the separation between "adequately assisted and protected growing-up situations and processes and situations without adequate assistance and protection" (Glauser 1990: 151). Once this threshold is breached by the child, his or her daily life grows increasingly decentered and away from the natal home.

As Glauser suggests is the case in Asunción, when Haitian street children cross the threshold into full street socialization, they do so gradually and rarely as a result of a sudden, conscious decision. However, whereas Glauser suggests that once Paraguayan children cross the threshold into street childhood, they rarely if ever reestablish themselves with their families, street children in Port-au-Prince continue to maintain many of their familial bonds, most often through continued, albeit sporadic, economic support of their natal households. Most children that I interviewed who still maintained contact with their families (*"m'konne fanmi'm,"* they would say—"I know my family") send some form of support back to their familial home, usually once or twice a year if they have completely removed themselves from their natal home, more often if they still sleep at home from time to time. Emmanuel, a twelve-year-old street boy from La Saline, indicated that he revisits his family village in Cazales (about twenty miles north of Port-au-Prince) twice a year to see his mother, usually bringing her money or a hen as a *kado* [gift]. Lajounou, a youth in his teens from Portail Léogâne, told me that he occasionally sends money back to his aunt in Léogâne through a market woman he has befriended who lives in his hometown and makes weekly marketing trips to Port-au-Prince and back. Another boy from the area, Jean-Paul, personally carries gifts of money to relatives in his natal home of Montruis several times a year, so that he can maintain his right to return home should he ever wish to do so.

Emmanuel, Lajounou, and Jean-Paul are children who by Glauser's standards have fully crossed over the threshold into complete street socialization, have lived at large on Port-au-Prince streets for a significant portion of their lives and have no intention of ever returning to their homes; but they nonetheless maintain economic relations with their kin. Other anthropologists who have worked with street children have also found a maintenance of economic ties between the street child and his familial home. Tobias Hecht, commenting on conclusions that he drew from his work in Brazil, argues that

> children who sleep in the street in different cities around the world are not necessarily cut off from their families. Many street children in Recife bring home money to their mothers. . . . Thirty-two percent said that they had been home over the past week, while 23 percent said that they had gone home only between a month and a year ago; a further 17 percent said it was more than a year since they had returned. The amount of time elapsed since the last visit home increases with age, with some of those 13, 14 or older not having been home in years (1998: 65).

Hecht's survey data confirms that the transition to street socialization is a gradual process marked by an incremental separation from home life, but Hecht also goes on to describe an emotional attachment that Brazilian street boys have to their mothers and how that attachment entails a sense of obligation to live a moral life on the street consistent with what they perceive their mothers would wish for them. Seen in this light, a street child's economic and emotional relationship to the natal family is generally more complicated than Glauser suggests, even given that most displaced children grow spatially and socially farther apart from their homes the longer they are on the street.

The life of the poor in Haiti is characterized by a communal ethic that fosters strong, collective social bonds. The sharing of resources, especially food, is fundamental to community vitality and crucial to individual survival, so it is unsurprising that a sociocentric perspective informs the cultural lives of most Haitians. Even the traditional spatial arrangement of the peasant *lakou*, with its several extended family households oriented in a semicircle around a common hearth, illustrates the significance of community in individual identity formation. As most urban street children ultimately originate from this rural, poor demographic, they too engage in a range of communal behaviors that reinforce communitarian ideals. Street children maintain complex networks of social support based on strong comrade relations that are revealed in virtually every aspect of their daily lives—as they work, play, fight, eat, and sleep with one another on the pavement. Perhaps nowhere is the sociocentric ethos of Haitian street children more manifest than in their economic relations.

Working the Boulevard

My previous work in Haiti (Bernat 1999, Kovats-Bernat 2000), as well as the work of others elsewhere (Ennew 1986; Aptekar 1988; Hecht 1998; Márquez 1999; Kilbride, Suda, and Njeru 2001) suggests that street children in various countries and cultural settings create, modify, and innovate adaptive economic relations and exchange networks on the street that are responsive to the unique nature of the informal economy that prevails there. While their capital resources and material possessions may be limited, street youth everywhere adapt to their surroundings sufficiently enough to carve out an economic existence that contributes substantially to the development of their cultural identities. It is within the domain of economic survival that we see most clearly the agency of *timoun lari.*

In Port-au-Prince street children establish and maintain their social agency through a complex network of comrade relationships and economic strategies that allow them to access capital, transform resources into usable goods, and distribute those goods among their companions for common survival. Contrary to appearances, Haitian street children labor more often than they beg, keep a number of objects that they value and regard as their own, and exchange commodities through simple systems of generalized reciprocity and egalitarian redistribution that guarantee that those who are valued as *zanmi*—allies, brothers, friends—are cared for and care in return through collective systems of sharing. The subsistence and especially the consumption patterns of street children in Haiti are the most compelling means with which they define themselves as social agents in relation to the larger civil society.

Street children are among the hardest working citizens in Haiti. Most rise very early in the morning and work well into the nighttime hours at jobs that are considered not only profitable to the children who perform them, but also valuable to the greater urban community that relies on their services as a given aspect of the everyday street economy of Port-au-Prince. While many kids do supplement their incomes through illegal activities such as selling drugs or sex or committing petty thefts, the overwhelming majority of street children engage themselves daily in licit service labor in the informal sector—washing cars, wiping windshields, loading parcels, shining shoes and other tasks worthy of a few dollars in tips.

Nonethnographic, sociological research findings with street children in other parts of the world have suggested that the reverse is true outside of Haiti. In 1994 a study was published by the University of Michigan-based Society for Research in Child Development, that offered a brief quantitative

Figure 4.1. Street kids in Port-au-Prince establish and maintain strong networks of support that guarantee the regular exchange of food and other goods with one another.

assessment of the daily activities of street youth in Belo Horizonte, Brazil (Campos et al. 1994). In addition to examining such variables as "social resources," "problem behaviors," and "institutional experiences," the research also provides tentative hypotheses about the different labor strategies of street children. The study presents data derived from a survey administered to 161 "home-based children" and 80 "street-based children" concerning the comparative rates of involvement in legal and illegal work for survival. Fifty-two percent of respondents reported earning money through legal activities only (including begging), 22 percent through illegal activities only (stealing, exchanging sex for money), and 26 percent through both legal and illegal activities. All told the study concludes that while only two-fifths of street-based youth worked at licit unskilled jobs to make money, a full 75 percent of street-based youth engaged in some form of illegal economic activity.

In September 1999 and again in January 2000, I conducted surveys of various street-child survival activities in Port-au-Prince that addressed variables similar to those scrutinized by the SRCD study, especially the relative rates of legal and illegal activities of street youth. In contrast to the findings of the Belo Horizonte study, the Haitian evidence indicates that virtually all street children in Port-au-Prince engage in legal economic activities (licit work, begging) and just over half engage in illegal economic activities (stealing, drug/sex sales). So while some kids supplement their income with illegal work, they rarely invest themselves full-time in illicit labor.

By far the most common means of making money for boys are wiping windshields, carrying groceries, loading and unloading parcels and passengers from trucks, and "guarding" cars for store patrons. Guarding cars is a creatively devious and clever means of making money. Some street kids wait outside convenience markets and look for a car to pull up to the curb, its driver entering the store. The children approach the patron and offer to *ap siveye* [watch over] that patron's car. The implication is clear: if the child is paid to watch over the car, he will guarantee that "nothing happens" to the unattended vehicle. Most take the child up on his offer for a few gourdes, mildly concerned over what might happen to the vehicle if the street child making the offer is declined.

Some street boys are also per diem helpers at small convenience markets, where they work for a part of each day breaking bulk for merchants. Some street girls also work on a per diem basis, securing work beside curbside food vendors, cleaning their fry pots and cooking utensils. The pay for such jobs varies based on the quality of work, the trustworthiness of the child, the relationship between the child and his or her patron, and the relative youth of the child. Younger children tend to make more for their unskilled labor, largely because the combination of their youth and their destitution is a source of sympathy that diminishes as the child matures. A child can make twenty-five to forty gourdes washing a car and five to ten gourdes for each windshield wiped. While washing cars involves a complete cleaning of the vehicle with buckets of water and sometimes soap, wiping windshields involves little more than spraying the windows of a vehicle with ammonia or a weak isopropyl alcohol and water mixture and cleaning them of dust and road grime. Because most motorists are more inclined to pay for the cheaper service, wiping windshields is a practice competitive with the more complete washing work.

At-large service labor is often a livelihood for street children. Children can make up to five to ten gourdes carrying and loading groceries for customers at a time and two gourdes per passenger helped onto the *tap-taps*—the colorful, rattletrap buses used by the poor as an inexpensive means of transportation about the city. A child working for a merchant breaking bulk and occasionally sweeping the front of the store can make anywhere from fifty to seventy gourdes for a half-day's work. Guarding cars will draw a fee of usually no more than five gourdes per vehicle; if the price for such a service grows too great, the child runs the risk of local alienation as an extortionist rather than as a shrewd service provider. Girls who work cleaning pots and utensils for street vendors can make fifty to sixty gourdes for a day's work and are typically fed as well. In general street children can earn a daily average of 110 gourdes and as much as 170 gourdes per day by exploiting various forms of licit work (Table 1). Given that the current legal minimum wage in Haiti is seventy gourdes per day, street children are able to make, through legal street labors alone, almost twice what they would earn were they employed in the formal sector in Haiti. This reality clarifies the economic rationale behind parental decisions to urge certain of their children from the household in order to work. The child who lives and works on the street not only frees up needed household resources like food and water, but is also capable of contributing substantially to the economic viability of the family.

Begging is engaged in by virtually all street children at least occasionally, but is generally regarded as very humbling and highly unpredictable and so it is not the preferred means of income on the street. Although most children disparage their inevitable need to ask for money, it can be a lucrative means of making money. While children rarely if ever ask for a particular amount when begging, they do expect to receive a minimum of five to seven gourdes from each donor. When children do ask for a particular amount, it is usually from foreigners and typically the request is an innocent demand of *"ba'm dola!"*—"Give me one [Haitian] dollar."[1] Smaller children profit more from their begging, because of the same inverse relationship between youth and sympathy observed by other anthropologists who have worked with street children (Hecht 1998, Kilbride, Suda, and Njeru 2001). Older children are increasingly regarded with suspicion as they mature and so are proportionately disadvantaged in their begging efforts, and girls of any age tend to make more than boys of any age. Cèlis, a street girl I befriended in Champ de Mars, explained to me that while she can on average make between forty to fifty gourdes per day begging, she prefers to work because it can be more lucrative, especially if she is able to do chores for merchants in addition to washing the pots and utensils of food vendors that she knows. Similarly Yves (a street boy of around eight years) remarked to me that while he can make as much as fifty gourdes per day *"ap mande lajann"* [asking for money], he prefers not to since he can make twice that amount wiping windshields. He usually only asks for money when he is too sick to work, though I have observed that Yves, like all street children, habitually extends an open palm to passersby who look as if they might be charitable.

Stealing, Dealing, and Selling Sex for Survival

Street kids who do work in the illicit sector are generally older boys in their late teens some of whom have explained to me that crime can be more lucra-

Figure 4.2. Many Haitian street children supplement their incomes by begging, though it is far more common among younger children like this boy, whose youth and smallness elicit a greater sense of sympathy from passersby.

tive than any other form of street labor. It also offers a supplement to their legal income when they grow too old to derive a good profit from begging. Indeed begging ceases to be a common occupation of youth who are past their early teens. Among older boys (over the age of fifteen or so) begging is considered very humiliating, and when I am infrequently asked for money by older youths, it is not by means of the open palm of the youthful mendicant, but rather by means of a secretive whisper into my ear.

The most common form of illicit income activity among street children is the practice of *de dwèt* [two fingers], which can mean either pickpocketing or cutpursing (using a razor to cut the strap of a woman's purse in order to snatch it), but usually refers to the former. While *de dwèt* can be lucrative business—one teen told me that he can steal hundreds of gourdes a day by surreptitiously reaching into the pockets of riders on crowded *tap-taps*—it is extremely dangerous. Aside from the very real likelihood of eventually ending up in the juvenile prison at Fort National if arrested by the PNH, most Haitians would be perfectly at ease beating down a young thief on the spot without bothering to summon the authorities, especially if the perpetrator is a street child.

Two street boys that I know from my work in Portail Léogâne are quite heavily enmeshed in marijuana trafficking in their neighborhood; neither of them would be considered proper dealers. Their role in the drug trade is that of intermediaries—they take money from an individual buyer or a potential dealer and purchase the marijuana from a supplier, keeping a modest cut of the cash as a fee. Depending on quality and demand, one-half ounce of marijuana sells on Port-au-Prince streets for around 140 gourdes. A street youth acting as an intermediary will customarily tack a thirty to fifty gourde fee onto this base retail price. Blanchet, a street teen who deals in marijuana sales from time to time, told me that this surcharge varies according to the youth making the run for the marijuana. "Some guys are very afraid of getting caught by the police," he explained, which will drive the intermediary fee even higher.

Selling sex for money is a common means of income for poor girls and some street boys as well, especially among those who live near the nightlife districts of Port-au-Prince and Petionville. While I conducted no extensive survey of prostitution rates among street children in Port-au-Prince, I did gather anecdotal data on the economics of the practice. While most are young girls in their early- to mid-teens, some are boys of similar age. Prostitutes generally constitute an economic class separate from street children, and they also suffer significantly higher rates of violent victimization, drug abuse, and disease as part of their work. They are rarely found in the areas of the city where street children congregate, instead working the bars outside the city center. Some child prostitutes work in the Palace Hotel on Rue Capois, a dubious tourist hotel across from the National Palace, as well as other

Table 1. Licit Street-Child Labor and Approximate Income per Task

Type of Work	Approximate Income per Task (in Haitian Gourdes)	
	Minimum	Maximum
Washing Cars	25.00	40.00
Wiping Windshields	5.00	10.00
Carrying/Loading Parcels	5.00	10.00
Loading/Unloading *tap-tap* Passengers	2.00	
Chores for Merchant	50.00[a]	70.00[a]
Guarding Cars		5.00
Cleaning Pots/Utensils for Street Vendor	50.00[b]	60.00[b]
Begging	60.00[c]	75.00[c]
Average Daily Income from Licit Street Labor	110.00	170.00

a. Per half-day.
b. Per day. This figure does not include the value of the food that is typically consumed as part of
   wages for such labor.
c. Per day.

Figure 4.3. Many street girls eventually find their way into prostitution as they reach sexual maturity. But this doesn't mean that until then they are protected from sexual exploitation. Girls as young as five have reported being sexually assaulted on the street, usually by older street boys.

destitute brothels in the market district. One street girl I know told me that she had at one time sold sex for money, but she was emphatic in claiming that she had done so only a few times and long in the past. She said that she was paid "five or seven" U.S. dollars for sex. This price seems to be the norm for such services, though somewhat low compared to the range quoted to me by an American acquaintance living in Haiti who divulged that he occasionally solicits sex from Haitian prostitutes. He indicated that he has paid between ten and twenty U.S. dollars for sex with prostitutes he is certain were mature women and not adolescent girls. In 1997 I was propositioned by a teenage street girl clearly under the influence of *siment* as I was leaving a bar in Petionville. She offered me sex at a price of ten U.S. dollars.

The sex trade in Haiti is dangerous business, as it is globally, and street girls speak with genuine fear about the grim prospects of a life devoted to prostitution. Among them, prostitution is generally regarded either as a last chance at economic survival or the eventual lot of drug addicts. One should keep in mind, however, that prostitutes generally constitute a social group separate from street children, and so my field experience with the issue of prostitution is generally confined to its status as a grim possibility, rather than as a workaday livelihood.

No matter how street children make their money, they generally regard their cash wealth as their own to dispense with as they please, though it is shared extensively, as most things are, among a child's *zanmi*, or comrades, close friends. When asked the question, "What sorts of things do you have that are your own?" most children begin their list with their clothes, especially their shoes if they own a pair. Food is invariably second if not first on the list, followed in almost all cases by *"lajann'm"* [my money]. Despite the widespread notion of currency ownership, money is almost invariably shared as a collective resource among *zanmi*. When I asked eight-year-old Ti Amos the question "Do you own money?" he replied with the sharp admonition that *"m'pa kapab posede lajann'm! Tout lajann se lajann pèp!"* [I can't own my money! All money belongs to the people!]. This notion of socialized wealth is common among street children and leads to a system of generalized reciprocity in which the sharing of cash and commodities is presumed within one's circle of *zanmi* and is tacitly understood by all members of a peer group to be essential to their common survival. A similar sense of communalism is described by Kilbride, Suda, and Njeru (2001), whose ethnographic research with street children in Nairobi revealed them to be considerably less tribalistic than the wider society.

Despite the readiness with which children share their money with their *zanmi*, the care they take in hiding it on their bodies (usually it is shoved discreetly into a deep pocket or down the front of one's pants, or in one's shoe, or in the case of girls sometimes down the fronts of their blouses) and the resistance they exhibit against those children who attempt to steal it from them, suggests that money is not indiscriminately distributed. Possession of cash wealth typically implies the right to purchase with it what one chooses, but it is not regarded as exclusively owned capital and is freely exchanged within the bounds of close comrade groups. As in most societies that rely on such egalitarian exchange networks, private property is acceptable among peers to the extent that it is not regarded as a reflection of ambition or selfishness. To purchase exclusively for oneself and to consume one's property conspicuously, especially in view of unfortunate peers, is considered among their lot to be in very bad form indeed. Selfishness is customarily controlled through the threat and occasional practice of ostracism.

Haitian street kids establish, solidify, expand, and maintain their social relationships with their closest friends and allies most often through the sharing of food. The considerable wages that they can make through their labor affords many street children the advantage of eating with a degree of regularity that can be almost twice that of the general adult population. The diet of Port-au-Prince street children reveals that they not only eat better but with greater frequency than does the greater population of the poor, as one considers that diet generally improves (however modestly) with increased income.

Food and Redistributive Exchange

Their relative food affluence in comparison to the rest of the starving majority should not suggest to the reader that street children are adequately nourished. To the contrary, by world standards the overall diet of street youths is considerably lacking. Nonetheless one can say that street children on average eat adequately, and at the root of this nutritional viability is their integrated system of redistributive exchange. At the end of each day, street children convene with their *zanmi* at their *baz fouaye* [home base] to pool their money and their food so as to ensure that everyone has something to eat in the evening. Fritznel, a street boy who sleeps on the steps of the Post Office near the Bay of Port-au-Prince, explains the redistribution that takes place this way:

> My daily activities consist of filling up public vehicles with goods and passengers. With this money I find something to put in my mouth. When I return with nothing, my friends at [our home base] share with me the loot of their day. (Desrosiers 2000: 1)

I have watched street children share food this way at the close of almost every day, and when the day's haul was particularly successful, the exchanges could take on the air of feasting. Never are street children in better moods and never do they tend to negate their lives of scarcity more readily than when they are rapaciously, heartily, animatedly eating. The social atmosphere within their circles at times borders on overconsumption, with purchased, begged, and foraged foodstuffs eaten with an ecstatic voracity reminiscent of the *raskol* feasts among poor youths in New Ireland, Papua New Guinea. Karen Sykes writes that those children

> devour tinned fish, rice, chickens—gorging themselves as if they were fat pork for participants at a ritual feast. The fraternity which is made by the shared act of over-consumption, even if members feel coerced into these convivial relationships, enables youths to assert themselves at least as a temporary ritual community against the national vision of "youth in crisis." Here the fraternity established in fake men's houses in the bush is pitted against that which is created by social planners for the political development of the nation. (Sykes 1999: 167)

A similar cementing of peer bonds among street children in Port-au-Prince is facilitated through communal eating rituals that also allow youths to rail against the dominant social paradigm that defines them as unsocialized brutes.

Solidarity among street children at the Lafanmi Selavi orphanage facility was often expressed through the sharing of food and illustrates my point. In 1995 I was joining the children for their supper, an activity to which I always looked forward because even within the highly sociable environment of the orphanage, the children were rarely as conversational and convivial as when they were enjoying their suppers. Mealtime rules at the orphanage required that all children refrain from touching their food prior to the communal recitation of grace. I watched as Ti Frankel's plate was taken from him by one of the orphanage staff because he had eaten a spoonful of rice during the prayer. Although the staff member intended to return the plate to the child's place after grace, a boy sitting next to Ti Frankel was not so sure. Before the prayer had ended, the boy had emptied half of the food from his plate onto the table in front of his friend.

It is important to understand that Haitian street children do not exist, nor do they envision themselves as existing, as individual economic agents bent toward autonomous survival. It is incongruous that we should so easily regard the endurance of poor, settled Haitian families as dependent wholly upon networks of social support and food sharing and yet suppose that the same collective strategies of survival somehow do not apply as readily to street children. Once it is understood that reciprocal exchange and redistributive practices are absolutely essential for the economic and nutritional vitality of street children, other social behaviors that underscore a group ethic among them emerge in greater explanatory context. As will be seen, it is that very sense of communalism that can provide the greatest protection against the interchild brutality that is also characteristic of Haitian street economics.

Fists, Knives, Rocks, and Razors

There simply isn't enough room on the Port-au-Prince streets for the thousands of children who have elbowed their way onto it following their displacement from the home. Densely overpopulated, virtually every square foot of living or marketing space is claimed by someone or something. Where there are not people or produce or structures, there are other things occupying space: rats, roaches, biting ants, stinging centipedes, stray dogs and cats, pigs, goats, roosters, rubble, broken glass, defecation, puddles of

Figure 4.4. Two boys share a plate of rice and beans in Port-au-Prince. Food sharing is one of the most common means of solidifying friendship and exchange partnerships among street children.

filth, piles of garbage, coils of razor wire, taxis, buses, *tap-taps*, other street children. Haitian streets are a clamor of bodies and matter all competing for severely limited and crumbling sections of pavement and macadam. The boulevards are contested spaces and people who choose to work, market, or live there are engaged in daily struggles for situation and existence. Occasionally those struggles, especially those between children, can become overtly violent.

Writers who have worked in diverse field settings have been documenting the phenomenon of youth responses to war and conflict for over ten years (Scheper-Hughes 1992; Reynolds 1995; Shiraishi 1995; Daniel 1996; Nordstrom 1997; Bourgois 1990, 1995a, 1995b; Lerer 1998; Olujic 1998; Scheper-Hughes and Hoffman 1997, 1998). But few researchers have directly addressed the immediate and pervasive issue of aggressive conflict *between* youths who live in distress (Hecht 1998 and Márquez 1999 are the rare exceptions). While it would be both irresponsible and probably impossible to formulate a quantitative assessment of such ill-definable variables as "aggression" or "conflict," I will describe here the fundamental elements of displaced-child violence as I have experienced it on the streets of Port-au-Prince.

Violence among Haitian street children begins at a young age and is typically used as a means to accomplish two sometimes separate, sometimes interrelated objectives: (1) territorial maintenance and (2) dispute settlement. The degree to which the violence will escalate in either case is dependent upon the particular circumstances of the situation, the relative desperation of the parties involved, and the sincerity of the motivations of the participants. Variability of degree aside, the justifying factors of interchild violence on the street are generally confined to the aforementioned two categories.

Given limited street space, the typically low regard for street children held by those citizens who actually notice them at all, and the high level of competition among street kids for work combine to create a contest for terrain on the boulevards that demands a certain degree of fortitude to endure and a certain degree of brutality to win. While there is little if any policing by street children of the perceived borders of their *teritwa* [territory], newcomers to a neighborhood are as conspicuous as any interloper could be. Street children are keenly aware of a competition for limited work and regard supernumerary street youths in their spheres of labor as overt and unwelcome rivals. This economic antagonism is largely responsible for the frequency with which young street children are beaten for their day's receipts by older youths who resent what they regard as profit loss to a competitor, even if the younger child's receipts were secured through begging and not work proper.

Street children own very little, often just the clothes on their backs and the few crumpled bills that they keep shoved down the fronts of their pants or blouses. So when things are taken from them, more often than not it is their money, and the thief's justification for these acts is usually a claim of economic rights to the cash being taken. Miko, a seventeen-year-old street boy who washed cars in front of the Bijou movie house in downtown Port-au-Prince, explained to me his reasons for stealing from younger street kids on the block:

Kovats-Bernat: You take from these [younger] boys often then?

Miko: Yes, yes. They collect for me for work that I am not doing.

Kovats-Bernat: What do you mean when you say that they collect for you?

Miko: Good. O.K. I mean that I wash cars up here, see? The little ones wipe [windshields] down that end of the street. At the end of the day I take some of their money, because they are wiping the cars of my customers, see? They work for me. They work for me because they are wiping cars that I would wash but do not. They do that for me.

Kovats-Bernat: Do the little ones ever not want to give you money in this way?

Miko: No. They give it to me all the time. They give it easily. Sometimes they leave without paying me money, but then I get them the next day for the money.

Kovats-Bernat: Has there ever been a time when a little one did not want to give you money like this, even later [the next day]?

Miko: Yes. Two boys. They wipe cars down the street and ran away without paying me. They didn't come back to this place. But we [Miko works with four other street youths about his age] saw them on [Avenue] John Brown and beat them and took all of their money, see? It was our money.

Miko explained that in exchange for giving him money at the end of each day, the younger street boys could come back and work again the next day, provided of course that they pay Miko's requisite "tax" again. This relationship is not regarded as mutually beneficial from the perspective of the children whose profits are taken at the end of each work day. Mati Ren, at around eight years old one of the "little ones" that Miko mentioned, saw the situation somewhat differently:

Mati Ren: They [Miko and his cohort] take our money. We work for something to eat, not for them. But they are bigger. They are bigger so they can take our money from us little ones.

Kovats-Bernat: Why do you work here then?

Mati Ren: We [Mati Ren works with Damièn, a friend about his age] work here because a lot of cars come here. We don't give those boys [Miko and his cohort] all of our money. We keep money in our pants and we take it to buy food for us during the day. Those older boys don't know that we buy food during the day with our money.

Kovats-Bernat: How much of your money do you give Miko each day?

Mati Ren: We don't give him all of it. Maybe I give him some dollars.

Kovats-Bernat: How many is that?

Mati Ren: Like this [he shows me a handful of twenty or thirty Haitian gourdes].

Kovats-Bernat: Why do you give him that?

Mati Ren: Why? No. I give him dollars because he takes it. I want my money for food.

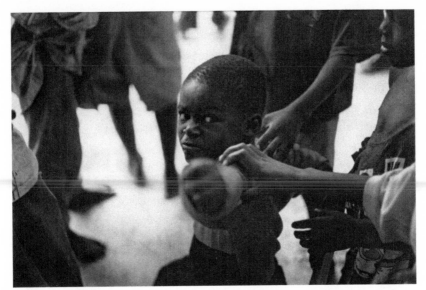

Figure 4.5. Haitian street kids live in a very violent social world. Fighting is frequent, usually among boys, and usually follows a graduated sequence of aggression from posturing, to shouting, to fisticuffs, and occasionally to rock throwing and razor fighting.

Those sectors that are clearly defined as "belonging" to a particular group of youths, those areas worth protecting as *teritwa*, are typically spaces in front of stores where one might work carrying groceries or guarding cars or on the tarmacs of petrol stations where children can always be found wiping or washing cars. In short it is the relative need for economic autonomy that determines what spaces will be coveted as *teritwa*. Contrary to Western suppositions about the territoriality of street youths, what constitutes "owned space" among street kids in Haiti is less often whole neighborhoods or even particular stretches of street. Typically one's *teritwa* is a mere twenty- to thirty-square feet of space that is worked for a particular purpose—begging or washing cars, for example. Most kids maintain *teritwa* on several streets of the city and move between them throughout the day.

While street children tend to avoid sections of town that are worked intensely by other youths, it is possible to carve a small space for oneself amid others, provided that such new settlement does not constitute an intolerable threat to the economic viability of those children already established in the area. The fact that Mati Ren and Damièn continue to work near Miko (even though the younger ones must pay Miko for the privilege) suggests that their presence as labor is quantifiable and in this case is not considered so great an economic threat as to invite any greater violence beyond exploitative intimidation.

Short of fisticuffs there are no uniform methods among street youth for defining territorial control and while there exists no predictable pattern as to how disputes concerning territoriality will be settled, aggressive posturing is typically sufficient for deterring outsiders from settling in areas where they are unwelcome. Rarely will established street children move beyond intimidation and posturing toward a particular newcomer right away. The activities of the recent arrival will typically be watched for several days in order for the established youths to ascertain whether or not he represents a serious enough threat to confront. But this is not always the case. In particularly destitute areas, any interloper to the informal street economy is greeted almost immediately with swift violence. Selejeur, a ten-year-old street boy in Portail Léogâne, illustrates this possibility with his own case:

> *Selejeur*: I was sick and could not work this day. I was vomiting but was hungry and needed some money to buy a little bit of rice and maybe some *bouyon* [broth]. So I walked to the *pòtay* [boarding place for the buses bound for villages outside the city] and stood where I could ask for money. People gave me things there before, so I knew I could eat something if I went there. After I got a little money an older boy who was wiping cars in the Texaco came and told me to give him my money. I told him no, but he beat me badly and took my little dollars. I was afraid and so I left that place and went to the *bar resto* [a nearby café/snackbar]. They gave me a little bit of food there.

On the steps of the National Cathedral, I spoke with Pitè, a sixteen-year-old street boy who described for me rather plainly how he dealt with a particular boy who made the mistake of taking up a piece of pavement next to him to beg:

> *Pitè*: I tell this boy, "This is not your place to be!" but he didn't listen to me. He was smaller than me, a little one. People give their dollars to little ones and old women and they give me nothing. So this one needs to leave and I tell him he needs to leave. But he stayed and would not listen. So I cut him with my *jilet* [razor] to make him leave.
>
> *Kovats-Bernat*: Where did you cut him with the *jilet*?
>
> *Pitè*: Where? [He looks quizzically, not understanding the question.]
>
> *Kovats-Bernat*: Did you cut him on his face, on his arm?

Pitè: I cut his leg with the *jilet*.

Kovats-Bernat: Did that make him leave?

Pitè: Yes. He ran away from that street.

Provided a given child does not interfere substantially with the economic yields of other street youths, he will be left unmolested. But this general rule cannot take into account the sheer opportunism of older, physically larger boys who do not "work" in the orthodox street sense of productive labor or begging, but instead make their livings beating younger children for their day's wages. These older boys, typically in their late teens, do not regard their *teritwa* as a static sector, but rather as a dynamic radius around themselves. They move through the neighborhoods in groups, intimidating and stealing from whomever looks vulnerable enough. It is likely this demographic of violent, predatory youths who contribute the most to the stereotype of the street child-cum-*zenglendo*. But even these predatory teens confine their attacks to their younger counterparts on the street and not the general public. Moreover their instruments of violence are typically their fists, not the handguns and machine pistols of the *zenglendo*.

The children upon whom these older boys prey are not afraid to solicit the protection of National Police officers, who are usually responsive to their complaints. Most officers come to know the street children that work in their jurisdiction and are willing to intervene on their behalf when they are threatened. Rozny, a National Policeman working Portail Léogâne, explained to me that as a part of his legal obligation to prevent violent conflict from erupting on the street, he ensures the status quo of street-child security against *malfektè* [troublemakers] as a defense against civil insecurity in general:

> *Rozny*: These children I know. I know them. These children work to eat. Sometimes I myself give them a little something. If they fight, I tell them to respect me and leave or I will arrest them. If they sniff *siment* I smack them easily. But I know them, and they do not always make trouble for people. When they come to me and tell me that boys are beating them, I say, "Where? Show me these boys," and when they show me to me, when they show me who is making trouble for them, I chase these boys out. The other ones, yes, not these boys. They are *atoufè* [vicious]. They are the ones who cause the problems for Haiti. They beat these boys. They beat them and they steal from everybody too. I don't like that so I look out for these kids. Those other ones are dangerous. Those ones are *atoufè*.

Beyond the conflicts that explode spontaneously between boys as an immediate protection of profit interests, the escalation of territorial disputes to intensified violence does not occur that often provided that everyone is working in their particular niche. Structural stability in the neighborhoods in which street children work is maintained by a common respect for each other's *teritwa*. When not working, most kids congregate in sections of town that are recognized as *disponib* ["free" or "open" spaces]. These "free areas" are usually noncommercial sectors of the city, residential areas or heavily policed public plazas like Champ de Mars, where opportunities for income through begging or working are sufficiently low as to make child labor less dense, reducing the opportunity for economic conflict. *Disponib* neighborhoods are also used by the kids the same way that they use the National Cemetery in downtown Port-au-Prince—as a social pressure valve. A street child who wishes to defuse an intensifying conflict with another child may opt to retreat to these safe spaces to let the animosities between the antagonists "cool."

Besides their keen awareness of the carrying capacity of the street market for child labor and strategies for avoiding conflicts that might emerge when a breach of that carrying capacity is threatened, street children also seek to avoid conflict and maintain a structural stability on the street in other ways. Most maintain some degree of mobility throughout the day, moving between particular streets on which they maintain *teritwa*, working mornings in one section of town and afternoons in another. They do this to avoid competition with one another on a given street as much as they do it to avoid wrathful merchants, areas of heavy police presence, neighborhoods likely to be swept by *arimaj*, and areas where there are dense populations of older boys who are known to prey on others. One boy with whom I spoke explained that he often moves out of an area when he begins to feel like *tiyo* [overflow].

Street children congregate according to patterns of age, gender, work or social lifestyle (in terms of sexuality or narcotic use, for example), creating a kind of "natural" segregation that serves to prevent explosions of violence that would otherwise no doubt erupt if such controlled associations and settlement trends did not obtain and street-child migration was thus less predictable. Younger children tend to work and congregate with other younger children in open, public places, usually not far from commercial areas where high pedestrian traffic means a higher police presence and thus a diminished chance of being beaten by older youths. These are also places where illuminated storefronts offer a modicum of light for solace while sleeping. Wonèl, a particularly young street boy of five years, confided in me that he sleeps close to the Big Star Market on Rue Capois because he is afraid of the dark and its entrance is lit throughout the night.

Street girls usually associate with one another in somewhat larger groups than boys and tend to sleep in similarly large groups in discreet but not isolated places like the back streets of residential districts or on the steps of the National Cathedral, which is quiet and somewhat safe after dark. The girls who work as prostitutes usually get much of their sleep during daylight hours and work the streets around bars and clubs well into the night. The children who sniff *siment* also tend to congregate in large groups with one another, if for no other reason than so that they might share the glue. Many of those with whom I worked could be found at the entrance to and inside the National Cemetery in Portail Léogâne, between whose crypts the children could hide quickly if the PNH or AGU was sweeping the area. Many Haitian cops harbor a special dislike for the *siment* sniffers.

Lagè Domi: Sleeping Rough in Port-au-Prince

While territoriality is somewhat important during working hours, concerns over the defense of space become less of a concern at night, when most street youth turn their attentions to the necessity of sleep and the spectrum of hazards that are unique to nighttime survival on the street. At dusk street children migrate back to their home bases where they regularly sleep, which are typically not the same places where they work. The architecture and landscape of street children's work spaces are usually ill-fit for sleeping, if for no other reason than because they are often in commercial areas that tend to be either quite filthy or too heavily policed by the AGU. Most children opt for communal seclusion, sleeping in clusters of two or three amid larger, allied cohorts of several dozen youths in a broader radius of space. Take for example the community of nineteen boys and eight girls who sleep near the entrance to the National Cemetery in Portail Léogâne. This particular group of children congregate together largely because of their shared addiction to glue-sniffing. Throughout the day they disperse alone or in pairs to different areas of the immediate neighborhood where they beg or wipe cars, making just enough money to buy *siment* or less often something to eat. They return to the cemetery frequently throughout the day to eat or to sniff, going back to the street when they need more money for glue or food. Beginning at around eight o'clock each night, the kids reconvene at the cemetery entrance to sniff, eat, and socialize until each grows tired and goes off to his/her respective areas to sleep. A pattern to their sleeping arrangements is apparent. Younger boys tend to doze off in the larger still-socializing group, to be roused when the teenage boys of the group move singly or in small clusters to separate sleeping spots against the walls of the cemetery. The younger boys usually follow their older counterparts, sleeping in clusters of three or four close to (but never up against) the older children, for protection. The girls of the group all sleep together, with two of the youngest boys in the group among them as well. I asked one of these boys, nine-year-old Bernestral, why he slept with the girls. He told me that he did so because it helps him to feel safe. "Like when I used to sleep with my sisters at home," he added.

Sleeping patterns based on age, gender, and interest group are observable among other groups of street children throughout Port-au-Prince as well. Within one allied community of about fifteen young street children in Champ de Mars, a handful of girls slept near a larger group of girls near the amphitheater, a few yards from two clusters of three and a single cluster of two street boys huddled near one another as they slept, each cluster a few yards from the next. Sometimes, though rarely, sleeping is an individual activity. In the market districts one can find children sleeping alone in the abandoned market stalls that line the streets. Many other children sleep in twos and threes in storefront doorways, not part of any other larger community of *zanmi* beyond the one or two comrades with whom they sleep. While over the course of my fieldwork in Haiti, I have met many boys who sleep alone or in isolated pairs or have done so in the past for a variety of reasons (usually, however, to hide from enemies who are familiar with their usual sleeping places); but never once did I meet a girl who slept in a group of less than three.

Confrontations between children that play out after darkness falls on the city are the most feared, because they are truly the most brutal and ruthless conflicts between street children. While daylight territorial disputes are common, they are somewhat mediated by geographic segregation and posturing and rarely do they escalate to deadly uses of violence, with most disputes resolved with a flurry of fisticuffs. Most of these conflicts carry shallow if any social meaning for the children involved. Beatings are not generally inflicted for symbolic purposes, nor are fistfights intended to carry some greater coded meaning concerning power relations on the street beyond the immediacy of the territorial conflict at hand. These are purely utilitarian confrontations bent toward either raw economic gain or personal vendetta and little more.

The relative intensity of particular violent acts among Port-au-Prince street youth, and the depth of cultural meaning that underlie them, are poorly measured against scales of escalation or explosiveness. The acts of interchild aggression that carry the heaviest weight of significance for street youth are usually not those spontaneous and sudden razor swipes, nor are they the escalating stages of posturing to fisticuffs characteristic of explosive confrontations over *teritwa*. The conflicts that bear out the most substantive cultural meaning are rather those protracted, low-intensity animosities between children that culminate in one punctuated act of brutality that marks a bloody, conclusive, and sometimes fatal end to hostilities. Emblematic of these confrontations are the *lagè domi*, the ritualized sleeping wars in which children exchange plastic burns and rock blows with one another in the dead of night, while the respective participants in the war are sleeping.

The *lagè domi* is rarely if ever employed for the settlement of territorial disputes. Rather it is considered by street youths to be a final solution to long-festering animosities that repeatedly emerge in the form of verbal insults and antagonisms and street scuffles. Its efficacy as a resolution to most serious disputes between children is generally considered to be effective but always brutal, given that many of the wars end at best in a serious wounding and at worst with the fatality of one of the protagonists involved. In this section I will explain the nature of the sleeping wars as I know them from my work with the youths who are veterans of them.

Making Sense of the Sleeping Wars

A sleeping war is by all accounts the absolute last resort to the resolution of otherwise unresolvable street child conflict, and all *timoun lari* understand the weighty consequences of involvement in such violent relations. Typically the nature of the dispute is one that might originate from any number of ultimate causes—persistent intimidation, leveled slurs, retribution for past beatings, sexual assault, suspicion of theft. It is important to point out however, that once a sleeping war is underway, the catalytic dispute is rarely cited by the kids as the reason for the ever-intensifying acts of violence over the course of the war. It is the escalating fear of both parties and their desire to put a conclusive end to the tension of the expectation of violence that is yet to come that leads the protagonists to ever more loathsome acts of brutality against one another.

The violence of the sleeping wars ultimately becomes a condition for its own reproduction. The combatants genuinely believe that the only event that can end the hostilities, and the terrible pain inflicted in the dead of night and slumber, is the annihilation of their opponent through insidious means—whether that annihilation comes as a profound maiming or a final deathblow. The *lagè domi* is therefore less a single event than it is an escalating sequence of violent acts that culminate in a final coup de grâce, an assault powerful enough to put a final and conclusive end to long-festering animosities between two street children. The final violent act is usually a blow to the feet, knees, or legs while the victim sleeps, though sometimes the head or chest will be targeted. The wounds inflicted are intended to be profoundly brutal but in fact are fatal in only a minimum of cases. On average one in every three street kids that I worked with has been involved in at least one war in their lifetime on the street and most of the rest have been witness to the sleeping wars of others, though were not themselves actors in the violence. Nadès and Gito are both veterans of *lagè domi,* and their experiences will serve well as an illustration of the patterns of violence that are characteristic of the wars.

Nadès is a teenager who was fourteen years old when he arrived on the street in Port-au-Prince from his natal village of Thomonde in 1998. He is a glue-sniffer who lives near the National Cemetery in Portail Léogâne. The year that he arrived in Port-au-Prince, he settled onto a piece of pavement on Rue Oswald Durand near the entrance to the Sylvio Cator Stadium, the grand soccer stadium adjacent to the cemetery, where he spent his time cleaning car tires and begging. After working the area around the stadium for several weeks after his arrival, Nadès had a run-in with a boy two or three years older than himself and whose name he could not recall. On one afternoon this boy (whom Nadès had never met before), attempted to steal his rags and a plastic bottle of gasoline that he was using to wipe car tires. Nadès resisted the other boy's grabs for his possessions, and the confrontation escalated into a brief scuffle that amounted to an exchange of shoves. The other boy left after the tussle, cursing Nadès as he departed, but returned later that afternoon and shoved Nadès hard from behind. Nadès suffered painful scrapes to his chin and the palm of his left hand as a result of the push.

Over the course of ensuing weeks, Nadès had several confrontations with his antagonist, none of which amounted to anything more serious than an exchange of glares and muttered curses directed at one another. Eventually, however, the glares and curses escalated to taunts, until finally the boys were embroiled in a fistfight that left both bloodied. The fight itself was disrupted by the intervention of a market woman who watched as the conflict escalated and who placed herself between the boys while shouting admonishments at both of them. Several nights after this, as Nadès slept against the wall of the National Cemetery, the other boy crept up on him and slashed the bottom of his right foot with a razor and ran. Nadès showed me the healed, four-inch scar that now runs along the side of the bottom of his foot and a quarter of the way around the right outer sole of his heel. It is straight and has healed cleanly, but retains that slightly raised appearance characteristic of a deep and painful wound. With the slashing of his foot, Nadès was drawn into the *lagè domi*.

After several days of watching his enemy, ascertaining where he slept and with whom, Nadès was poised for his retribution. This time it was he who crept up on the other boy as he dozed in his sleeping place behind a parked car on a quiet side street off Rue Oswald Durand. Heating the mouth of a plastic juice bottle to melting, Nadès shoved the hot plastic into the sole of the foot of his enemy. Nadès recalls being very afraid as he ran away from the screaming boy. He also recalls being fearful of what would come next:

> *Kovats-Bernat*: Did you believe that this boy would leave you alone after this? Did you hope that the boy would stay away from you after you did that to him. After you hurt him with the bottle, I mean.
>
> *Nadès*: [pause] No.
>
> *Kovats-Bernat*: You didn't think that he would stay away?
>
> *Nadès*: I knew that he would hurt me now. I was afraid because he would come. I slept *je klè* ["with one eye open," with a drowsy vigilance].

Despite Nadès's fears, the boy did not come back for him. After the incident with the bottle, Nadès in fact never saw the boy again.

Gito's experience with the sleeping wars was brief but brutal. In 1999, when Gito was fourteen years old, he was involved in a fistfight with a street boy about his age named Samwel. Though Gito was not *zanmi* with Samwel, he did work with him from time to time washing cars near the Bijou theater. Gito says that the fight began when Samwel hit him in the mouth with a plastic bottle that he kicked as part of a game he was playing with another boy. Gito was infuriated when Samwel added insult to his injury by laughing at his misfortune and taunting him. After exchanging several blows, Gito threw a punch into Samwel's chest that knocked him onto his backside. Samwel leapt from the ground and produced a small knife that he brandished at Gito. Gito relented and ran from the scuffle. The next night Gito came upon Samwel as he slept, stomped him hard in the small of his chest, and ran. Several nights later Samwel sought out Gito's sleeping place against the wall of the Casernes Dessalines, the former military prison and barracks of the Haitian army located just behind the National Palace, and dropped a heavy concrete rock onto his legs. Gito suffered painful swellings and probably fractures that went untreated as well. He now walks with a pronounced limp as a result of his wounds. Fearful of escalating the animosities beyond what they were, Gito sought no further retribution. He still sees Samwel from time to time, but Gito says that they both avoid one another. Their conflict is apparently over.

Nadès's and Gito's experiences with the *lagè domi* illustrate just how unimportant the original dispute is to the final outcome of the sleeping war, beyond its nature as the catalyst of the protracted confrontation. In Nadès's entire account of the war, he mentioned the attempted theft of his rags and gasoline and the subsequent shove to his back only at the outset and seemed to draw little significance around its role as a causal factor in the continuation of the war. Likewise Gito mentioned Samwel's ridicule of his injury as an instigation for the fistfight, but did not cite it as the rationale for the escalation of violence between the two boys. What then is the reason for the *lagè domi*?

First, the sleeping wars act as the great equalizer between street children of differing sizes. Many *lagè domi*, like the ones cited here, originate in rather one-sided assaults. Nadès was shoved brutally from behind by his antagonist, and Gito delivered a sound punch to Samwel, knocking him breathless. Blak Lovli (whose experience with the sleeping wars was addressed in the Interlude section preceding chapter 3) solicits the assistance of larger friends in pummeling his nemesis—an act that draws him into a *lagè domi*. Though these wars originated with violent beatings, they all eventually end with powerful assaults that require a minimum of strength in exacting a maximum toll on an enemy who sleeps unawares: a razor slash, a plastic burn, a dropped block of concrete. So the sleeping wars permit even the most frail child an equal advantage in inflicting trauma or even death on a larger, physically stronger adversary. In this respect the wars level the playing field, stripping away some of the advantages that would typically allow a more powerful opponent to brutalize at will. In fact the very possibility of the equalizing violence of *lagè domi* is enough to keep bullying on the street at least somewhat in check. Even the most predatory of older street boys have told me that there are some small children who they will not beat for money because they are known veterans of *lagè domi* and despite their size have demonstrated that they are capable of easily inflicting dismemberment and death on adversaries within the bounds of a sleeping war.

The value of the *lagè domi* is its capacity to rapidly negate one's enemy as a threat, settling once and for all disputes between two street youths that otherwise would continue to reemerge in the form of low-intensity scuffles that fail to resolve the conflict with any satisfaction for either party and persist to the economic disadvantage of both parties involved. In all cases the desired end result of the *lagè domi* is a complete end to the hostilities between the antagonists as soon as possible, so that both children can get back to the business of making a living.

It is clear that in some sleeping wars, hostilities between the protagonists escalate to the point where only the outright killing of one's enemy is considered sufficient to end the conflict. Maria, a sixteen-year-old street girl in Delmas, explained in detail how her boyfriend (a street teen who hustled marijuana and picked pockets for a living) settled a sleeping war by dropping a large rock onto the chest of his enemy, killing him outright. While these kinds of homicides are not common, they do occur. I have collected a handful of accounts of homicides that have ended especially protracted *lagè domi*, but their rare occurrence is indicative of the fact that few street children intend to inflict mortal wounds on their enemies, though they easily could. Indeed, in the stories that the children tell of sleeping wars that end in fatalities, a heavy stigma is attached to those who take the lives of their adversaries. Even Maria spoke disparagingly and fearfully about the demonstrated homicidal capacity of her boyfriend, and when she told her tale, the five or six children gathered around shook their heads and clicked their tongues with disapproval of her boyfriend's lack of mercy on his enemy. In short the intent of the sleeping wars is not to kill, but to inflict just enough pain on an adversary to convince him that his attacker is *capable* of killing and that conceding the conflict is in the best interest of all concerned.

Though the wars cited above did not end in mortal assaults (though I suspect that in Gito's case he was trying to kill Samwel when he stomped his chest and Blak Lovli's attack on his adversary was clearly intended to be lethal), they were effective in putting an end to any more aggressive acts between the parties involved. In the cases cited the protagonists were able to return to working the street effectively *only after the sleeping war was conclusively over.* Gito explained to me that until he received the rock to his legs, he was too fearful to work in his usual places, because he did not want to get into any more fistfights with Samwel, who washed cars with a gaggle of friends who were much bigger than he was. After he sustained the wounds to his legs, Gito knew that it would be up to him to strike next or to end the conflict by doing nothing to avenge his injuries. In short he suffered last but reserved the right to end the conflict in the interest of his own economic survival. That the two boys continue to maintain a tense but stable détente in the interest of working without fear of one another is testimony to the fact that the sleeping wars are an effective means of ending violent hostilities that otherwise would go on without end, interfering with both parties' ability to make enough money to eat from day to day. All that is required to get back to the business of street work is the concession of victory to one's enemy by not protracting the conflict any further beyond one's own victimization, and few street children value their egos over their economic survival.

As ritual violence the *lagè domi* is a socially regulated symbolic relation between street children that begs an interesting question—why do the children who fight the wars adopt the same methodologies of violence? After being shoved to the ground, Nadès received a slash to the bottom of his feet, which he avenged by burning the foot of his tormentor with molten plastic. Gito stomped Samwel's chest with his foot, but then himself suffered the agony of a large block dropped onto his legs. Blak Lovli suffered plastic burns to his feet during the course of his sleeping war, which he avenged by dropping a chunk of concrete onto the head of his victim. While many other accounts of *lagè domi* suggest that the head and chest are frequently targets of adversarial blows, virtually all of the accounts involve descriptions of significant individual assaults directed at the victims' feet and legs. Though not involved in a sleeping war, even Pitè slashed the leg of another street boy in order to defend his economic territory. Why do the children target particular parts of the anatomy when they attack one another during the wars?

I suggest that the common intent in inflicting wounds in the sleeping war is to incapacitate one's victim long enough to cause him economic hardship, the effects of which—hunger, infection, fever, incapacitation, helplessness—are far more humiliating and frightening to a street child than even the risk of abrupt death. Assaults to the feet and legs are the kinds of wounds that guarantee the best chance of ending the war as soon as possible, short of the stigma of murder. Street kids aren't generally afraid of being killed in the sleeping wars; they are afraid of being maimed. Indeed every child on the street wakes each morning to the very real possibility (indeed, likelihood) of their death at the hands of countless other violent causes—gunfire, traffic accident, disease. What is genuinely frightening is the possibility that their only source of autonomy and survival—the ability to labor—will be taken from them painfully by another street child.

Whether they make their living as thieves, beggars, shoeshines, package handlers, or car washers, street children rely very heavily on walking to get around the city in order to make money, as is also suggested by the considerable value that street kids place on the ownership of shoes. Disabling injuries to the feet or legs can precipitate painful days or even weeks of immobilized recovery without the ability to make money for food outside of the humiliation of begging. Such assaults are in fact regarded by the kids as more devious than fatal ones, because hunger and helplessness are regarded as worse than a quick death. Whether the attack is directed at the feet, legs, head, or chest, it is clear in all cases that a long recovery from the wounds inflicted is a given outcome of the assault. And that recovery is likely to involve a severe limitation on one's ability to work.

Viewed in this way, the sleeping wars serve a larger socioeconomic purpose. They are a ritualized means of maintaining a delicate economic balance on the boulevards of Port-au-Prince. Recognizing that the violence of the wars is directly related to the labor strategies of the combatants goes a long way toward destabilizing the dominant ideology of street children as wild mongrels, bent to an irrational, asocial tendency toward senseless violence. Street children in Haiti are engaged daily in a struggle for physical space as well as a space in the local economy that supercedes all other considerations, because that space carries with it the same degree of personal identification that our homes and places of work do for us. Perhaps more so, because the street in this case is not only the locus of their domestic, economic, political, and social realities, but it also represents space that lies in the public domain and is therefore contested. Little wonder that street children defend their small space of it so desperately. Little wonder that the mere occupancy of space on the street and within its economy carries with it the occasional burden of brutality and victimization.

It is important to note that the children who fight in the sleeping wars do not speak of the wounding of their enemies as an offensive measure but rather as a deterrent to further hostilities and as such these wars are best understood as defensive measures. None of the veterans of these conflicts ever gave me any indication that their motivation for fighting the wars was anything other than to end the existing dispute as quickly as possible so as to avoid any further harm to themselves and to get back to working the street without fear.

Methods of Protection and Strategies for Defense

Confrontations over territorial integrity and the violence of the sleeping wars occur with enough frequency to prompt street children to adopt routine strategies for protecting themselves as they socialize, labor, and sleep. The most effective means of safeguarding one's well-being is through the careful observance of street norms. There are few children who negotiate the city streets alone or sleep in isolation, for example, guaranteeing at least a modicum of strength in numbers while they work, play, and doze. Smaller street children are averse to congregate in areas frequented by older street boys, who are typically the most opportunistic aggressors given their size and strength advantage over their smaller and younger counterparts. All street children are sensitive to their possible encroachment into others' *teritwa*. Most avoid unnecessary confrontations, often considering it more feasible to yield to an aggressor's demands for money rather than fight back. But mere membership in a larger community of associates and careful adherence to appropriate street behavior are not enough to guard oneself against the host of threats that stand to jeopardize one's security while on the street.

A street child's vulnerability is never more heightened than when he or she is sleeping. Girls run obvious special risks, given the fact that their gender places them in a special category of potential victimization. Rape is not at all uncommon on the street and both girls and boys have confided in me that they had been raped by older street boys. Street girls tend to sleep in larger groups than boys, for the express purpose of protection from rape while they sleep. Younger street boys tend to sleep in larger clusters as well, ostensibly as protection against assaults by older street youths.

The threat of attack during the night prompts some communities of street children to adopt strategies for group identification based on who sleeps where and with whom. Some children wear like colors when they sleep, so that they can identify who is friend and who is foe in the murk of night. One teenaged boy named Dèjwi explained that he, like the girls and boys with whom he sleeps, wears a white T-shirt at night to give indication to his *zanmi* who may not recognize him in the dark that he belongs there among them. He intimated to me that this method of identification also protects him and his friends from theft and abuse by members of his own group who are prone to engage in such violations against outsiders who sleep nearby.

While some children regard a well-hidden sleeping spot as sufficient protection against victimization while sleeping, some make a habit of changing their sleeping place regularly to avoid adopting predictable patterns that could be exploited by observant, predatory street youths. This practice is especially the case among children who are embroiled in active sleeping wars, as Gito explained:

> *Gito*: All the time I move where I sleep. When he [Samwel] was trying to hurt me, I moved even every night!
>
> *Kovats-Bernat*: Did your friends move with you?
>
> *Gito*: No, no, no. I don't want them to come with me. He knows my friends. He knows them so I don't want to sleep with them. I sleep in good [safer] places if I sleep by myself. It's good to sleep with these guys, but it can be a bad thing. I hide better alone.

Sleeping in groups, wearing clothing that identifies one as friend rather than foe and changing sleeping locations frequently and unpredictably are useful strategies of defense while sleeping, but no community, color, or hiding spot is ever sufficient to guard against all threats. It is for this reason that many street children sleep very lightly and most indicate that they wake frequently throughout the night. Most kids sleep *je klè* [with one eye open], ever alert even in sleep, ready to leap to self-defense when necessary. Among gaggles of girls who sleep together, alertness throughout the night is of even greater importance, given the constant threat of sexual violence by street boys. Claudette, a young street girl of around twelve years explained how the responsibility for staying awake and aware while the rest of the girls sleep rotates throughout the course of the night. She called the girl who acts as the sentinel *"djal siveye"* [watch-out girl].

Nearly all street children arm themselves in some way, either all of the time or only when they feel threatened. The most common weapon carried is a *jilet*, a small disposable razor blade scavenged from street dumps, and I have seen both girls and boys with them, though boys tend to produce them in disputes with greater ease and frequency. Even among the children that habitually carry them, the blades are regarded as weapons only in times of need. Most children use the *jilet* as a grooming instrument for shaving their head or trimming their fingernails. Street children fight with one another almost constantly, though their disputes more often than not are verbal arguments accompanied by aggressive posturing suggestive of the potential for violent outburst. Occasionally, however, these confrontations do escalate and the children (usually the boys) are apt to produce the razor as a threat. I have watched children swipe at one another with the blades on several occasions, and a few times have seen them draw blood. A typical incident occurred in Portail Léogâne in 1999. On that occasion two teenage boys whom I did not know were engaged in a heated argument on a side street off Rue Jean-Marie Guilloux near Sylvio Cator Soccer Stadium that resulted in one of the boys swiping his *jilet* at his opponent's raised arm. The blade caught its target's wrist and hand, drawing blood as the boy drew back from the swipe. Though the wounded boy spat rebukes through his sobs as the two continued to curse one another, the confrontation ended without any further assaults from either.

While razors are carried by many street children, few of the children have actually used them in anger. Nearly all of the children that I have known, however, have used rocks as weapons. They are perhaps the weapon of choice among street youth, given that fist-sized chunks of concrete are found everywhere on the streets of Port-au-Prince. Kids use rocks as weapons in a number of ways. Two street girls explained to me that although they do not throw the rocks at enemies the way some kids do, they have held them

Figure 4.6. Street girls begging in the capital. The very real risk of sexual assault prompts most street girls to travel and sleep in large groups. They will often rotate the responsibility for sitting sentinel (on the lookout for predatory street boys) while the larger group sleeps.

rocks = common weapon

in their hands and swung them in their fists at other street girls with whom they were fighting. Other children have indicated that they have thrown rocks in their retreat from fights or beatings. Two older boys told me how they threw rocks at soldiers of the Haitian army during the most recent coup d'etat (1991–1994); the younger of these two boys also claimed to have thrown rocks at National Policemen in the sprawling Cité Soleil slum after the coup as well, in retaliation for the beating of a street boy at the hands of a policeman in the slum earlier that week.

Large rocks and chunks of concrete block are the preferred weapons of the *lagè domi*, probably because they can inflict massive damage to the body and as such afford the attacker the greatest chance of ending the dispute abruptly and conclusively, thus effectively defending himself against further attacks. Samwel dropped a concrete rock onto Gito's legs. Blak Lovli dropped a concrete block onto the head of his enemy, and Maria's boyfriend killed his foe by dropping a rock onto his chest. When I asked Gito and Blak Lovli how they chose the weapon that they used in their respective *lagè domi*, both explained that they picked up the rocks at the scene of the assault (as opposed to bringing the rocks with them), indicating that they chose their weapon

Figure 4.7. A street boy practices his karate moves, which he claims is his best defense against attack on the street.

on the spur of the moment just prior to the attack, rather than calculating in advance exactly how they planned to wound their target.

While many street children are apt to use weapons to defend themselves when they feel threatened, most children recognize that the National Police can be a source of protection for them. When I asked street children, "Do the National Police protect you?" most responded that they do. Many of these same children however listed the National Police (and their multiple paramilitary subsidiaries such as the AGU) as a threat to them as well. Nonetheless street children generally believe that they can go to a National Police officer if they feel threatened or are harassed by other street children or if they are in need of medical or other emergency assistance. The children do not, however, seek out the police as a first line of defense, because they correctly acknowledge that the protections that the PNH offer can only ever be temporary. Officers are not bodyguards and cannot watch out for the welfare of all street children all of the time. That said, street children are more inclined to defend themselves against everyday hostilities with flight, fists, or weapons before they seek out the protection of the National Police.

The best defense against the hostilities of the streets is obviously to get off them altogether, but few street children have the opportunity to do so. Some shelters are available throughout Port-au-Prince that offer street children at least a modicum of haven from the dangers that obtain on the boulevards. In the next chapter I will detail the social history of one such shelter, the ill-fated Lafanmi Selavi orphanage facility in the Pacot section of Port-au-Prince. While in its form Lafanmi Selavi was very much like the many other street-child outreach centers in the capital, providing food, clean water, and a bed to displaced youth, the facility was unique in its mission as a political institution, offering to mold the cultural identity of street youth toward the formation of a new generation of Haitian nationalists. While Lafanmi Selavi represented an ambitious social project that enjoyed some early success, the reality of its complete history calls into question the contradiction implicit in its stated claim to offer a safe alternative to street life on the one hand and its pedagogy that both advocated and stimulated often dangerous youth political action on the other. As will be seen, the material, political, and cultural conditions at the facility eventually deteriorated to such unlivable conditions that children began to leave the facility in droves by the late 1990s, preferring to take their chances on the street rather than continue to cope with the violence, scarcity, filth, and political hypocrisy that came to be emblematic of the Lafanmi Selavi orphanage complex in Port-au-Prince.

Tifrè is eleven years old. I sit beside him on a splintered sheath of plywood lying in the courtyard of Lafanmi Selavi, at this time a vibrant, very loud street-child outreach/orphanage in the middle-class Pacot section of Port-au-Prince. There is a gaggle of seven other boys huddled in close around him, intently watching what he is doing. They are chattering back and forth at one another as they observe Tifrè at his craft. Beside his left foot is a pile of foraged bottle caps, beside his right is a pile of bottle caps that he has pounded into flat disks with the rock he is now using to work another cap in front of him. He is bending the flattened caps onto one another. Over time I see that he is making a small table and chairs.

He has an oversized Band-Aid on his forehead over his left eye that covers a scratch he suffered in a scuffle with another street boy named Jean-Robert in the orphanage courtyard the day before. They were playing soccer when Tifrè accidentally tripped Jean-Robert. The two fought and were eventually broken up by two of the teachers, but not before Tifrè suffered the deep cut above his eye from Jean-Robert's jagged fingernail. Explosive encounters like this are common at Lafanmi Selavi and expected, given that the facility is home to over two hundred street boys who spend most of their waking day learning, eating, cleaning, playing, and working as one large group. Most often, their clashes end in a flurry of punches before they are broken up, but sometimes they go unchecked and end up bad. Last week, I watched the back end of one such fight between two of the older boys. I arrived as one of them was drawing a small razor blade from his pants. In an instant he had slashed a long gash down the arm of his adversary. The offending boy was ousted from the orphanage and never returned. The wounded boy required dozens of stitches to close the wound.

Few of the boys ever have such serious problems with Tifrè, though. In an abstract but fundamental way, he is different from the others and the others know it, though I don't think that Tifrè does. He is very soft-spoken and, rare in the often violent world of Haitian street kids, decidedly pacifist. He never attended school before he arrived, by chance, at Lafanmi Selavi in 1994. He had been displaced from his mother's home and onto the street in Bon Repos when she fell ill and could no longer work to care for him and his three other brothers and one sister. Tifrè and his eldest brother were sent onto the street to work to help support the household.

Tifrè spent his days shining shoes and selling penny-candy, returning each night to give his day's receipts to his mother, who would save some and give the rest to his sister to fetch food for the family's one meal each day. At first Tifrè spent every night sleeping in his mother's house. Then he fell in with a few other street kids in Bon Repos who spent their nights sleeping behind parked cars. Soon Tifrè was returning home only every few nights. Eventually he stopped going home altogether and moved to Port-au-Prince, where the work was believed better.

After a severe beating that he received at the hands of a soldier in the Haitian army during the Cedras regime, Tifrè made his way out of the city center to Pacot, where he wandered past Lafanmi Selavi and was invited in by one of the facility's teachers who was arriving for work as Tifrè was approaching. He has been at Lafanmi ever since.

Tifrè is, like most of the others, illiterate but he is exceptionally bright and possesses a peculiar knack for the principles of mechanics and physics. He seems to always be fashioning some little thing from scraps of this and pieces of that which he has foraged from the street dumps. Today I am eating a breakfast of toast and goat milk (a typical morning meal at the facility) in the orphanage clinic and am approached by Tifrè, who asks me for a battery. I take a AA cell from my camera flash and give it to him. He pulls me out into the courtyard to show me what he wants to do with it. As is typical he has a small project nearing completion that a gaggle of boys has crowded around, anxious to see what Tifrè's newest creation will do when energized by the battery. On the ground in the center of the group is a strange contraption made up of salvaged street-junk: a scrap of wood that is serving as a base onto which is fastened a small motor connected to bits of frayed wire, which are in turn attached to small scraps of aluminum cans that will power a Popsicle-stick propeller once the battery is secured in place.

Tifrè wedges the battery between the aluminum-can-scrap contact points, bending the metal to accommodate the size of the battery. Dramatically, a proverbial hush falls over the onlookers. Tifrè takes hold of one of the pigtail wires, touches it to one of the contacts and the Popsicle stick begins to twirl. It sputters on-and-off at first as he makes the proper adjustments and then the propeller twirls into a blur. A wash of dust from beneath the contraption whishes away. A gleeful cheer of approval goes up from the gaggle. It is an admiring, approving boyish kind of cheer. It seems to shout, "Tifrè has done it again!" Some of the boys pull at my shirtsleeves and say excitedly to me, "*Sa se helikopte! Sa se helikopte!*"

"Yes," I think to myself. "It is indeed a helicopter."

And then Tifrè does something very typical of Tifrè. He picks up the contraption and unceremoniously hands it to a small boy of eight whose squeals of glee at the spinning toy clearly suggests that he is most impressed with it.

"*Sa-a pou ou,*" Tifrè says to him as he hands it off. "It's for you."

5

Lafanmi Selavi

"The Family Is Life"

There are outreaches of many kinds in Haiti, especially in Port-au-Prince, many of which are specifically aimed at alleviating the immediate dangers to the physical (and in the case of the mission orphanages, moral) well-being of street children. By far the most common type of facility for street-child outreach is the orphanage. Hardly any of them are publicly funded and few are secular. Most are Christian church-affiliated, clergy-run institutions that extend valuable immediate aid and services like food, potable water, clean beds, vitamins, and some education to the burgeoning street-child population in the capital. There are a handful of exceptions to the parochial rule. Centre d'Action is a small, privately funded, secular outreach center near the Carrefour-Feuilles section of Port-au-Prince. It offers food, security, and primary schooling to around one hundred street children (both boys and girls) in the surrounding community. But as is always the case in Haiti, the needs of the many far outstrip the charity of the few. Centre d'Action is financially limited and has only enough space to house eighty children comfortably, though they do manage to find enough room for the one hundred in residence today.

Margaret, the center's director, advocates a pragmatic strategy for addressing the needs of street children. She believes that an orphanage in Haiti must first fill a child's belly, provide the children with clean water, give them a comfortable place to sleep, and teach them to at least know how to read street signs and write their names. Like most Haitians in her line of work, Margaret also believes that a child's susceptibility to danger is heightened by his/her complete exposure on the street, and she's right. For this reason and for others, Margaret does not see a value in encouraging children to act out politically in the streets. This perspective is one that has been shared by nearly all of the other orphanage outreach centers in Port-au-Prince, public or private. All in fact, but one.

Lafanmi Selavi was conceived as not merely an orphanage, but as a new template of Haitian citizenship, built on a foundational ideology that would support the pillars of the new postcoup nationalism: justice, reconciliation,

democracy, and poverty with dignity. Firmly rooted in Haiti's liberation theology movement, the orphanage was home to over four hundred boys and
girls at the height of its success, all with greater or lesser degrees of experience with the street (or in the case of some of the girls, harsh treatment in
domestic service as *restavèk*). With successive martial regimes shaping the
backdrop of its early history, the Lafanmi program actively sought to raise
the political consciousness of the children it served, allowing the introduction of child identity as legitimate terrain for the settlement of often violent
political differences in Haiti.

Though Lafanmi Selavi would grow in child population as well as in the
scope of its ambitions throughout its early development, it ultimately succumbed to the attrition of successive political attacks, administrative corruption, and material destitution—the hallmarks of Haitian bureaucracies.
The underlying philosophy and function of the Lafanmi Selavi orphanage
program and the children who would be beaten, raped, disappeared, and
killed as a result of their affiliation with it, raise serious questions as to
whether the cultural identity and political agency of children should have
any place in the violent arena of Haitian nationalist conflict at all. If not, then
what can be said about the rights and agency of children in general?

"The Family Is Life"

The Lafanmi Selavi orphanage began in the mid-1980s as the nationalist vision of Jean-Bertrand Aristide, then a Salesian Catholic priest and pastor of
St. Jean Bosco church in the Port-au-Prince slum of La Saline. At the time,
Aristide was one of the few prominent individuals in Port-au-Prince who
risked public expressions of discontent and disgust with the totalitarian regime of Jean-Claude Duvalier (1971–86), heir to the repressive government
of his father, François (1957–71). Through his antityrannical preaching and
homilies of dissent against the Haitian military and the brutal Duvalierist
civilian militias, Aristide had helped to create in the capital a climate of civil
unrest and impatience that had made the departure of Duvalier absolutely
necessary. By the time the dictator had left for exile in February 1986, Aristide was one of the most visibly prominent of the many priests, sisters, and
laity who together formed Haiti's *ti legliz*—the "little church" of liberation
theology. At odds with the Vatican and in line with other populist forms of
radical Catholicism practiced throughout Latin America and the Caribbean,
ti legliz is an ideological and ritual revolt against the colonial teachings of
the Church, perceived to be instructing the poor to accept their poverty
and scarcity as God's will and with a guarantee of salvation in the afterlife.
Opposed to these and other Catholic doctrines believed to be at once de-
featist and in support of foreign interests, *ti legliz* is founded on the belief

that Christ does not want the poor to accept their wretched lot in life with passivity. Arguing that Jesus lived very much like the poor of Haiti— destitute, criminalized, and persecuted by a repressive army—Haiti's liberation church instructs its parishioners to follow God's command to bring Heaven unto Earth through social revolution. Aristide would in fact become the first prolific exponent of Haitian liberation theology, outlining the fundamental doctrines of *ti legliz* in his *In the Parish of the Poor: Writings from Haiti* (1990). It was through this radical theological base that he succeeded in raising the social consciousness of the urban poor, as well as the violent ire of the state apparatus.

Rather than work within the bounds of programs for the poor already established by the Salesians in Haiti, Aristide opted to initiate his own projects, most notably the Lafanmi Selavi orphanage. Its name means "the family is life," and it was instituted in July 1986 in order to provide housing, food, and vocational and literacy training for the emerging number of street boys roaming around La Saline (Tifi Lafanmi Selavi would be added to the orphanage program in 1996, providing services to *restavèk* and girls living on the street). The Lafanmi program was originally situated on the grounds of the parish church of St. Jean Bosco in the Port-au-Prince slum of La Saline. At that time Aristide was welcoming street children from the community into the church courtyard to eat, sleep, and receive informal instruction in literacy.

Aristide's sermons against the abuses of the Haitian army and their death squad proxies would inevitably lead to the infamous government massacre of parishioners at St. Jean Bosco. On September 11, 1988, as Aristide said Mass, a government hit squad launched a firebomb and machete attack against the worshippers as retribution for Aristide's outspoken preaching. The attack resulted in the near-complete destruction of the church and the hacking deaths of seventeen parishioners, one a pregnant woman. In the aftermath of the attack, it became clear that if the safety of the street boys was to be a priority, the Lafanmi Selavi program would need to be relocated to a safer neighborhood. With the financial assistance of several international donors (Caritas, France-Libertés, and Danièle Mitterrand among them), Aristide purchased a small house with a walled compound in the bourgeois Pacot section of Port-au-Prince. From this base community on Camille Léon Street, Lafanmi Selavi's middle-class neighbors were afforded an intimate vantage on the everyday lives of Haiti's youngest dispossessed, as hundreds of street children played, slept, ate, and regularly visited at the new orphanage. By 1989 Lafanmi had also begun to extend the services of its *klinik pòv* [clinic for the poor] to the lower-class communities surrounding Pacot. The relationship between Lafanmi Selavi and its neighbors was a good one and several physicians living in the area extended their services to the clinic.

The violent exile of Lafanmi Selavi from its original location in La Saline to Pacot resulted in a dramatic increase in the number of children served by the program. Prior to the move from St. Jean Bosco, Aristide was administering on a regular basis to less than fifty street children. Once the program was moved to the Pacot center, the number of children (nearly all of them boys) escalated to over one hundred by 1990 and to over two hundred by the end of the following year. From 1989 to 1991 Lafanmi Selavi also broadened its programming, formalized its elementary education system, and expanded its vocational training. Though secondary schooling for those promoted to that level was unavailable at Lafanmi Selavi and had to be pursued outside the orphanage, Lafanmi provided financial support to children who wished to continue their schooling at the secondary level.

Over the course of 1990 and 1991, amid tumultuous social and political upheaval, government violence against citizens, and systematic antidemocratic terror, Lafanmi Selavi emerged as a political safe haven for street children who had become active, participatory agents of democratic change in the days leading up to Aristide's unprecedented election to the Haitian presidency in December 1990. Their visibility and vocality against state authority would make them specific targets for repression in the years to follow (Bernat 1999). By 1991 Lafanmi Selavi had emerged as a vehicle for the political voice of children in social discourse and as a nucleus for responsive action.

In the early morning hours of September 30, 1991, Aristide (in office for little more than eight months) was ousted in a coup orchestrated by Army Chief-of-Staff Lieutenant-General Raoul Cedras. Understanding that popular support for Aristide could effectively hamper the usurpation of presidential power, the army moved to prevent the populace from gathering, from erecting barricades, and from ultimately unleashing a popular insurrection against the coup. Before organized demonstrations could assemble, the military was dispatched throughout the capital and the rural sectors of the country, firing weapons indiscriminately, and killing scores of civilians in the first few hours of the putsch.

The military was assisted in its takeover by the *attachés*, the descendant factions of Duvalier's notorious *tontons makout*. Keenly aware of the historical propensity of the Haitian army to act as the executors of coup d'etat against heads of state, François Duvalier chose in the late 1950s to consolidate his executive power with the creation of the *makouts* as a paramilitary counterpoise to the army, a secret police organization answerable directly to the National Palace. The *makouts* borrowed their name from the *tonton ma-*

kout of Vodou folklore, a malevolent creature that lives in the countryside, coming into town after nightfall to snatch up "bad" children, carrying them off into the night to eat them. Duvalier's *makouts* became the most ruthless implementers of political terror, acting on behalf of the state as informers, neighborhood bosses, extortioners, executioners, and all-around thugs. With many former *makouts* filling their ranks, the *attachés* enjoyed greater support and cooperation from the Haitian army under Cedras. Aside from their respective nom de guerre, the only real difference between the *makouts* and their descendant *attachés* was the nature of their respective relationships to the FADH. Whereas the *makouts* were completely independent of the military by design, the *attachés* were supplied and supported by the army and coordinated many of their civil terrorist activities in concert with them. So not only were the *attachés* better organized than their predecessors, but they carried better weapons as well—automatic rifles, machine-pistols, and hand grenades. Many *attachés* were also full-time FADH soldiers.

With the cooperation of the *attachés* and the army, Cedras completed what would turn out to be the bloodiest coup d'etat in recent Haitian history. Terror was carried out methodically and in brutal form toward the discouragement of any popular reaction and the young, politically mobilized partisans of the pro–Aristide Lavalas movement were its specific targets. By the time the coup had ended with a U.S.-led United Nations invasion in September 1994, well over three thousand Haitian civilians had been executed or disappeared, many of the victims the young, poor residents of the staunchly democratic Port-au-Prince slums.

Characteristic of the Cedras regime was the resurrection of makoutist tactics of political coercion, carried out by both the army and death squad *attachés*. By its unique extremism, *makoutinaj* permitted the profound penetration of state power into the intimate affairs of the civil sector. Emblematic of the violence was the deconstruction of traditional, cultural constraints on the state's use of coercive force, including the targeting of clergy, women, nonpolitical groups, the elderly and certainly, children (Trouillot 1990)—notably those at Lafanmi Selavi.

During the coup the army and the *attachés* were represented in the Haitian parliament by the Front Révolutionnaire pour l'Avancement et le Progrès d'Haïti [Revolutionary Front for the Advancement and Progress of Haiti] or FRAPH, a political party that served as the de facto regime's democratic facade. FRAPH, like the *attachés*, hinged on the support of the Haitian army, which protected their political power in exchange for parliamentary support of the regime. FRAPH was instrumental in the suppression and neutralization of popular challenges to the de facto regime, centralizing and legitimat-

Figure 5.1. The outside wall of the Lafanmi Selavi orphanage facility in Pacot, 1998. The graphic in the center reads, "I love you." Also shown is the emblem of the clinic for the poor, which depicts a farmer, a beggar, a street child, and a nursing mother climbing up to sit around the "table of prosperity," a common theme of the Aristide political movement.

ing violent state coercion. Because of the work of FRAPH and the *attachés*, the Cedras regime lasted longer than anyone could have anticipated in late 1991.

Given that the martial law of the coup regime criminalized prodemocratic institutions like Lafanmi Selavi, it is not surprising that the orphanage and its children bore a brunt of the political attacks against Aristide's supporters, especially given the historical prominence of street children on the front lines of the anti-Duvalierist street demonstrations. Political rapes, disappearances, firebombings, torture, and executions were the principal means by which the state and its *attaché* proxies sought the suppression of youth resistance movements to prevent such movements from undermining de facto legitimacy.

Through murder, thuggery, assault, and intimidation, the Cedras regime was able to completely arrest the programmatic development of Lafanmi Selavi until the coup was ousted in 1994. By the end of 1992 many of the children had deserted the orphanage after repeated political attacks on the facility by the supporters of the de facto government. The orphanage was a primary target for antidemocratic violence because of the vocal dissent and active resistance to the coup advocated in the education program and because of the facility's close, intimate relationship to Aristide himself. A February 1991 firebomb thrown by *attachés* through the window of Lafanmi's dormitory killed five children as they were sleeping. A second firebombing in June of the following year wounded scores of children and destroyed the clinic for the poor, the pharmacy, and the administration house, which contained the children's dossiers, the only real evidence of the children's identities ever compiled.

In July of 1993, amid rumors that Aristide would be returning to Haiti behind a U.S. invasion, several *attachés* rented a house near Lafanmi Selavi and established a local headquarters there. For twenty-two weeks the *attachés* routinely entered the orphanage compound brandishing automatic weapons, grenades, and machetes, beat and harassed the children and pressed several of them into *restavèk* servitude at the rented house. Under the stress of *attaché* persecution, the orphanage's population dwindled to its nadir, with fewer children staying at the facility since its relocation to Pacot. The number of street boys at Lafanmi Selavi had been reduced in a single year by half—from close to two hundred and fifty in the spring of 1992, to less than one hundred and twenty in the summer of 1993 (Table 02). In an interview that I had with him in 1995, the executive director of Lafanmi Selavi described the summer and fall of 1993 as the worst period in the orphanage's history. During that time Lafanmi was barely operational. The entire staff of teachers, counselors, mentors, and administrators had gone into hiding, neither the clinic nor the pharmacy had yet been rebuilt after the 1992 bombing, and the children wandered in and out of the facility uneasily, uncertain as to whether it was safer to stay at Lafanmi or return to the street. Throughout July and into August of 1993, the *attaché* presence in the neighborhood was tantamount to an "occupation" and was in fact described to me as such—*lokipasyon*—by a number of the children who had resolved to stay at the orphanage during that time. By September 1993 less than a hundred boys were staying at Lafanmi Selavi.

Restored to the Haitian presidency with the 1994 U.S. invasion, Aristide moved to dissolve the Haitian army in order to break the endless cycle of military-led coups that had plagued Haitian politics since the mid-1940s. Lafanmi Selavi took advantage of the fragile democratic space that was created to rebuild the facilities that had been destroyed throughout the coup and to resume its services to street children in Port-au-Prince, and the street-child population at Lafanmi began to rise once again. By 1995 over 175 street boys were once again eating, sleeping and taking classes at Lafanmi Selavi, and its programmatic recovery was nearly complete. The administrative house had been reconstructed, the clinic and pharmacy were once again operational, the elementary and technical school programs were reinstituted, and by the following year the child population at the orphanage was approaching 190 boys. A week-long planning session of Lafanmi Selavi's General Assembly (made up of teachers, staff, and children) in mid-1995 produced an aggressive five-year plan for the orphanage program. The first phase of the plan looked to the expansion of the existing Pacot facility to serve more children in the capital, especially street girls and *restavèk*. The second phase of the plan anticipated the expansion of Lafanmi Selavi services into the countryside to aid the thousands of displaced children there. Finally the plan sought the eventual establishment of formal Lafanmi Selavi chapters throughout the world (starting in Latin America and moving outward), which would serve as an international network of voice and support for the rights, needs and values of dispossessed youth worldwide. It was an ambitious agenda and for a while it seemed as though it might be possible.

In 1996, recognizing the need for expanded space and desiring to implement as soon as possible the outreach to girls, Lafanmi Selavi purchased a house immediately adjacent to the Pacot facility for boys. In preparation for the opening of its new program for at-risk girls, Lafanmi staff members toured Port-au-Prince each Saturday in June and July, recruiting girls who were living on the street or were in otherwise desperate situations. The girls were brought to the facility, washed and fed, and invited to stay for the day to play with the other children, allowing them time to familiarize themselves with the program before deciding if they would like to take part in it. In April

Table 2. Street Children in Residence at Lafanmi Selavi, 1986–1999

Years	Number of Children[a]
1986–1988	50
1988–1990	100
1990–1991	200
1991–1992	250
1992–1993	115
1993–1995	175
1995–1996	190
1996–1997	350[b]
1997–1999	400

a. Numbers are estimated averages based on Lafanmi Selavi records and head counts by the author.
b. Tifi Lafanmi Selavi opened in April 1997 with 160 girls in residence.

Figure 5.2. Tifi Lafanmi Selavi opened in 1997, and at its peak boasted over 160 former street girls and *restavèk* in residence.

1997 Tifi Lafanmi Selavi formally opened its doors to young girls for their primary schooling and twice-daily meals. The new facility was ill-equipped for dormitories, so Tifi Lafanmi Selavi remained a day program only. The combined child population at Lafanmi Selavi reached its all-time peak that year at 190 boys and 160 girls and this before the inclusion of dozens of other street youths who would simply wander in and take advantage of Lafanmi's nonresidence resources (meals, clean water, toys, games, a safe place to rest) on a per diem basis. Lafanmi Selavi had become *disponib*—an area collectively claimed, a space not balkanized into individual children's *teritwa*.

By 1997 the orphanage program was expanding its enterprises beyond the Pacot compound. The Lafanmi Selavi Agricultural Initiative was launched the prior year as a program for reconnecting urban street children to the land and to the socioeconomic lessons of Haitian farming. Occupying eleven acres of precious arable soil just outside Port-au-Prince in Tabarre (near the Ministry of Agriculture), the initiative permitted children from the orphanage to visit the farm weekly, accompanied by agronomists and local farmers,

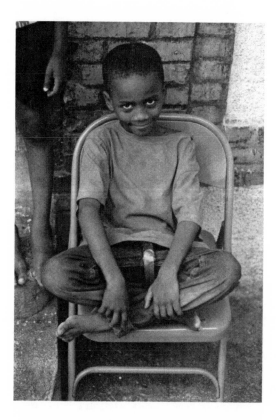

Figure 5.3. A former street boy sits in the courtyard of Lafanmi Selavi in 1996. By 1997 the facility was providing food, clothing, medical care, and schooling to over four hundred boys and girls.

where they cultivated twenty thousand banana and plantain trees and hundreds of rows of corn, melons, okra, sweet potatoes, and *melojen*. A rapid growth crop, *melojen* is a variety of squash that ripens at a foot and a half long in less than four months. The plant had not traditionally been grown for local consumption, but rather was cultivated for export. In October 1999 *melojen* was introduced to Port-au-Prince's local market by the Lafanmi Selavi Agricultural Initiative, which featured the vegetable at the Ministries of Agriculture and Social Affairs's food festival honoring national dishes and locally grown produce. The crop was a success and became a symbol of the bounty that could still come from Haiti's arid soil. Today some call the crop *lafanmi*, both because of its domestic introduction by the orphanage's farming initiative and because it is regarded as a large enough foodstuff to feed an entire family.

Through the Agricultural Initiative, Lafanmi's children learned to till, irrigate, and harvest crops grown from Haiti's hardscrabble soil. The produce also helped to feed the several hundred children in residence at Lafanmi

Selavi, reinforcing a principle that in Haiti is revolutionary: farmers should be able to directly reap the benefits of their labor. Surplus crops were sold to the local community through the orphanage's affiliated produce store at market-competitive prices. Lafanmi was also cultivating a reputation—as an urban institution that wisely acknowledged that the true wealth of the country is in the countryside.

Launched in 1996 Radyo Timoun [Children's Radio] accelerated the development of Lafanmi's reputation as a political institution and facilitated a broader dissemination of its agenda throughout the country. A low-frequency, all-children's radio station broadcast from the main compound in Pacot, the station provided Lafanmi's street children with a voice in national debates surrounding poverty, literacy, democratization, and children's issues. With close to three-quarters of Haiti's population functionally illiterate and in a political climate that afforded the print press few real freedoms, the radio broadcasts provided Lafanmi Selavi with a broad audience for the dissemination of its platforms, especially among the poorest classes, Radyo Timoun's target audience. By 1999 the station was broadcasting fourteen hours of programming a day, consisting of a decidedly unpolished format of extensive in-depth news reports, social analyses, interviews, music, commentaries, and agriculture reports. In 1998 Radyo Timoun was complemented with the addition of TeleTimoun [Children's Television]. Relying on over fifty child-correspondents and broadcasting much of the same material disseminated on their radio frequency, the television station (also housed at the main compound in Pacot) further broadened the media reach of Lafanmi Selavi.

The Lafanmi Selavi Car Wash on National Route 1 near the International Airport opened in 1996 and allowed each child who volunteered to work there the opportunity to make 225 gourdes per week—125 gourdes of which they received in cash and 100 gourdes of which was placed in a bank account set up in the child's name so that they might establish a savings. The car wash would be the site of a political attack in 1997, which would serve as a vivid reminder of both the persistence of state terror even in the absence of the army, as well as the continuing political significance of Lafanmi Selavi.

Late in the evening on September 11, 1997, nine years to the day after the *makout* massacre of parishioners at Aristide's St. Jean Bosco church in La Saline, vandals (later identified as supporters of the demobilized Haitian army) tore a triangular section of sheathing from the roof of the car wash office, ransacked the interior and stole equipment. Oil and grease were smeared over the clean outside stucco walls of the facility, as well as in and throughout the office, and several threatening messages were left at the scene. Some of the messages denounced the leadership of the newly formed National Police. The attackers had scrawled *"Aba Piè Belize!"* [Down with Pierre Belize!] on the walls of the office. Belize had just been named the head of the PNH. Other slogans scratched into the walls professed allegiance to former army officers. One of the messages, a threat to the children of Lafanmi, was repeated in several places in and outside the car wash office. The threat originated with the demand that Aristide convince then-president René Preval to pay the army officers their pensions, which were suspended two years prior when Aristide disbanded the army. The threat concluded with a promise to *"boule"* [to burn] Lafanmi Selavi if the demand was not met. Specifically the threat read: *"Si Aristide pa fe Pwèval pèye nou menm ansyin gaol yo nou pwa boule La Fanmi Selavi nan Kamilèon!"* [If Aristide does not make Preval pay the former soldiers, we will burn down Lafanmi Selavi on Camille Leon!—the street on which the orphanage is located]. The messages were all signed "FADH" and were written in media suggestive of flammability and fire—grease and charcoal writing splashed with motor oil and kerosene—a subtle and intentional underscoring of the threat. Following the incident Canadian U.N. soldiers mapped out the Lafanmi compound in Pacot and used the map to identify vulnerabilities in the facility's defense. They spent the next few days on sentry duty in the Pacot compound and patrolling the neighborhood around the orphanage. The vandals' demands were never met, and to the relief of Lafanmi's personnel, the threatened fire-bombing of the orphanage never actualized.

The Decline of the "Family"

Over the course of the years following the car wash incident, I watched as the physical and social conditions at Lafanmi Selavi steadily deteriorated, at the same time that Aristide's political career was climbing. The children at the facility were increasingly unsupervised, went about in filthy and ripped clothing, and were now occasionally beaten by the staff. There was no longer any adult control being exerted over the movement of kids between Tifi Lafanmi and the house for boys, and some of the children were being sexually victimized by older youths. The abuse of smaller children by bigger ones and sometimes outright rape had always been an infrequent but persistent problem at Lafanmi. Because only the house for boys included overnight dormitories, the majority of cases of sexual abuse occurred between boys in the middle of the night. The risk of this was reduced with the assignment of an overnight mentor who slept in the dormitories with the children, but by the end of 1998 the kids were again sleeping unsupervised. Some of the children had begun to tell me about the sexual abuse of the girls by some of the older boys, who passed without interference into the compound of Tifi Lafanmi Selavi.

During this time the children were no longer mandated to eat in the refectory above the school and so little was being done to assure that all were fed adequately. A scarcity of plates and utensils forced many of the children to eat from dirty sheaths of cardboard or plywood. Some ate with a common spoon from large, dented aluminum bowls, intensifying the spread of viruses and oral contagions. No longer was anyone checking to see that the children's hands were washed after defecating and before eating. Sickness ran rampant through the child population—influenza, ringworm, amoebic dysentery, cholera. Everyone seemed to have diarrhea. Several kids were running incredibly high fevers for days on end. Infections were not being treated, and many of the kids were suffering from purulent and weeping wounds on their arms, hands, feet, and legs. Lafanmi's doctor (the kids called him "Dr. Max") continued to come weekly to the facility, but was often unable to treat the children adequately due in part to the scarcity of proper medical supplies like intravenous hydration bags, suture kits, syringes, bandages, Tylenol, hydration salts, and antibiotics. Dr. Max donated a great deal of time and services, but was overwhelmed even in the best of times. The majority of Lafanmi's intravenous saline bags bore expiration dates from the 1980s and oral antibiotics were rare. I cleaned and dressed open wounds when they were presented to me, though the bandages rarely stayed clean for long, and I ultimately did not have any more resources, supplies, or time than did Dr. Max to continue treating all of the children who needed care. The handful of HIV positive kids at the facility did not receive any treatment at all for the virus, because Lafanmi never did have the budget for AIDS drugs like AZT; even if it did, these drugs are less than scarce in Haiti and they might as well not exist at all for the poor.

By 1999 the physical conditions of the place had deteriorated to their lowest point since my first arrival there four years prior. Lafanmi Selavi had become a nightmarish slum of childhood and adolescence. The kids' sleeping quarters were filthy and ridden with rats and roaches, the kitchen was infested with flies, the classrooms smelled of urine, and trash and garbage had begun to pile up in corners. Virtually all of the children were wasting, their arms and legs beginning to show the knobs of their bones beneath their skin. The stomachs of some were distending. Some of the children were running about completely naked, while others wore little more than rags. Some were defecating in the grasses of the drainage ravine just behind the compound, others were drinking downstream. They were going hungry and begged me

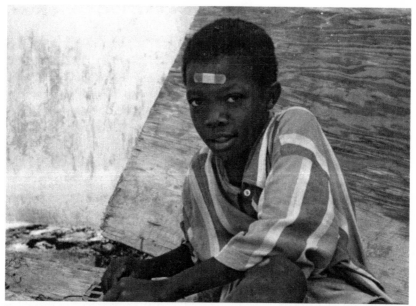

Figure 5.4. A former street boy at Lafanmi Selavi repairs a toy truck that he made out of metal scavenged from the streets. As the living conditions at the facility steadily deteriorated, many children reported that the street was cleaner and safer than the courtyard and dormitories at Lafanmi.

for food whenever I was around. "*M'grangou*," they would say, over and over again, "*M'grangou*." I am hungry. I am empty.

The abysmal living conditions at Lafanmi Selavi were in large part the result of administrative corruption, the characteristic mark of unmonitored Haitian institutions. Increasingly monies were being diverted from Lafanmi's treasury to the Aristide Foundation for Democracy (AFD)—a national assembly of peasant groups and democratic activists who provided the essential base of Aristide's political support, what would eventually become his Fanmi Lavalas party—the "family of the popular flood." Misappropriation of funds had been going on since at least 1996 and was made apparent to anyone in the know in 1998 when Lafanmi money was used to build a sprawling auditorium in Tabarre; when construction was completed, it was "donated" to the AFD. The following year, Lafanmi's only vehicle—a rattletrap minibus—was given to the AFD by the executive director of Lafanmi, a close boyhood friend and political ally of Aristide. This director also had the audacious habit of parking his Mercedes in the Lafanmi compound and instructing the children to wash it. In March the director went chronically delinquent in paying the teachers and staff and many left the orphanage for good.

By the summer of 1999 Lafanmi Selavi resembled nothing like what it had been during the height of its professionalism and charity in 1995. It was clear that little financial investment was being devoted to educational programs and facility upkeep and some children remarked that living at Lafanmi was not much different than living on the street. Some who left the facility at this time pointed out that the street was actually cleaner and safer than Lafanmi.

Like many street children some of the Lafanmi kids had locatable kin. A few families knew that their children were staying at the orphanage, believing that it was the best opportunity for their child to receive an education. But when word of the living conditions at Lafanmi Selavi reached them, several came to reclaim their children. Nonetheless the vast majority of Lafanmi's children either did not have family or were not in contact with them and had only the street to which to return.

The only quantifiable investments being made at the orphanage from 1998 to 1999 were drastic improvements to Radyo Timoun and TeleTimoun, which by then had become little more than media outlets for the dissemination of pro-Aristide propaganda. The Lafanmi Selavi orphanage program had clearly become little more than a political front and money-laundering mechanism for the Aristide electoral machine. A close friend and informant who was a teacher at Lafanmi throughout the 1990s remarked that his impression of Lafanmi Selavi in 1999 was that it was little more than a "*machin pwopagann politik*" [political propaganda machine]. This disillusionment eventually trickled down to most of the kids who remained at the orphanage. By mid-1999 several of the older boys at Lafanmi had become disenchanted with the failed promises of literacy, work, and an at least dignified poverty made to them by Aristide and they began to plot a revolt.

One of the oft-touted missions of Lafanmi Selavi since its beginning was to prepare the oldest children at the orphanage for their integration into the Haitian economy two years before their actual outplacement. Aristide himself had stressed that the boys should be taught a skill while at Lafanmi, be placed in an apprenticeship program, and be given assistance in finding housing and a permanent job in the trades. Many former graduates returned to their hometowns in different parts of the country to work after processing out of the Lafanmi program, while others chose to stay and work in Port-au-Prince where they might live with fellow Lafanmi graduates. But since 1998 the vocational program had declined into neglect along with the rest of the orphanage programming, and no plans at all were made for the several dozen older boys who were approaching the end of the Lafanmi program. In the spring of 1999 a cohort of thirty-four of these older boys was approached by the orphanage director and told that they could no longer sleep at Lafanmi Selavi. The boys protested, pleading that the orphanage's vocational outplacement program had failed to secure them jobs and that without an income they would have no alternative but to revert back to the street.

The boys continued to sleep at the orphanage and asked for a meeting with Aristide that took place at the Lafanmi compound in May of 1999. The boys' spokesman, a youth named Nado, argued on behalf of his own case, the cases of his cohort, as well as those of the younger children in residence at the orphanage. He reported to Aristide that the facility's conditions had deteriorated such that "the children were dirty, had no clean water to drink, were being fed irregularly, and were inadequately clothed." Though unmoved by Nado's concerns about the unsanitary conditions at his orphanage, Aristide did arrange jobs for all thirty-four boys in Nado's cohort, who would work at the wharves in Port-au-Prince, Léogâne, Mountruis, and Saint-Marc. The employment offer was contingent upon these thirty-four boys leaving Lafanmi Selavi immediately. All of the boys assented.

Several days after the meeting, some of the boys received their letters of introduction, signed by Aristide, that were needed for their employment. At least seventeen of them did not. Frustrated with what they perceived as yet another false promise made by Aristide, these seventeen returned to Lafanmi Selavi and began sleeping there again during the second week of June 1999. Their ability to slip into the dormitories at night was made easier by the utter lack of staff supervision and by the absence of the director, who had resigned the previous month after a dispute with Aristide over embarrassing and accurate public speculation that he had been skimming orphanage funds.

A younger boy staying at Lafanmi at this time told me that these seventeen youths had begun to *fè plan* [make plans] to take over the facility and demand justice for their cause. They had also begun to solicit the support of other children at the orphanage who were sympathetic to their cause and troubled with their unsanitary living conditions.

At around nine P.M. on June 23, the seventeen conspirators wrapped bandannas around their faces to mask their identities and began to throw rocks and bottles over the orphanage walls and into the surrounding neighborhood, hitting cars, private homes, and a few pedestrians. They had also begun to stone the windows of Radyo Timoun. With some of the boys brandishing machetes, they cut the telephone lines and the electrical cables feeding the radio and television transmitter. One of the boys involved told me that the telephone lines were cut in order to prevent anyone from calling the AFD. The boys apparently were not as worried about the police as they were of Aristide.

The morning following the start of the uprising, the cooks and some of the staff arrived at the orphanage compound for work but were barred entry by the youths inside. After successfully turning away the staff, the boys resumed their rock-and-bottle assault on the surrounding neighborhood from within the walls of Lafanmi. By now the original seventeen youths who had initiated the melee were joined by about a dozen younger boys. At some point a vendor who sold candy and cigarettes from a stand outside of Lafanmi Selavi was struck in the face with a rock. She was blinded permanently in her left eye as a result. Despite her injury (she now wears a patch over her blind eye), she continues to sell her wares just outside the facility's gates.

News of the incident was broadcast on Radyo Metropole (a national station) at noon on June 24, the second day of the siege. By this time troopers from CIMO, the PNH's riot control unit, arrived on the scene and had been told by Aristide supporters who convened on the location that *zenglendo* armed with grenades, machetes, and pistols had taken the orphanage's children hostage. Some of the boys involved in the incident later told me that the riot control troops were told that those involved were *zenglendo* because Aristide's people needed to protect the interests of the Fanmi Lavalas party, the reputation of which would be tarnished by this incident because of the political proximity of Aristide to Lafanmi Selavi. Dany Toussaint, though once a *makout* and an officer in the Haitian army and today a senator, had by this time become Aristide's public spokesman and a senatorial candidate. He issued a statement to the Haitian press in the midst of the standoff: "*Gason yo se gang malfèktè*" [These boys are criminal gangsters].

Throughout the day the older boys inside the compound were yelling to the press who had gathered on the other side of the wall behind police barricades: "*Yo te manti nou!*" [They lied to us!] and "*Aristid ap fè chita poutèt nou!*" [Aristide is making a fortune off us!], a reference both to Aristide's increasing political strength and his conspicuous wealth.[1] On Aristide's orders the riot troopers fired tear gas into the facility on the afternoon of the siege and stormed the compound wearing gas masks and riot gear and wielding batons and automatic weapons. Over twenty youths were arrested at the scene, but some escaped apprehension by crossing the ravine at the back of the orphanage compound. Those that were arrested were handcuffed with plastic ties and held shirtless and on their knees outside the compound until they were transported to Fort National, the juvenile prison in Port-au-Prince. By the close of the standoff, two riot officers had been wounded by

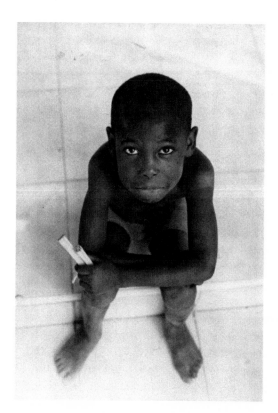

Figure 5.5. In June 1999 an uprising of street children at Lafanmi Selavi called national attention to the abysmal living conditions at "Aristide's orphanage" in Pacot. Tactical units of the Haitian National Police staged a standoff with the children for several hours before firing tear gas over the wall and storming the facility. Aristide ordered the closure of Lafanmi Selavi, and over four hundred children were turned out onto the streets of Port-au-Prince.

rocks and several of the children inside had sustained minor injuries when troopers stormed the gates and entered the compound. The fifty or so children in the courtyard when the tear gas was fired into the compound suffered from lachrymator inhalation and were treated by Dr. Max, who had arrived after hearing word of the standoff on Radyo Metropole. Ten PNH officers stood surveillance over the facility, and the several hundred kids who were now assembled in the Lafanmi compound. The residue of the gas lingered on the ground and in the air like chalk dust, as children milled around the compound holding cut lemons beneath their noses to neutralize the burn of the lachrymator.

The gassing of the orphanage effectively marked a public end to the short-lived legitimacy of the use of child agency in Haitian politics enjoyed during Lafanmi's early years. The orphanage's outreach programs and school were closed for good on Aristide's orders later that day, and the children were ordered by the National Police to vacate the premises. With close to two hundred boys and a hundred and eighty girls in residence at Lafanmi

Selavi at the time of the standoff, the population of displaced children on the street in Port-au-Prince burgeoned overnight by almost four hundred kids. Though some left the city and dispersed throughout the countryside to return to their hometowns, most stayed in Port-au-Prince, returning to the boulevards where they started when they were first taken into Lafanmi by Aristide. That was long before Aristide became a *gwo nèg* [big shot] in Haiti.

Machin Politik: Lafanmi Selavi Since 1999

Today Lafanmi Selavi is no longer an orphanage, an outreach, a clinic, or a school. But it does still broadcast both Radyo Timoun and TeleTimoun as media outlets for Aristide's political propaganda. Though no street children live at the compound, a handful of youths, maybe a dozen in all, work at the stations, maintaining the illusion that "Children's Radio" and "Children's Television" are still for and by street children. Whereas in the past street children chose their stories and wrote their own copy for broadcasts, today information liaisons for Aristide wield a heavy hand in deciding what stories are written, how they are written, who is interviewed, and what is said in the broadcasts concerning Aristide and his politics. Lafanmi Selavi truly is little more than a *machin pwopagann politik*.

I returned to Lafanmi only once since the siege, in January 2000. When I arrived outside the gate of the compound, the main door was slightly ajar. I knocked and announced myself in the custom of those who approach doors as strangers. As I knocked I called out *"onè"* [I come honorably]. The desired response from the party on the other side of the door is the one that I received now—*"respè"* [enter with my respect]. I knew that because most of the teachers, staff, security, and nearly all of the children that I knew were no longer at Lafanmi, it would be best to approach the situation with delicate caution.

Because of the political significance of the orphanage since the time of its inception, Lafanmi Selavi has always been very heavily guarded. Since 1994 Aristide has arranged with the Haitian National Police to have officers on duty at the compound gate during daylight hours. They are relieved each night by private, professionally trained security agents whose weapons are frequently of better quality and greater firepower than those of the police. Following Aristide's return to the presidency from exile in 1994, security at Lafanmi's gates was further bolstered by the addition of agents from the Presidential Guard, a highly-trained special forces unit instituted by Aristide for his personal protection as president. Today they function as little more than a palace militia and are answerable to no one but Aristide. In their cult loyalty to Aristide they are comparable to Duvalier's *tonton makout*.

The security agents opened the gate for me, allowing me inside. An older guard was on a telephone in the guardhouse, just right of the entry vestibule. He waved me into the courtyard, but it was clear that I would need to identify myself before proceeding any further. After stepping into the guardhouse that led into the courtyard of the compound, I greeted the seven guards present. This number is far more than was typical when Lafanmi functioned as an outreach. I identified myself as a friend of Jonas, a former Lafanmi teacher who I knew still worked at Radyo Timoun. None of the guards were uniformed, but it was clear from their demeanor, posture, and weapons that at least three were Presidential Guard and the rest National Police (PNH officers assigned to the Lafanmi detail would often be out of uniform while on duty). All of them were very heavily armed. Aside from the service revolvers that all of the guards wore holstered in their belts, I counted two Uzis, a combat shotgun, an M16 assault rifle and two automatic machine-pistols (held by the men I suspect were Presidential Guard).

I was searched and run over with a handheld metal detector. Such rituals are common when entering any place considered worthy of attack in Haiti, which nowadays could be anywhere, but principally banks, government offices, hotels, schools, and even some bars and most dance clubs. My satchel, camera, tape recorder, and a sheathed pocketknife were confiscated, to be returned to me on my way out. I was permitted to keep my notebook and a pen.

The older guard who had been on the phone when I arrived waved for me to follow him to the office. As we walked toward the old administration building, I noticed how immaculately clean the facility was. The children's writings that had been scrawled across the walls had been painted over with battleship-gray paint, the concrete ground was swept clean of dust and dirt, and not a single stone or piece of loose concrete was to be seen. Completely devoid of children, the compound looked sadly neat and tidy. It was also eerily quiet.

When I entered the office, I greeted a receptionist and several boys, two of whom recognized me and greeted me by name. After we exchanged pleasantries, I asked if Matien was there. Matien is one of the first boys that I befriended at Lafanmi. He arrived at the orphanage, filthy and hungry, in 1992. He managed to keep himself out of trouble for his entire tenure at Lafanmi and threw himself wholeheartedly into Radyo Timoun. Today he is an articulate young man in his late teens, who speaks both Kreyòl and English fluently and artfully. His mild disposition and likable manner affords him the chance to continue working at the radio station as a broadcaster. I was told he was upstairs in the radio booth and was led to him.

The radio station consists of two booths separated by double-paned Plexiglas. One is the control booth with transmitting and sound equipment and the opposite booth is an interview room with a plywood counter, several folding chairs, and a microphone. An on-air call-in show was in progress. In the interview booth was seated a functionary of Aristide's Fanmi Lavalas party, who was fielding phoned-in questions about his party's platform concerning literacy in Haiti. Matien was seated at the sound board in the control booth, managing the broadcast and fielding the phone calls. Another teenage boy was also in the sound booth, preparing his copy for a news brief. It was printed in pen on two sheets of loose-leaf paper in a child's hand and bore several edits throughout in what was clearly adult handwriting. All briefs read on the air are first cleared by Fanmi Lavalas personnel.

After the call-in show, the politician came into the control booth, greeted me, thanked Matien, and departed. The other boy then went into the interview booth and read his news briefs, interspersed with cassette recordings of on-street interviews with children commenting on what they would like Aristide to provide for them if he were to again become president.[2] The news broadcast included a long feature story concerning an AFD program that promised education for all Haitians. Finished with his work in the booth, Matien suggested that we go outside and talk.

We sat on the ledge in the courtyard outside. I asked what was going on next door at Tifi Lafanmi Selavi. Matien asked if I wanted to see it and I said yes. He remarked with the hint of boastfulness that I know Matien to indulge from time to time that I could see anything I wanted if I was with him, which suggested that not only had Lafanmi Selavi again become a politically sensitive area where access must be restricted, but that our movements about the compound were being watched.

We went around the back of the main administrative building, through the old wood-shop, past the kitchen (padlocked), and up the steps past the old dormitories and classrooms. I asked Matien what was in those rooms now. He remarked flatly, *"ryen ap nan la"* [nothing is in there]. We moved around the hallway at the top of the steps and into the Tifi Lafanmi Selavi compound. The first thing he showed me was a room that I remembered to be a classroom, the one in which Aristide's wife, Mildred, used to teach from time to time. Inside the room now was a very large, very black, and very nasty rottweiler. It was kept in the room by a barred gate that certainly was not there when the room was used for classes in literacy. Matien explained to me that the dog was brought down by "Aristide's people" from the United States a few weeks earlier. He said that the dog is let out at night to roam the compound for security. He explained to me that this dog was *"pa bègwè kou chen Aysien"* [not stupid like Haitian dogs]. He elaborated by saying that Haitian dogs bark and bark at anything in the night, but this dog, which has no name, is quiet at night as it roams but will viscously attack any threat. The animal was clearly professionally trained and, unlike most Haitians, was healthy, robust, and well-looked after.

We moved up the steps of the main house in the Tifi Lafanmi Selavi courtyard and it too was immaculate and well kept, completely unlike it's condition just two years earlier when the stench of urine and feces hung in the air and dirty little girls crowded every corner, hand-washing laundry and braiding each other's hair. Matien, completing the tour, remarked with a hint of melancholy, *"Fè yon ti gade. Piès moun"* [See, look about. No one is here].

Politics, Violence, and Child Identity

Aristide never hesitated to emphasize the political underpinnings of Lafanmi Selavi, frequently pointing out that the destitute condition of street children in Haiti is the result of the extreme stratification of Haitian society into a hierarchy of impossibly rich and impossibly poor in uneven proportion. He has always isolated the Haitian state apparatus itself as responsible for the everyday violence of life on the boulevards and avenues of the capital, thus vocalizing the frustrations of the poor majority, most of whom live on, in, or about the street.

In a talk given at a meeting of priests and laity at Chimbote, Peru, in 1968, the liberation theologian Gustavo Guitiérrez identified three types of poor in Latin America: "the stranger rejected by a nationalist people, the woman who has no one to support her, and the orphan, left without aid of parents" (Guitiérrez 1995: 75). He went on to argue that it is in encounters with and emancipation of these poor that God, liberation, and social justice resides. Aristide followed Guitérrez's model and early on identified street children—displaced and rejected as vagabonds and criminals in nationalist discourses—as crucial to social justice and liberation in Haiti. He also recognized the religious significance and political potency of well-organized and directed youth. Aristide proclaimed that street children are the truest manifestations of God on earth, and he envisioned the political potential of integrating them into a Christianized program of social liberation:

I often saw these children on the main street of Port-au-Prince, not far from our house at St. Jean Bosco. Their presence had challenged me for a long time: how could we speak of God and leave God wandering in the streets? It was all the more poignant because these were children, innocents subjected to every kind of corruption just to survive. What could we do *with* these children?—with them and not for them. (Aristide 1993: 73, italics in original)

Haiti had glimpsed the power of adolescent action in the prominent role played by street children on the front lines of popular mobilization against the Duvalier dictatorship in 1986. These were children who stood to gain significant security in their daily lives with the removal of the Duvalierist paramilitaries and the *makouts*, who many of the older children said could "*kraze tèt*" [break heads] with greater brutality than even the PNH's paramilitaries, who continue to do so today. In youth demonstrations against the Duvalierists, Aristide was able to glimpse the possibility of adolescent power in Haiti, and it led him to believe fervently that the most devout commitment to radical political change would need to originate in the youth of Haiti. He writes that,

I have participated in many struggles in my life, but none has pained me so greatly as the struggle within our church over the depth of that Church's preferential option for the poor of our parish. There are those of us, usually younger and eager for change, who believe that commitment should be total, unrelenting, intransigent. . . . In my heart I am sure that the way of total commitment is the right way. (Aristide 1990: 18)

Aristide advocated the mobilization of youth through a Christianized politic of social justice. He saw *ti legliz*, Haiti's liberation theology movement, as the force that could, if carefully applied to political action, lead to dramatic democratic change for Haiti. Lafanmi Selavi was an attempt to establish a Christian base-community composed entirely of children, a first for Latin American liberation theology. Phillip Berryman defines such communities as "small lay-led communities, motivated by Christian faith, that see themselves as part of the church and that are committed to working together to improve their communities and to establish a more just society" (1987: 64). Lafanmi Selavi would be the social model upon which post-Duvalier Haiti and Aristide's political fortunes would be based:

I had the feeling that I was acting as a theologian in order to give direction to a political struggle: the eruption of the poor onto the social scene. . . . Lafanmi Selavi was an experience and a symbol of realized Christian faith genuinely shared. The new frontiers we were discovering together rendered the anachronistic repression engulfing the country all the more odious. We proved to the skeptics that it was possible to live differently in our society (Aristide 1993: 75).

That Aristide modeled Lafanmi as an extension of Haiti's *ti legliz* liberation theology movement is not in doubt. What is in doubt is the efficacy of liberation theology in alleviating the human suffering it so vocally abhors. Was Lafanmi Selavi successful in raising the social consciousness of the children upon whom this Christian base community was constructed?

Intended Success, Unanticipated Outcomes

Representing itself as a cultural counterpoise to the routinization and political impotence of street children, Lafanmi was truly unique in its ambition to raise the political resolve of citizen-children, rather than simply feed them. This is a daunting mission in a country where 60 percent of the population is under the age of twenty-five, 40 percent of whom are under fifteen, many of them living or working in or about the street.

The artistic expressions of the children at the orphanage provide some evidence of the effectiveness of Lafanmi's endeavor to stimulate the social resolve of street children. In early 1998 the children were encouraged by the Lafanmi Selavi staff to decorate the rather bland interior of the wall surrounding the orphanage compound with a mural that would reflect the social issues that the children considered to be of most pressing importance to Haiti's social reconstruction in the wake of the Cedras coup. The adult staff was conscientious in not influencing the children's decisions about what they wanted to paint. The result was a colorful, thirty-foot-long mosaic of Port-au-Prince life through the eyes of street children. Punctuating the visual imagery of the mural were statements and interrogatives that were reflective of the social attunement of the children who wrote them. One declaration commanded *"Pa koupe bwa!"* [Don't cut down trees!], a reference to Haiti's almost complete deforestation. A child's rendering of Cité Soleil, one of Haiti's most destitute urban slums, figured prominently in the mural. Beneath the image of the cramped shantytown is a caption that challenges, *"Eske tout sitwayen panse a Sité Soley?"* [Do you know the entire situation in Cité Soleil?]. Beneath this, an illustration of two children asleep in the street. Below them is the legend, *"Si timoun yo ap dòminan la ri ki sa n'ap fè pou yo?"* [What are the children who sleep in the street to do?].

While my discussions with the kids corroborated the evidence suggested in the mural, that street children were genuinely developing a complex understanding of the causes and consequences of social problems in Haiti, many of the painted images and slogans in the mural seemed to simply parrot the political rhetoric of Aristide's Fanmi Lavalas. One slogan painted several times throughout the mural was "*Tout timoun se moun*" [All children are people of worth], an adaptation of the Fanmi Lavalas slogan "*tout moun se moun*" [all people are people of worth]. Elsewhere on the wall was written the question, "*Eske timoun bo tabla?*" [Are children seated around the table?], above a depiction of a table laden with bowls of food, behind which sit several people. In a largely illiterate society like Haiti, verbal imagery can be an effective means for the transmission of political ideas, and Aristide is unarguably a competent weaver of metaphor. During the course of his election and subsequent presidency, Aristide reiterated the allegory that only the wealthy elite and politically powerful (including the army) were "*bò tabla*" [seated around the table] of prosperity, while Haiti's poor majority were kept "*anba tabla*" [beneath the table], feeding on the scraps that fell from the gluttonous meal above them. In his bid for the presidency in 1990, Aristide demanded that all Haitians be seated around the table, eating as a more egalitarian community. So influential was the metaphor that the symbol of the Fanmi Lavalas party today is a large table around which sit a businessman, a farmer, a middle-class woman, and a poor woman holding a child.

Some of the key tenets of Haiti's *ti legliz* movement were easily integrated into the Lafanmi program, while others were more trying. The nationalist theme of "reconciliation" proved to be an especially difficult concept to develop among the children at Lafanmi. Reconciliation—in this sense, unilateral Christian forgiveness of the army, *makouts,* and other aggressors following their legal justice at the hands of the Haitian human rights courts following the coup—has been a fundamental pillar of Aristide's political platform since 1994. If Lafanmi Selavi was to provide an institutional model for a new Haitian citizenship, then the idea of civil contrition had to be implemented in both the orphanage pedagogy as well as in its school yard. While at times challenging, the idea of reconciliation was integrated into the day-to-day disciplinary decisions at Lafanmi. Lafanmi's boys fought among each other with a fair amount of frequency. These confrontations would run the full scale of escalation, from angry exchanges of words, to threats and posturing suggestive of ferocity, to in some cases physical violence. Many of the boys at Lafanmi Selavi kept with them the razors they carried on the street before coming to the orphanage, and their readiness to produce them in arguments was unnerving. In 1997 a school yard confrontation erupted between two of the boys over a game they were playing, when one of the boys suddenly leapt forward and slashed the back of the other repeatedly with his razor. The offending boy was ousted from Lafanmi Selavi by the administrators and spent a number of weeks working, begging, and sleeping at the International Airport before returning to the orphanage to seek forgiveness and reentry to the program. Lafanmi's director had a private meeting with the boy and after a number of punitive punishments and corrective measures had been decided upon, the boy was readmitted to the program. The case exemplifies the orphanage's early determination to incorporate the liberation ethic of reconciliation into its pedagogy and disciplinary philosophy.

While Lafanmi Selavi's devotion to a new nationalism through the empowerment of children may have been novel and revolutionary, and inasmuch as it was successful in instilling a sense of social potency in many of the children, it also proved to be a very dangerous endeavor at a time when democratic stability was at best tenuous and fragile. Perceived as haughty and ambitious by the powerful foes of Fanmi Lavalas, Aristide's Lafanmi Selavi did not endear itself to the martial states that emerged in the wake of the collapse of Duvalier's regime in 1986. As a result its children paid profoundly under Cedras and over the course of the years that followed for both their ties to Aristide and their active participation in prodemocratic discourse.

For most of the children who had come to Lafanmi Selavi, the Cedras coup was the background against which their childhood identity was formed. With Cedras's seizure of power from Aristide, martial law was put into place and democratically oriented institutions like Lafanmi Selavi became criminalized. Political attacks on the children of the orphanage became commonplace and were an effective means by which the regime sought to stunt youth resistance in Port-au-Prince. Even with the fragile restoration of democratic order following the 1994 invasion, *makoutist* violence against the politically mobilized children of Lafanmi Selavi continued.

Some Implications for Theory: State-Civil Relations in Haiti

The method, form, and practice of *makoutinaj* as it was exercised against Lafanmi's children raises important theoretical questions about the culture of national politics in Haiti, as much as it challenges our assumptions about the role of children in state-civil relations. Any examination of state-against-street child in Haiti must originate from a theory that embraces the impact of violence on the everyday lives of street children and then proceeds to identify the ramifications of that violence on their formation of social identity. The amalgam of social realities that are intrinsic to a political economy of the street—hunger, scarcity, poverty, criminalization, displacement, abandonment, isolation—in conjunction with the symbolic and institutionalized violence of the modern, even democratizing Haitian state contributes to an everyday kind of violence. During the Cedras coup, political terror was added to this culture of violence. Today it is *zenglendinaj*.

Carole Nagengast (1994) identifies conformity within narrow political ranges as among the primary goals of the modern state. Also among these goals is the creation of a societal consensus about which categories of individuals are legitimate and which are not. The ideal state attempts to ensure conformity of the civil society through the formation of diverse cultural forms that assist in the determination of the range of tolerated social, political, ethnic, and national identities and thus expound a negative definition of criminalized groups and individuals. Those identities that fall outside the range of acceptable norms are marginalized and persecuted as threats to social and even cultural stability. Such has been the case in Haiti, where street children have become acceptable targets for violence, insofar as they are cited as largely responsible for the escalation in Port-au-Prince's street-level woes.

Some modern states have developed the ability to persuade and influence the civil sector through less overtly violent means than other modern states, but Haiti is not one of them. Talal Asad (1992) has argued that repressive states like Haiti share the pretense of virtually all states to intervene profoundly in the civil sector, but have failed to sufficiently develop the administrative and social control infrastructures necessary to effect such penetration in less extreme manners. They are essentially weak states, resorting to physical coercion and terror because they cannot secure political ends through the more subtle, symbolic, and manipulative practices of power associated with predominantly northern "surveillance" societies—those relying more heavily on suggestive political persuasion than the use of overt force (Gledhill 1994). The repressive alternative to softer forms of state persuasion and control is a direct attack on citizens—arbitrary arrest and interrogation, imprisonment, and finally torture, mutilation, killing, and disappearance. It should be remembered though that even the most stable of northern surveillance states may resort to threats or even open violence against "disorderly" or "criminal" social groups when institutions of social consensus are weakening or changing (Scheper-Hughes 1992).

Haitian government lacks every essential aspect of a stable bureaucracy recognized by social theorists since Max Weber—a continuous organization of official functions bound by rules, an organization of offices that conforms to a principle of strict hierarchy, standardized acts and rules, administrative impersonality, strict and systematic discipline and control in conduct of office, an impartiality in policy. A strong tendency toward plutocracy is the only aspect of Haitian government bureaucracy that would be recognizable to Weber. If a weak state is one without a strong bureaucratic tradition of social control; if it is one in which the people are alienated from the means to read and therefore to understand the laws of their constitution, then Haiti is a weak state, indeed, and always has been. As authorities of an intrinsically weak state, the martial agents of the Cedras regime *had* to kick in doors, and sanction and support the activities of death squads; that is, if they wished to see certain political ends met. They invariably did. Seen in this light, the Anti-Gang Unit, as much as the *zenglendo* they pursue, is just the next evolution in Haitian political power, preserving both the terror and the efficacy of its antecedents.

The crisis of the modern Haitian state originates in its variable ability to monopolize social power and from the nuisance of peripheralized groups who challenge state definitions of who and what should be repressed (Nagengast 1994). We must be reminded that the exercise of state power is always violent and that the state always claims a monopoly on force. The relations between the state and the civil society are therefore always power relations. They emerge as a particular arrangement of groups and institutions in the midst of social and ritual relations. Political violence *ritualizes* power. It deploys it symbolically and is often the preferred tool that states use to enforce themselves and to maintain power. But the *makouts*, as the *zenglendo*, demonstrate how state violence need not be primarily applied by the state apparatus itself. It has been seen throughout Latin America that statist activities, including the exercise of political terror, may be undertaken by groups independent of the government in power and often by civilian proxy. *Makoutinaj* and *zenglendinaj* are but two examples. The collaboration of civil police, appointed by local politicians, with hired *pistoleríos* and *justiceiros* employed by plantation estate owners in the operations of extrajudicial Brazilian death squads has been documented as well (Scheper-Hughes 1992).

Several theorists (Foucault 1977; Scarry 1985) remind us that the goal of state violence is not merely the infliction of individual pain and suffering, but rather is the social project of creating punishable categories of people, forging and maintaining boundaries around them, and building consensus about those categories that specify and enforce state-desired behavioral norms. The violence is a *process* of legitimating and delegitimating specific groups, and is a function of the kind of power that state's use to facilitate a docile and passive civil society. Simply put, the goal of the violence is not so much exploitation of the targeted "other" as an enemy of the state, as much as it is the other's mere consciousness of the possibility of total domination by the governing body politic (Simmel 1955). It is a unique exercise of the state's monopoly on force—one that looks toward the terrorization of society into conformity.

David Riches (1986) has argued that violence need not be perceived as merely practical, visible, or physical, but that it may also manifest as symbolic, invisible, or emotional. Alongside instrumental definitions of political violence—the use of physical coercion, bodily harm, torture, the infringement of property or dignity—there is also the dramatic *portrayal* or *representation* of any of the above: the threat of physical force, the public exhibition of executed political targets, threatening political graffiti. Such violence forms "a backdrop for everyday life and confirm[s] [the community's] worst fears and anxieties—that of losing themselves and their loved ones to the random forces and institutionalized violence of the state" (Scheper-Hughes 1992: 229–30). The drama of the violence, the *performance* of terror, is itself a social domination measure, one that moves beyond the physical bloodshed to destabilize social norms, community sustainability, and cultural viability. No act of political terror is ever an act intended to destroy a single individual, not even a case of torture of one man by one other; it is always an act intended to undermine an entire body politic (Robben and Nordstrom 1995). The grotesque display of an executed political target shatters the mirage of an ordered and just world, at the same time making the community a witness that is now party to the terror. The immediacy and the proximity of the violence is evoked by "tortured and abandoned bodies, corpses out of place" (Warren 1993: 31). It is a jarring, secondary kind of violence, especially in those regions where one's home community, now the impotent witness to the crime, is the very fulcrum for cultural identity. John Gledhill (1994), reflecting on Sri Lankan political terrorism, writes that the nonburial of the dead and the public display of their dismembered corpses also victimizes living relatives, permitting the violence to penetrate into the very fabric and core of social relations. Even acts of political rape (a custom of political conflict in Haiti since the late 1950s) are not just examples of the politicization of gender with violence, but are also intimate reminders of the state's extreme ability to penetrate civil society, even into the profoundly private realms of femininity, sexual identity, and marital sanctity. Political violence is not just a literal threat to the individual singled out for punishment, but is also a *representational* threat to the civil society's vulnerability writ large. We would do well to consider this argument as we recall the terror wrought on street children by AGU today. Their blitzkrieg sweeps through street-child communities, their baton brutality, their tear gas, and their extrajudicial imprisonments are tactics that move well beyond individual victimization and extend the violence into the greater community of the poor.

Lafanmi, Criminalization, and the Political Culture of Haiti

While social constructions of street children in Haiti cast them as dangerous *social* threats, perceived as supernumerary nuisances and criminals, the democratic activism of street children has also drawn the ire of a Port-au-Prince community fearful of their dangerous potential as *political* agents. The criminalization of Haitian street children leads logically to a denial of human and civil rights that would otherwise be extended to them. This negative conception of rights denies those perceived as non-citizens, living outside of social norms or civil law. Haiti's paramilitaries of today represent aspects of a political culture in which terror continues to be reproduced and sanctioned for the preservation of a socially constructed perception, a facade, of civil stability.

The structural basis for the criminalization of street children was widely recognized by the kids at Lafanmi Selavi. Consider these lyrics of a song written by Lafanmi's all-children musical group, *Seròm* [Lifeblood]:

We live in a country, we don't have freedom of speech.
We're always fighting. We're not making progress.
We are children, just like any other children.
God created us.
If we are suffering, the big shots are responsible.
All over Haiti there are children going to school and living their lives.
But the street children are considered troublemakers,
And society always sees them as guilty.
We are children, just like any other children.
God created us.
If we are suffering, those in authority,
Those with power,
Are responsible.

Expressions of child agency in political conflict are corollary to social identities that emerge in cultures of violence. Like the child soldiers of the Palestinian *intifada* and adolescent stone-throwers in Belfast, the street children of Haiti's Lafanmi Selavi were living examples of the profound ability to rouse the political consciousness of children, or at least manipulate it, in states of unrest. But just as the uncertainty of violence relates to a summoning of fear, terror, and confusion, so too does violence provoke innovations in resistance, survival, hope, and creativity (Robben and Nordstrom 1995)—especially on the part of youth who live in conditions of extreme scarcity and who therefore are among those with the most at stake in social transformation. The contribution of children and adolescents to political change ought not be discounted. Youth agency in social and political processes are frequently the by-product of the construction of childhood in highly volatile state formations.

The sociopolitical agency of children, including participation in strife, resistance, victimization and social witness, also finds material basis in the economic realities and general life conditions in which they live, as is the case with adult political agency. In conjunction with scarcity, displacement, criminalization, and civil abandonment, poverty may in fact be identified as at the root of street children's alienation from their civil liberties. From this bottom-up vantage, adolescent political agency in Haiti might best be understood as arising from the children's identification with certain cultural rights to which they are entitled and a realization of those rights denied them.

When Lafanmi Selavi was invited to participate in the 1997 Youth Summit in the United States, two young girls from the Tifi Lafanmi Selavi project were selected to attend. They identified school, a home, and health care as the absolute rights of all children; rights that could not be claimed by Haiti's street-child population. Because street children almost always identify school attendance as the distinguishing factor between themselves and sheltered children, education frequently appears high on all of their lists of rights that should be extended to street kids.

The adolescent mobilization for democracy that originated in the Lafanmi Selavi program did find at least some of its impetus in the children's identification with fundamental cultural rights denied them for whatever reason, thus provoking the initiation of their civil challenges to state legitimacy. The foci of the commentaries on Radyo Timoun and TeleTimoun (in the early days when the children drafted their own copy) were clearly influenced by the liberation politics advocated at Lafanmi. How much of that emerged from genuine consciousness-raising and how much of it was merely recitation of the Fanmi Lavalas agenda will never be fully known. The child staff had broadcast daily commentaries on a range of volatile political issues, from the newly formed PNH, to ongoing discussions of why education should be truly free. A special report that Lafanmi's street kids aired in 1997 addressed the plight of children in Haiti's prison system. Eighteen-year-old Laronce, who arrived at Lafanmi Selavi in 1991, talked on the air about his life on the street and his recognition that he was somehow being deprived of rights that should be accorded him:

I remember when I was living on the streets. My heart would break when I saw other children going to school and participating in activities myself and other children living on the streets could never do. It's humiliating, because people who see you on the street treat you like an animal and you can do nothing to defend yourself. Instead you feel very sad and the sadness never leaves you. . . . We need laws to force the government to take care of these children. They have a right to live like children who have parents. I would like other street children to have the chance to become the man I am today. I say this in the hope that children in all countries can live.

Not overlooked by the children at Lafanmi Selavi was the contradiction implicit in the promise of democratization and the failure of that goal to actualize. One twelve year-old boy remarked in a 1996 Radyo Timoun broadcast that

we need to be able to freely elect a government that's noncorrupt. That's a fundamental right and only a noncorrupt government will prevent the killings by the [former] army. My family was beaten and raped and many of us were murdered in the streets by the *makouts*.

While the Lafanmi Selavi program was promoted as a social haven providing children protection from the abuse, battery, and exposure characteristic of life on the streets of Port-au-Prince, there are glaring contradictions implicit in the facility's professed mission as a locus for the children's security on the one hand and an institution of politicization on the other; not the least of which is the question of how the support of child involvement in dangerous political mobilization can contribute to the specific conditions under which children are nurtured and protected. Clearly Lafanmi Selavi recognized child identity as legitimate ground upon which the fight for political and economic justice in Haiti should be waged. The high level of political importance accorded Lafanmi Selavi resulted in it being specifically targeted as an institution of liberation theology, its children specifically targeted as active agents of political discourse, and its educational program specifically targeted as promoting political resistance. The high-intensity political violence perpetrated against these children as a result lends credence to the argument that the children at Lafanmi Selavi were a considerable threat to the longevity of the Cedras government and continued to be a tacit antagonism to antidemocratic elements in Haitian politics thereafter, as evidenced by the continuation of its targeting long after the return of Aristide.

Most significantly it was a profound political act—the rock-and-bottle standoff between the Lafanmi youth agitators and agents of the Aristide protostate—that led to a greater social recognition of the squalor and hypocrisy of the orphanage program and of Aristide's larger political agenda. Ultimately it was an all-children's popular uprising that led to the violent closure of the facility that had originally taught the children to act as political agents to preserve their dignity and secure their rights in the first place. In what respects then are children, as symbols of what is at stake in contests over cultural identity, pivotal in the structuring of a Haitian democratic order?

Lafanmi Selavi helped to make street children vocal participants in the democratization discourse, rather than its passive witnesses. And in this respect, these children need to be viewed as active agents of change, not as mere spectators to or victims of violent government suppression or pawns in adult political maneuvers. The social refusal to acknowledge the political potency of children is not just manifest in the literature on child rights, but is also increasingly argued to be detrimental to the understanding of certain cultural realities of state formation. Pamela Reynolds (1995) advises that to ignore youth interpretations of political oppression is tantamount to demeaning their contributions to social opposition and to deny their inventiveness inherent in processes of change. Further, Tobias Hecht contends that the denial of child agency in greater sociopolitical contexts is the result of dehumanizations and delegitimizations that have come to be socially embraced. He also points to the consequences of such denials:

> Stripped of human agency and placed in a pantheon of faceless victimhood, street children become objects in a largely adult debate that does more to enhance the status of those who crusade in their behalf than to shed light on the myriad ways children in fact live violence. (1998: 122)

For better or worse, the Lafanmi curriculum led many of its children to structure the design of their cultural and political identities from the precedents of the past, to participate in political discourse, and to clearly state the terms upon which each will express his or her intentions in contemporary Haitian society. The lyrics of a song written by Ti Soni[3] (the lead singer of the orphanage musical group) illustrate the point:

> Forget, we will never forget.
> It's freedom we're asking for, freedom.
> Why can't we have freedom?
> Why did Aristide have three years of coup d'etat?
> Because he was struggling for us to have justice.

Since he has returned, we must say democracy lives.
Why then, when the street children suffer,
Don't you join hands with them?
If you do that, you won't lose anything.
You must join hands with them, for them
To be recognized as people with dignity.
Why did they kill Father Jean Marie Vincent?[4]
Because he wanted us to have democracy.
Today we must call for freedom.

Despite repeated violent attacks against them and the unquestioned freedom that they had to come and go from the orphanage as they pleased, nearly all of the children at Lafanmi Selavi did choose to stay until the facility's closure in 1999. Many indicated to me that they were proud to be participatory in Haiti's continuing transition to democratic order and most recognized that the basis of their social empowerment throughout the 1990s was their membership in the Lafanmi program. This was an empowerment that they themselves acknowledge they did not have on the street. One young boy named Clovis told me that,

> when I used to be at my house, I had nothing, nothing that kept me from the street. . . . I had to steal because I was living on the street. . . . I went to seek help and found it at Lafanmi Selavi. They showed me what I can do as one person for Haiti's tomorrow.

Another boy commented to me that he "lived in misery [on the street]. I had no one to help me, only Father Aristide and some others. They say that I can work for liberty, that I don't have to steal."

The children at Lafanmi Selavi clearly developed a unique composite identity that was shaped by their own sense of individual rights, the ideologies of the Lafanmi Selavi program, the influences of a politically active peer group, and their solidarity as both displaced street children and political targets. Many of the children recognized a continuity in political consciousness and action both laterally among their comrades and longitudinally through past generations of street-child activists. Most of my interviews with Lafanmi children strongly suggested a deep sense of solidarity with others in their cohort, while the life histories of some revealed that political activity (civil disobedience, demonstrations, church-based empowerment, community organization, radio-based vocal dissension, illegalized labor cooperation) was typical among their parents and older kin under the Duvaliers. Their common awareness of intrinsic cultural rights including education, health care, housing, work, protection against hunger, and other economic and social necessities was unquestionably heightened by participation in the Lafanmi Selavi project, and was instrumental to the development of their civil and political identity.

The violent end of the orphanage and the continuing use of it as a facade of child activism through Radyo Timoun and TeleTimoun reveal the dangers implicit in the utilization of child agency for political ends. Whatever sense of empowerment the children felt while at Lafanmi Selavi was utterly and permanently shattered when the state's gas canisters were lobbed over the compound wall in June 1999, effectively marking the end of Lafanmi's legitimacy as an institution tolerant of adolescent political expression. The orphanage now represents a material and purely symbolic space, not only as a failed salvo to the everyday violence of street life, not only as an engine for child manipulation in the culture of Haitian politics, but also as a terrain of social witness to and child agency in the changing state of Haitian nationhood.

Dezalin

Dezalin, now thirteen, has been on the street since he was around eight years old. He tells me that he has no father, that he never knew his mother, and that he is an only child. Before ending up on the street, he lived with an aunt in Les Cayes, but he left that household because she beat him. Although he has extended family, including other aunts and uncles in Port-au-Prince, he does not stay with them because he does not believe that they can afford to care for him.

When living with his aunt in Les Cayes, Dezalin attended a Salvation Army-run elementary school. After leaving his aunt's household he left school and ended up sleeping on the streets of Les Cayes–in his words, "for a long time"—before leaving for Port-au-Prince. Once in the capital, he quickly associated himself with a handful of friendly street boys with whom he slept and still sleeps for protection. Among them is Blak Lovli, Dezalin's *bon zanmi* [his closest comrade]; both boys frequently refer to one another as "fre'm" [my brother]. Dezalin slept on the street full time until he wandered and was admitted into Centre d'Action–a small outreach program for street kids near where he used to sleep in Carrefour-Feuilles. At the center Dezalin eats twice a day (usually rice with bean sauce) and is provided with clean water to drink and a mattress upon which to sleep. He is required to participate in several hours of schooling each day. Although he can write and spell his name and a few other short Kreyòl words, he is still, from all practical standpoints, illiterate.

Dezalin does not always take advantage of the services offered to him at Centre d'Action. He spends the better portion of any given day on the street and with a close group of seven other boys who also take varying degrees of advantage of the services offered by the center. He often uses his own money to buy food and sometimes sleeps with his friends on the street in Champ des Mars near the National Palace. These other boys live a lifestyle not unlike his own and are his coworkers on the avenues as well as his *zanmi* in exchange relations.

Like most street children, Dezalin exploits a diverse array of economic opportunities offered by the busy urban streets. Though he prefers to work—usually washing cars or wiping the road dust from them with a chamois rag—he relies on begging as a secondary means of support. He typically asks for money when he begs, but he points out that he very often supplements his day's diet with handouts from café patrons from whom he solicits table scraps.

His personal possessions are starkly limited. When I ask him to list for me everything that he owns, he starts by jokingly listing his head and then the clothes he is wearing, the sandals on his feet, his money, a small steel-bead chain that he found in the street and cleaned and now wears as a necklace, and a razor blade that he uses for shaving his head and trimming his fingernails. He is generous with most of what he has. If he feels hungry and if he has enough money, he will buy *ti manje* [a little something to eat] throughout the day, which he will share with his friends with whom he works the street. He says that he shares with these boys "as if they are my brothers."

For a boy of thirteen who has lived the past four years mostly on the street, Dezalin is in very good health. He has had fevers in the past, sometimes accompanied by vomiting, but has never taken medication for these ailments that have always passed after several days. He has never been to a hospital and as far as he can remember, he has never seen a doctor. None of this is to say that Dezalin has never been in need of medical attention. On one occasion he was sleeping on the top of a large truck making an overnight delivery of produce from the countryside to Port-au-Prince, when he was thrown from the vehicle after it hit a rut in the road. The fall injured his legs and left him seriously bruised. He was helped by some passersby who saw what happened and gave him a medicinal tea infusion to drink for the pain. On another occasion he was bitten by a stray dog in Port-au-Prince. The threat of rabies is a very real one in Haiti, which has one of the highest rates of incidence of any country in the Western Hemisphere. He cleaned the wound himself but developed a fever over the course of subsequent days thereafter. He did not seek any medical treatment and fortunately the fever passed.

When I ask him what scares him the most about street life, he answers immediately: he is afraid that *lapolis* [the National Police] will arrest him or that other street children will kill him. His greatest fear is of *gwo timoun lari* [older street boys] who might beat or kill him while he sleeps. Dezalin acknowledges his extreme vulnerability to threats, but despite his resignation to the physical power that these threatening entities hold over him he does what he can to protect himself. When he sleeps on the street he typically does so as part of a group and secreted away from open view. Nonetheless he, like all street children, is keenly aware of his inability to be completely invisible.

Against some threats there is simply no best defense. Dezalin regards all *zam* [weapons] as the most dangerous aspect of life on the avenues regardless of who carries them—*zenglendo, lapolis, gwo timoun lari*. He worries that he is too skinny to protect himself against such deadly force as that brought down by machetes, pistols, batons, and cinder blocks. He carries no weapons himself, save for his razor, which he regards as a tool for grooming and not an instrument of violence. His lack of even the most rudimentary artifact for his effective self-defense beyond this, coupled with the fact that he is known among other street children as a boy who makes good money washing cars, makes him an easy target for abuse from the older street boys, whom he fears most of all. He says that he has few problems with these boys, at the same time that he easily recalls a number of incidents in which he was seriously beaten and robbed of his little bit of money by them. Dezalin knows that he has few options for his defense against the predation of these older boys. Teenaged street boys often outnumber their younger counterparts in many neighborhoods, and these older boys are keenly aware of the advantage that this holds for them over younger, weaker boys like Dezalin. Like most Port-au-Prince street youth, teenage boys travel the city in groups; but unlike all younger street kids, some older boys make a living as thugs, exploiting their comparative size advantage by routinely beating, intimidating, and stealing from smaller children.

Dezalin understands the options available to him when confronted by a group of older boys bent on hurting or stealing from him, and they run the gamut from submission to flight to resistance. His most effective defense against predatory street teens is the one he employs most often—he runs from them and when he is a safe distance away he may throw rocks at them. In most cases, however, he opts for the most pacifistic route and simply flees.

On only one occasion that he can remember has Dezalin sought the assistance of the National Police. This after he was involved in several scuffles with older boys, who during the last fight threatened to kill him. The police responded to his requests for protection and arrested the threatening boys, who were held at the juvenile prison at Fort National for several days before being released. Dezalin fled the neighborhood where the scuffles transpired while his antagonists were incarcerated and he hasn't been back since.

While Dezalin believes that the police can protect him and although he has successfully sought their protection in the past, all of his descriptions of police responsibilities imply an intrinsic aggression against street children. He explains that the primary duty of Haitian police officers is to *"kembe ak kale ou si w'ap batay"* [arrest and beat you if you are fighting] and to *"fèmen ou sinon touye ou si ou menm vòlè sa bagay"* [put you in jail or kill you if you steal something]. His negative impression of the responsibilities of the National Police is probably derived from the rather limited utility its officers have for him. He himself has been arrested twice for pilfering fruit from market stalls. He has little reason to regard the police as anything more than a force of subjugation (whether to his advantage or not) and often, humiliation. When still living on the street in Les Cayes after he had fled the household of his aunt, Dezalin had taken to sleeping in an abandoned *tap-tap*, one of the many that have toppled into the steep roadside ravines on the high-speed run from

Port-au-Prince to Les Cayes along National Route 200. These vehicles commonly provide sociable and usually safe shelter to rural street kids. One evening Dezalin and two other boys were sleeping on the roof of the vehicle because some other child had days before defecated inside the bus. Two National Policemen arrived a short time after Dezalin had fallen asleep and, after having searched the *tap-tap*, ordered the boys down from the roof. The officers were looking for an armed bandit who had been operating in the area at night and, angered at the street boys for living "*tankou chen*" [like dogs] and "*ap gate*" [spoiling, contaminating] Les Cayes, they arrested the three boys and took them to a detention facility in town. Once there Dezalin was forced to stand on one foot for thirty minutes while the officers laughed and spat on him. Though not beaten he was held in a cell with other street boys overnight and for all of the following day without food or water before being released.

He has thus been spared harsher experiences of police violence through a formula of pragmatic decision making, opportunism, and fleetness of foot. He stays away from dangerous areas of the city like Portail Léogâne because he is afraid of the gangs of street children who live there, because he is wary of the consequences of associating with those who engage in illicit behaviors like habitual glue sniffing, because he is fortunate enough to have recourse to Centre d'Action, and because he is wise enough to know when to run and throw rocks from far afield of danger.

6

Aprè Dans, Tanbou Lou

After the Dance, the Drum Is Heavy

It is my hope that the preceding chapters have served to make at least one thing clear: while Haiti's poorest, most vulnerable, and exposed children—her street children—may in fact be living in the most unenviable of circumstances, their existence, survival, and autonomies are far more meaningful than what their victimization has to say about the state and the civil society that have neglected them or have otherwise failed to safeguard their welfare. Not a single child that I have known living on the streets of Port-au-Prince has ever given any indication of resignation to the death that would come easily to them should they choose to give up the struggle for survival. To the contrary, each and every one of them has provided evidence for their determination to work, to love, to share, to fight, to eat, to sleep, to live, and to be in the world with their dignity intact and with their destiny all their own. While I as much as anyone else would like to see the numbers of street children dramatically reduced, a decade of work with Haitian street children has convinced me of at least one certainty: while few children would choose to live on the street, those who do demand recognition of their power to act, both in their own interests and in (and sometimes against) the interests of others.

But the agency of street children in Port-au-Prince has always been and continues to be mitigated by the structural conditions in which they live, and perhaps never before in Haitian history have their rights to self-determination been more threatened than now. Haiti is now nearly lost in the deepest economic, political, and environmental nadir that the country has ever known. Deflation, famine, starvation, disease, lawlessness, and warfare are all that can be seen on the horizon, and the apocalypse may already have begun.

The purpose of this and the next chapter is to outline the major crises that are plaguing Haiti today and to demonstrate how they are further compromising the survival of the country's street children. Perhaps most importantly, these final chapters will argue that the plight of Haiti's street children is intimately linked to a global system of economic inequality, political destabilization, and postcolonial militarization that not only feeds the very roots of transnational terrorism but, just as significantly, puts the children of the least developed world disproportionately at risk of unnecessary suffering and miserable death. Let's begin the analysis where the end results of this global system are starkly illustrated: on the streets of Port-au-Prince that have become the frontlines of nothing less than a civil war that began in 2004.

A Prelude to War

On January 1, 2004, Haiti celebrated a lie. It was supposed to mark the joyous bicentennial of the declaration of Haitian independence from French rule. After a hard fought revolution against slavery and brutality, Jean-Jacques Dessalines proclaimed the liberty of the Haitian people. The rout of Napoleon's legions from the island signaled the end of the first and only successful slave revolution in world history. But independence and liberty are merely ideas in Haiti. Cash-strapped and saddled with a labor-intensive plantation economy that required trade in order for it to be sustained, Dessalines militarized the agricultural system. He turned the victorious Haitian army on his fellow citizens, and ordered them back to the cane fields. The Haitian tradition of using military force to govern was born, and two hundred years later nothing has changed. The Haitian bicentennial was a lie. While blue and red crepe was being strung around the palace, Haitians were starving to death, the government was slipping ever deeper into corruption and repression, and war was on the horizon.

The living conditions on the streets of Haiti since the reelection of Aristide to the presidency in 2000 (amid opposition electoral boycotts, disputed results, and accusations of fraud) have deteriorated dramatically. As the economy has continued its seemingly endless descent, so too has the popular despair and the public confidence in the government to alleviate the suffering of the majority poor. By January 2002 the tentative stability of the Aristide government began to crumble. Prime Minister Jean-Marie Cherestal resigned at the start of the year over mounting criticism of his government's failure to alleviate the country's economic and political woes. In the north of the country, Aristide's popular base had eroded significantly. In Haiti's third largest city of Gonaïves, strongman Amiot Métayer, the local chief of a fiercely pro-Aristide street clan called *Lamè Kanibal* [the Cannibal Army], was arrested by the National Police in July 2002 in a crackdown on street violence. Métayer's men had been firebombing several buildings in town associated with a rival clan rumored to be supported by former FADH

Figure 6.1. Street boys pose with their bicycle. The lives of Haiti's poorest children are intimately linked to the lives of the poorest children elsewhere in the least-developed world. A global history of colonialism, small arms trafficking, structural adjustment, unilateral military interventionism, and skyrocketing debt conspires to keep the children of the poorest countries of the world in a state of utter desperation.

officers. His shocking arrest was intended to rebut opposition accusations that Aristide was using unruly street gangs and hired thugs to affirm his control of the country. Métayer's detention would not last long. A month after his arrest, members of the Cannibal Army used a tractor to break through the wall of the Gonaïves prison, freeing Métayer along with 158 of the 221 violent inmates interred there with him.

The political situation then grew ever more rapidly out of the government's control. In Gonaïves, by then a stronghold of anti-Aristide insurgency, dissidents clashed with whip-wielding pro-Aristide gangs in a messy confrontation that left dozens injured. Sporadic violence throughout the north reached frenzied proportions in 2003 when Métayer's bullet-riddled and mutilated corpse was found on an isolated road twenty-five miles south of Gonaïves. He had been shot at point blank range in both eyes, and his chest was hacked down the midsection with a machete. The graphic political overtones of the killing enraged members of the Cannibal Army, who accused Aristide of ordering Méyater's assassination because of the incriminating leverage he could bring against the Fanmi Lavalas government that imprisoned him the year before. Dozens were killed and wounded in angry riots that raged for days after the discovery of Métayer's body. Amiot Métayer's brother Butteur assumed control of the Cannibal Army, rechristened it Front de Résistance de l'Artibonite or FRA (the Artibonite Resistance Front), and turned it aggressively against the Aristide government. Civil war was now imminent, and would begin with an FRA uprising against the National Police in Gonaïves, less than five months after the discovery of Amiot Métayer's mutilated corpse.

The War Begins

In early February 2004 four bystanders were killed and twenty wounded when the FRA, armed with an assortment of handguns and old (some rusty) bolt-action M14s left over from the last century's army, overran the PNH barracks in Gonaïves. The attack touched off an already-brewing war between supporters of then-sitting President Aristide and his opponents, who contend, along with most of the international community, that the elections that won Aristide the National Palace and his Fanmi Lavalas partisans thirteen of the available fifteen seats in parliament, were rigged.

In its vehement turn against the Aristide government, the FRA had orchestrated a series of terrorist attacks and violent demonstrations throughout the towns and cities in the country's north, which left scores dead and hundreds wounded between September 2003 and the February 2004 attack. The FRA easily overtook Gonaïves after the poorly armed and utterly overwhelmed police fled their posts under the onslaught. FRA rebels cut cellular and landline communications in the area and erected barricades of rubble, tires, and flaming vehicles around the city limits, intermittently blocking roads and bridges leading from the capital—a defense intended to slow government response.

From his base camp in Gonaïves, Butteur Métayer broadcast a call over the radio to anti-Aristide factions throughout the country to take up arms against the Fanmi Lavalas government and the National Police, now widely seen as an institution loyal to the president. Out of hiding and exile came a host of rebel groups including the "New Army," a still-active faction made up primarily of former members of the FADH. One of their leaders was former army sergeant Louis Jodel Chamblain, whom Haiti's Truth and Justice Commission had suspected of engineering the 1987 massacre of over thirty voters who lined up to cast their ballots in a civilian-run election. In 1993 Chamblain helped to found the viciously anti-Lavalas Front Révolutionnaire pour l'Avancement et le Progrès d'Haïti, or FRAPH [Front for the Advancement and Progress of Haiti], a terrorist organization based in Port-au-Prince with Duvalierist and FADH support. FRAPH (the acronym is pronounced "frap" and echoes the pronunciation of the French verb *frapper*, meaning "to strike" or "to hit") has been held responsible for the killing of hundreds of Aristide loyalists during the Cedras coup. In 1994 Chamblain fled to the neighboring Dominican Republic after it became clear that he was to be held accountable for the 1987 voter massacre. He returned to Haiti with his former military colleagues to take the northern city of Cap Haïtien on February 23, 2004.

Chamblain drank rum and danced in the streets that day with Guy Philippe, a former FADH soldier who fled Haiti for Ecuador after the Cedras coup government was ousted from power by U.S. forces. Upon his return to Haiti in 1995, Philippe was integrated into the fledgling police corps, and served as the police chief of Delmas and later Cap Haïtien. He fled to the Dominican Republic after a warrant for his arrest was issued for his role in plotting a failed coup attempt against Aristide in 2001. Philippe reentered Haiti in February 2004 to merge his own crew of rebels with New Army forces. After the seizure of Cap Haïtien, Philippe took command of the now-confederated New Army, christened them the Front de Libération d'Haïti or FLA (Front for the Liberation of Haiti)—a name that never really caught on—and began plotting an assault on the National Palace to arrest Aristide on charges of corruption. After this the plan was explicit: to reinstitute the Haitian army, which the Front claimed had been illegally dissolved by Aristide in violation of the standing constitution of the Republic.[1]

Port-au-Prince Burning

As the north seethed, the sprawling capital of Port-au-Prince was put under a state of siege. By the time I arrived in the capital in early March 2004, martial law had been declared, and government forces presided over all auspices of social life in the public domain, preparing for a showdown on the streets of the capital. Clad in the dichromatic drab of Haiti's paramilitaries (all gunmetal-black and khaki) the troopers remain the very spectacle of Creole colony, a fusion of autochthonic authoritarian police labor equipped with hypermodern hardware imported from the United States. Unlike the postcolonial army of the past, Haiti's paramilitaries are outfitted with state-of-the-art matériel that ten years of foreign military aid (ostensibly intended to support a stronger civilian police force) can buy. Sporting riot helmets, face shields, gas masks, Kevlar vesting, composite plastic knee and elbow pads, combat shotguns, machine pistols, hand grenades and steel-spring batons, tactical units of AGU, CIMO, GIPINH, and the PNH braced themselves against the walls of the government district as fiercely pro-Aristide gangs calling themselves *chimere* (a folkloric, two-headed, fire-spitting monstrosity—part lion, part goat, and with a serpent for a tail), whose weapons were issued by Fanmi Lavalas partisan bosses, littered the streets of Port-au-Prince with flaming barricades. The noxious smell of burning tires fed to these blockades settled into the very fabric of street life in the capital, gagging the city with black soot that mixed with the choking smog of auto exhaust and charcoal smoke that has long been typical of the city's ecological woes. As I made my way around Bel Air on the eve of the impending rebel assault on the neighborhood, a street boy named Mathias whom I had known from years before ran up to me and gleefully waved a fistful of gourde notes.

"Kwis! Kwis!" he called to me, "If my eyes did not tell me so, I would believe you were not really in front of me! It is a bad time here, man. You will not be able to work here now. Its crazy. The army is back, Kwis. The police are frightened. The people have no security, nothing."

I asked him about the money he held in his hand. "Are you working while this is going on?" He had always made a decent living on the street washing cars.

"Oh yes, man. There is much money for us [street children] to have now. These men came to me, they are with Titid [Aristide], see. And they find me and Jimmi and Ti Jean—they are kids that you know, Kwis. We were wiping cars in Delmas and they say to us, 'come with us to Rue Capois [the large boulevard near the National Palace] and you will make a lot of money.' Now they pay us to work the barricades. We throw tires on the flames, we keep them burning. Look at my money—I make a lot of gourdes now!"

We talked some more, and he wished me good courage before running back to work the barricades. As I watched Mathias take up his post with other boys beside the fires, I thought about how few cars there were on the street, and how few motorists in this time of war would stop to get their car wiped down by a street boy. Mathias had already adapted well to the conflict economy.

War Without End

Since January 2004 a fragmentary coalition of students, political dissidents, merchants, civic organizations, church groups, and businessmen known as *Groupe de 184* [the Group of 184] had been agitating for Aristide's resignation and had clashed with armed *chimere* in several skirmishes and demonstrations-cum-riots in which people have been killed and wounded in the ensuing exchanges of gunfire. The PNH and the paramilitaries routinely fired into the crowds, often panicking and fleeing as the crowds turned ugly and against them. Despite the arrival of international peacekeeping forces in February 2004, violent confrontations among *chimere*, rebel clans and their sympathizers, the PNH, paramilitary troopers, student demonstrators, and partisan street clans have continued, and have been added to the matrix of social violence already woven with the crimes of the *zenglendo*, FRAPH terrorists, FADH loyalists, drug gangs, and vigilance brigades. This before we consider the sporadic attacks of homicidal vengeance and sexual brutality that now may opportunistically pose as political, rather than pathological, violence. And this too before we also consider the loss of civil rights, human dignities, and life suffered by the civilian casualties of the sum of Haiti's economic woes.

As the rebels moved from village to town during the early days of the uprising, they sacked and torched police precincts and private homes, freed hundreds of violent prisoners from criminal detention, and seized stores of automatic weapons, uniforms, and helmets from the provincial arsenals of the PNH.[2] Markets and schools throughout 60 percent of the country, some in regions that remain rebel-held territory outside of government control, are still shuttered because many farmers, vendors, teachers, and students are unable or unwilling to travel dangerous roads to return from their places of internal exile in the country's west and south.

A full-scale New Army assault on the capital and a certain civilian massacre was only averted when Aristide, under strong pressure from the United States and France, resigned his duties as president and quit Haiti for Jamaica on February 29, 2004, later to take up exile in the Central African Republic and then in South Africa. An advance contingency of U.S. troops arrived in the country the day following his departure, in support of the Marine units already defending the embassy in downtown Port-au-Prince. They were later joined by Canadian, French, Venezuelan, and Argentine peacekeepers, and were eventually replaced by a Brazilian contingent that arrived in mid-2004 to assume control of the entire U.N. Multinational Intervention Force (UNMIF).

Since March 2004 The United Nations Stabilization Mission in Haiti (MINUSTAH), UNMIF, and the PNH have been engaged in the long and treacherous task of disarming a civilian population with tens of thousands of illegal sidearms, semiautomatic rifles, and machine guns. To date they have collected little more than two hundred firearms; to place that number in proper context, the Geneva-based Small Arms Survey (SAS) recently estimated that there are close to 209,000 small arms and light weapons in Haiti, nearly all of which are in the possession of non-state-armed groups and civilians (Muggah 2005: 27–30). The job of disarmament is made all the more difficult now that vast stores of police hardware and uniforms are in the possession of rebel insurgents. In some villages in the north, rebels have completely replaced the National Police and are dressed in the full uniform of the PNH—badges, weapons, and all. They have since assumed a semiofficial role in security operations, their activities condoned though not overtly supported by the provisional government, which has come close to full paralysis under the onslaught of pro-Aristide violence and police and paramilitary retaliations. Days after U.S. troops arrived in March, a fierce gun battle erupted in the seaside Port-au-Prince slum of La Saline as rebel soldiers attempted to disarm a gang of *chimere.* Several civilians were wounded in the exchange of gunfire. Neither the PNH nor the peacekeepers were anywhere in sight. Since September 2004 two U.N. soldiers have been wounded in clashes with the *chimere,* and during the second week of October 2004, five beheaded bodies were discovered on the streets of the capital. They remain unidentified: erased, deleted, edited out, made invisible.

It is difficult to tell if there can now or ever be a public trust in the Haitian police, regardless of who is wearing the uniform. The colored history of the PNH and its disparate and fragmented paramilitary units has caused nationwide uneasiness over their tactical similarities to the old FADH. Their tenuous grip on authority and control in the country has been severely compromised by the rebel insurgency, and this has led to the restoration of what is essentially martial law in the capital where the struggle to regain state control is presently at its fiercest. The New Army is energized and mobilized, empowered by the failure of anyone to disarm or contain their return to the political arena. The upshot is that Port-au-Prince has acquired the now-hallmark characteristics of large cities in postindustrial, postoccupation, democratizing nation-states in the developing world: an utterly militarized public domain, irreconcilable political polarization, upstart neighborhood warlords, criminal opportunists, incipient opposition parties, authoritarian governance, a profound scarcity of basic resources, and legions of poor, disaffected, and unseen citizens who are every day reconstituting their broken worlds—social, cultural, familial, moral worlds—that have been left bleeding and fragmented on the pavement in the wake of political terror.

No Way Forward

When I arrived on the street in Port-au-Prince in early March of 2004, most of the city was still largely outside the control of the government. Little has changed. Since Aristide's resignation and exile, the state's paramilitaries have been hunting down the *chimere* and other armed factions of the Fanmi Lavalas party. A concentrated New Army initiative to reinstitute the FADH is well underway, with an active recruitment of new soldiers and their outfitting with new uniforms financed by wealthy families with an interest in restoring the pre-Aristide status quo.

Factions of heavily armed *chimere* are also on the offensive, and the city has descended into near-anarchy. The Haitian National Police, routed by the rebels just about everywhere in the northern two-thirds of the country, continue to fire their weapons indiscriminately into civilian crowds. Arson, riot, looting, and summary execution have once again formed the lexicon of political conflict on the streets. Vigilante bands and entrepreneur assassins roam the Port-au-Prince slums of Bel Air, Cité Soleil, and La Saline with Uzis, semiautomatic handguns, combat-grade shotguns, assault rifles, homemade "creole" firearms, bayonets, whips, and machetes. Amid the chaos and a state of siege on the streets and in the complete absence of legal authority, political scores are being settled alongside violent acts of personal vengeance. Summary executions are being carried out on roadsides, the bodies littering the streets with single bullet holes through their foreheads.[3] Dozens of others are being killed in less formal ways, their bodies machine-gunned, hacked to death, decapitated, mutilated, burned alive. Some victims of the conflict have been disemboweled, some strangled with their own underwear. There are rumors of a young girl from the militantly pro-Aristide Cité Soleil slum having been raped to death by rebels after the departure of Aristide. Since October of 2004 pro-Aristide gangs have been systematically beheading PNH officers under the rubric "Operation Baghdad." The war has come to Port-au-Prince, and it is not being fought around the civil society as much as it is being fought directly through it. At the time of this writing, there have been over eight hundred Haitians killed in factional clashes since the fighting began in earnest in late February 2004.

While the government has imposed a curfew and urges residents of the capital to seek shelter indoors when shooting is heard, the truth of the matter is that when a bullet is fired in Port-au-Prince there is little difference between inside and outside; here, especially in the most volatile slums, most homes are made of cardboard and tin. Haiti's violent history of successive coups d'etat has shown how political conflict can become a civilian bloodbath when the fighting reaches the capital, even when people do stay indoors. There appears to be no end to the violence in sight. Though the rebel army had pledged to lay down their arms after the UNMIF force arrived in 2004 to reestablish order, they have shown little real interest in doing so even as MINUSTAH continues to conduct disarmament and policing operations throughout the country. Outfitted in new fatigue uniforms and brandishing automatic weapons, members of the New Army depart daily from their Petionville headquarters and descend on the capital down the hill in a show of force intended to quell the pro-Aristide gangs and assuage the concerns of a business elite growing impatient with the insecurity and the toll it has taken on their commercial interests.

Ordinary Lives, Extraordinary Circumstances

The destruction of the war in the capital is superimposed onto an urban landscape already devastated by the crushing poverty of the Western Hemisphere's most destitute economy. Long the poorest country in the Western Hemisphere, Haiti was recently further crippled by the floodwater obliteration attributed to Hurricane Jeanne, which struck the island in September 2004 and claimed over three thousand lives while leaving two hundred thousand homeless. In the northern town of Gonaïves—the first to be routed by the rebels in February 2004—the floodwaters caused a hunger crisis like never before seen. Mothers picked through the muck to salvage fallen fruit, washing it in septic water before feeding it to their starving and emaciated children. Men chopped away with machetes at collapsed shanties, searching for what remained of their families' homes. In the third week of October, some in the north had not eaten for three weeks. The New Army stepped forward in Gonaïves, brandishing their weapons at international relief workers whom they charged were ineffective at the distribution of food aid, which was increasingly looted from World Food Program warehouses. Everyone involved in the relief effort agreed then that insecurity was the greatest obstacle to feeding the victims of the floods.

In Port-au-Prince, where even moderate rains result in the overflow of raw sewage into the homes of the poor living in low-lying slums, street boys zombified by their glue-sniffing habit and suffering from oozing vapor burns around their noses and mouths sleep against the wall surrounding the National Cemetery. That wall is itself scarred with the dimpled craters of gunfire, and is covered with a cacophony of vicious political graffiti and counter-graffiti, variously in condemnation or support of the deposed president. One of the street girls congregating there in March 2004 told me bluntly, "I am beyond hungry. I am already dead." Inside the cemetery, tombs have been looted, caskets smashed, corpses strewn about. I stoop down to examine the splintered coffin of a child, wedged between two mausoleums. Some of the small corpse is inside, but much of it has been scattered about the space, here and there among the bones of many others. In these times the desecrations are as often the work of political partisans targeting the tombs of opposing families as they are that of the common grave-robber or less frequently still, the necromancer.

In the sprawling slum of Bel Air, I step through gutters filled with raw sewage mixing with coagulated blood from an earlier street shooting. The upside-down shells of burned out cars line streets obstructed by heaps of smoldering garbage, some as high as ten feet. In one such car the charred skeleton of the driver sits bolt upright in his seat, his blackened skull grimacing at the Armageddon playing out before him. In the first days after the departure of the deposed president, bodies and pieces of bodies in varying states of decay could be found stuffed in trash-clogged drainage culverts and thrown like so much litter against the side of the city morgue. Formidable roadblocks of burning tires, often manned by armed and masked factions and occasionally street kids, stop traffic and pedestrians searching for victims and valuables. The cityscape is a wrecked vision, the absurd and impossible but nonetheless real consequence of a profound civil destruction imposed on preexisting urban disorder. The war in the capital has left chaos and mayhem in the middle of a slum constructed not by logic or symmetry but by human necessity and the struggle for space in which to live, eat, love, reproduce, and die. For the poorest Haitians who depend everyday on the city for life itself, the ruination of Port-au-Prince writ large has completely shattered an already cracked mirage of an ordered and just world, as it has compelled entire communities to again bear witness to the carnage of machine-gun politics. Since February 2004 spectacular acts of violence in the capital, a place where well over two million people are crammed into the least amount of space per capita of any other city in the Americas, have made close to one-quarter of the city's population direct witnesses to and thus participants in the violence. Even this troubling statistic betrays the reality of the hundreds of thousands more who in one way or another are suffering because of the incidentals of war.

Somehow Haitians manage to maintain a semblance of normalcy even as their social and cultural worlds are crumbling around them. Street children recover from the loss of their friends to gunplay by expressing firm and certain knowledge of their understanding of what has happened to them. They impose a logic born of the war-torn conditions that frame their lives of poverty, scarcity, fear, and death. Some say that their friends were taken to be made into *zombi*. Others say that they were *manje* [eaten, consumed, exhausted, destroyed, disappeared] by monsters, which is not so far from the truth. But they also recover their comrades by speaking their names and telling stories of their good friendship and humanity. Social and cultural lives go on. Women give birth, vendors sell candies and cigarettes on street corners, welders ply their trade on the sidewalks in front of their shops, *tap-taps* carry passengers between markets and homes, children make their way to school, street kids wipe the hoods of passing cars. Laborers lay cinder block around a memorial commemorating Haiti's two hundred years of independence from French rule; the year 2004 marked Haiti's bicentennial as well as its descent into anarchy and war. They are seemingly undeterred by the bullet holes that already mar their work from yesterday. In these and many other ways, Haitians in Port-au-Prince are demonstrating the resilience, resistance, and creativity that anthropologists are increasingly realizing are qualities characteristic of communities transformed by violent conflict. The business of everyday life must go on even in a civil war zone, where a facade of the ordinary masks the reality of lives lived under truly extraordinary circumstances.

The unspeakable violence and devastating misery that afflicts Haiti inevitably leads one to ask: how did all of this happen to Haiti? The answer to this question is contained in the answer to the question: "If all we knew about the state of the world was what we know about Haiti's poorest children, then what would we know?" To pose such a question is to undertake a perspective on global political economy that is almost vengefully ground-up. It is to see and to interrogate the world from the knee-high vantage of children living at the low-water mark of security, health, and dignity. The view, unsurprisingly, is not an auspicious one.

The streets of Haiti—filthy, disordered, destitute, violent as they are—hardly embody conditions conducive to healthy child development. They also are not unique to Haiti. Here, as elsewhere, children are struggling not simply to survive but to carve a small space for themselves to work, to eat, to sleep, and to foster hopes for a better future. It is particularly dangerous and irresponsible to believe that these struggles are localized ones, just as it is to believe that the causes of the odds against which poor children everywhere struggle are any more local than the struggles themselves. In the next, concluding chapter, we will explore the ways that the desperation of Haiti's street children is fatefully linked not only to the desperation of other children living amid similar conditions worldwide, but also to global political and economic processes that catalyze, reproduce, and perpetuate the scarcity, misery, and conflict that defines the backdrop of their adolescence, wherever they may live.

7

All That We Know

The Poorest Countries and the State of the World

What if we were to ask the question, "If all we knew about Haiti was what we know of her poorest children, then what would we know?" The answer to that question would surely be grim. The steady maintenance of some of the highest rates of child mortality and morbidity in the world do not bode well for an assessment of the country's health care system, and the comparably low rates of school enrollment and child literacy speak volumes about the multitude of failures of the nation's educational system. Reports abound in Port-au-Prince of the participation of children in political gun violence, including child soldiering, in direct contravention of the U.N. Convention on the Rights of the Child, to which Haiti is a signatory. This coupled with the fact that children and youth are disproportionately victimized by gun violence in Haiti would seem to suggest that here is a country where "political partisans" and "political targets" are defined in the abstract and with little regard for customary cultural constraints on violence that serve to protect the very young from participation in or victimization by political conflict. The fact that children can be found in legion in the adult courts and the adult penitentiary system suggests a Machiavellian legal culture that gives new and sinister meaning to the concept that all are equal in the eyes of Haitian law. Port-au-Prince children are everyday rebuked and marginalized by businesspersons and passersby as they seek a living on the street. Hundreds of thousands of *restavèk* labor under conditions of postcolonial servitude in the homes of the moderately poor. Middle-class and working-class men avoid the question of age when selecting prostitutes outside of Petionville bars.

If all we knew about Haiti was this, we might be excused for believing that it is a country whose children have little recourse but to a predestiny of resigned suffering. But this is not all that we can know about Haiti, nor is this all that we can know about her children. The problem is not that the situation in Haiti is not grim (indeed it is) or that her poorest children are not living under extremely difficult circumstances as a result, because they are. The problem is in the belief that we can understand Haiti by understanding the plight of Haiti's poorest children, which we can't. A better question than the one that opened this chapter might be this: "If all we knew about the state of the world was what we know about Haiti's poorest children, then what would we know?" It is a question worth asking, because the dismal conditions amid which these children are living are inextricably linked to a complex network of capital exchanges and political machinations that transcend Haiti as they spread brutality, war, and destitution throughout the least-developed world, guaranteeing lives of anguish and agony for the vast majority of children not killed outright by its immediate consequences. Put another way, the suffering and violence faced by the poorest of Haiti's children is part of a *global system* that reproduces and maintains the same suffering and violence faced by children in scores of other impoverished countries.

It is axiomatic that children bear the brunt of health and social distress throughout the developing world, and children in least-developed countries suffer at a rate consistently higher than those throughout the rest of the world. Studies conducted by the World Health Organization and data contained in UNICEF's annual report on the State of the World's Children (2005) consistently verify this claim:

· 42 percent of the population in least-developed countries has no access to clean water and 65 percent have no access to adequate sanitation facilities. For comparison, UNICEF data suggest that virtually every citizen in the industrialized world has access to clean water and adequate sanitation facilities.

· The infant mortality rate for least-developed countries is nearly twice that for the rest of the world and nearly twenty times that for industrialized countries.

· The under-five mortality rate for least-developed countries is nearly twice that for the rest of the world, and almost twenty-six times that for industrialized countries.

· 4,312,000 children in least-developed countries die before their fifth birthday every year. That number represents 40 percent of annual under-five deaths worldwide, and is sixty-six times more than the number of annual under-five deaths in industrialized countries (65,000).

· 18 percent of babies born in least-developed countries are of low-birth weight, a percentage consistent with the worldwide rate of 16 percent. For comparison, 7 percent of babies in industrialized countries are of low-birth weight.

- 36 percent of children under the age of five in least-developed countries are moderately-to-severely underweight, 10 percent are moderately-to-severely wasted, and 42 percent are moderately-to-severely stunted.

- 21 percent of one-year-old children in least-developed countries are not vaccinated against tuberculosis, 32 percent are neither vaccinated against diphtheria/pertussis/tetanus nor polio, 33 percent are not vaccinated against measles, and 80 percent are not vaccinated against hepatitis B.

- The gross ratio of primary school enrollment in least-developed countries is 15 percent lower than that of the rest of the world, with only 64 percent of primary school entrants reaching the fifth grade. Worse still, the secondary school enrollment rate for children in least-developed countries is less than half that for the world's children.

- Thirty-four of the fifty least-developed countries in the world (see Table 3) have witnessed political violence, open warfare, factional strife, or acts of domestic terrorism in the past twenty-five years (Afghanistan, Angola, Bangladesh, Burkina Faso, Burundi, Cambodia, Central African Republic, Chad, Congo, Eritrea, Ethiopia, Guinea, Guinea-Bissau, Haiti, Laos, Lesotho, Liberia, Mali, Mauritania, Mozambique, Myanmar, Nepal, Niger, Rwanda, Senegal, Sierra Leone, Somalia, Sudan, Tanzania, Timor-Lesté, Togo, Uganda, Yemen, and Zambia). The conditions of childhood in all of them is the same: poor, desperate, dangerous, and short.

- The World Health Organization has estimated that there are as many as 100 million street children worldwide, most of them in the developing and the least-developed world (2000: iii).

The combined negative effects on health and social development that scarcity and violence bring to bear on children in the least-developed world is further aggravated for the poorest of those children, those who have been displaced from their homes and onto the streets where they often subsist and survive wholly in a world of limited resources and unlimited insecurity and uncertainty. These children are canaries in the coal mine, harbingers of a rapid decline of the human condition in the most destitute of the world's economies. What is explicit in the dismal data is a close association of the health and welfare of children with the inability or unwillingness of the least-developed states of the world to administer to the needs of their most destitute citizens. What is implicit in the dismal data is a set of global conditions

and processes that are to blame for the misery of many alongside the affluence of the few. In other words, none of this is coincidental.

A Global System of Desperate Childhood

When viewed in isolation, the war in Haiti seems very much a local conflict
between political factions, much in the way that the crisis in Darfur does,
and much in the way that the genocide in Rwanda did. Similarly, the pervasive corruption of the Bangladeshi government, the starvation of Timorese
under Indonesian occupation, the Maoist insurgency in Nepal, the degraded
infrastructure of Cambodia, the low level of primary school enrollment in
Burkina Faso, the low literacy rate in the Solomon Islands, the low life expectancy in Zambia, the economic torpor of Guinea-Bissau, all of it seems so localized, so isolated from larger global processes. Indeed all of this and more
stands in stark contrast to the affluence, stability, and growth characteristic of the industrialized world that few would believe, in this age of global
capital and multinational conglomeration, are phenomena isolated from

Table 3. The Least-Developed Countries of the World, 2005

Afghanistan	Madagascar
Angola	Malawi
Bangladesh	Maldives
Benin	Mali
Bhutan	Mauritania
Burkina Faso	Mozambique
Burundi	Myanmar
Cambodia	Nepal
Cape Verde	Niger
Central African Republic	Rwanda
Chad	Samoa
Comoros	São Tomé and Principe
Democratic Republic of the Congo	Senegal
Djibouti	Sierra Leone
Equatorial Guinea	Solomon Islands
Eritrea	Somalia
Ethiopia	Sudan
Gambia	Timor-Leste
Guinea	Togo
Guinea-Bissau	Tuvalu
Haiti	Uganda
Kiribati	United Republic of Tanzania
Lao People's Democratic Republic	Vanuatu
Lesotho	Yemen
Liberia	Zambia

Source: U.N. Office of the High Representative for the Least Developed Countries, Landlocked
Developing Countries and the Small Island Developing States.

worldwide networks of economic exchange. The fact of the matter is that the instability and poverty in the least-developed world and the stability and abundance of the industrialized world are the manufactured, intertwined, and codependent products of a composite world system of colonialism, unilateral military intervention, small arms and light weapons trafficking, debt and structural adjustment that ensures underdevelopment by maintaining global inequities in civil freedoms, economic participation, health, and security. And as is so true of most power imbalances, it is children who suffer the most. It is to this system, and its disproportionate effects on the poorest children of the world, that the balance of this chapter is devoted.

COLONIALISM

All fifty nations listed as "least developed" by the United Nations have had some degree of experience with colonialism by the world's industrialized powers, most of them European or American. Once the Industrial Revolution mechanized the conquest of foreign territories, the United States, United Kingdom, France, Germany, the Netherlands, Spain, Portugal, Belgium, Russia, Italy, China, Japan, and others accelerated their quest to subjugate previously autonomous regions of Africa, South Asia, the Pacific Islands, Latin America, and the Caribbean. These colonial territories generated fabulous wealth for their metropolitan master states, most often through aggressive extractions of wealth from the land through mining and plantation agriculture. In either case, the infrastructural consequences have invariably provided the foundation for economic dependence and agricultural unsustainability.

As colonial endeavors, both mining and plantation agriculture, were aggressively undertaken by European and eventually American powers during the roughly three hundred and fifty years between the seventeenth and mid-twentieth centuries. Given that the goal was the rapid extraction of wealth to be sent back to the metropolitan centers, little effort was invested by colonial administrators in preserving the land base. There was rarely the desire on the part of the occupiers to settle the colony beyond the time and space needed to harvest resources for export, whether those resources were gold, bauxite, diamonds, iron, copper, coffee, sugar, tea, indigo, or cocoa. As a result colonial mining and farming were notoriously unsustainable, with the drive to generate profit in the shortest order possible leading inevitably to rapid and permanent land degradation in either case. Colonial mining fostered soil erosion and water contamination, while plantation farming of cash crops encouraged uninterrupted planting-and-harvesting cycles with few fallow periods during which the soil might rejuvenate itself.

Centuries later the effects of these strategies of wealth-generation are most apparent in the lack of arable soil in the least-developed countries that at one time served as the world's most profitable colonies. Following the discovery of diamonds in Sierra Leone in the 1930s, British colonial authorities began aggressively mining them, eventually establishing a contract with DeBeers giving the company exclusive prospecting and mining rights in the colony. Illicit production nonetheless persisted, the methods ranging from hand-digging the earth and washing and sifting the ore to the use of more intensive equipment including water pumps and excavators. Whether legal or illicit, colonial mining practices led to the permanent clearing of crop land and water contamination on a large scale. Today, two-thirds of the population relies on small-scale farming for survival, though only 7 percent of the soil is arable.

Haiti's exhausted soil, massive deforestation, devastated rural economy, and consequential deluge of rural migrants into the already overcrowded capital are a direct result and extreme example of the long-term damage of colonial cash-cropping. Less than 20 percent of Haitian soil is considered arable, and much of that land was concentrated in the private property holdings of the Haitian-American Sugar Company (HASCO), an American-owned corporation forged during the 1915–34 U.S. Marine occupation of the country, until it closed its doors in 1987.

A litany of other woes in least-developed countries are also directly related to their history of colonization by industrialized states. The exploitation of discrete ethnic or racial populations as forced or coerced labor in some colonies has since resulted in broad disparities in the quality of life and distribution of wealth between descendant ethnic or racial populations. Today, in those countries where Indian or African slavery was deployed as the colonial labor base, social class inequities are paired with racial disenfranchisement—a legacy of the color politics and blood quantums that directed social stratification under such regimes.

The sudden withdrawal of metropolitan powers from their former colonies has all too frequently resulted in vacuums of political power in newly independent states that are rarely peacefully filled. A more typical consequence is political instability and factional warfare, which in turn is often used to justify unilateral military intervention by neighboring states. Worse still, in some cases the departing colonizer leaves behind repressive apparatuses that ensure civil pacification at the expense of human rights. When the U.S. occupation of Haiti ended in 1934, the Marines left behind the *gendarmerie*, the predecessor to the modern Haitian army that Michel-Rolph Trouillot has indicated would "kill as many Haitians during the second half of its 122-year-long history as it had Frenchmen during the war for independence" (1990: 105). What the *gendarmerie* and its descendant FADH did ensure (besides the misery of the Haitian people) was political stability; as well as a half-century of puppet presidencies, coups d'etat, popular suppression, and an economic climate (high unemployment and low wages) favorable to U.S. business interests.

UNILATERAL MILITARY INTERVENTION

The use of self-interested, coercive force by one sovereign state to bring about a change of policy or government in another sovereign state without the strength of multinational coalition-building is another means by which a system of global inequity between the industrialized and least-developed worlds is reproduced. Clearly a mandate for the use of force by the United Nations Security Council carries with it the greatest authority of legitimacy, insofar as the motivations and likely outcomes of intervention are debated openly in an international forum that necessarily includes the voices (if not the votes) of the nation to be invaded and other interested states. The danger of unilateral as opposed to U.N. multilateral intervention lies in the possibility of a state's use of its industrial military might to advance its own interests to the detriment of the target state's civil society.

A bloody coup in 1978 executed by the communist People's Democratic Party of Afghanistan (PDPA) led to the establishment of a Marxist revolutionary government there. Relations with Moscow rapidly soured as the PDPA shunned Soviet guidance on how to establish stability and consolidation within the regime. The realities of Cold War politics made the potential loss of Soviet hegemony in Afghanistan an intolerable option. By the end of 1979 Soviet troops conducted a massive unilateral invasion of the country, seizing control of Kabul and sparking a grueling ten-year guerrilla war that eventually led to the deaths of 14,500 Soviet troops and over one million Afghans. The war destroyed the Afghan economy and immediately catalyzed factional violence and widespread scarcity that continues to plague the Afghan civilian population in ever more dastardly fashion, now that the United States is itself engaged in massive, ongoing, unilateral military operations in the country.

In the earlier twentieth century, the United States sought to impose its vision of manifest destiny on the sovereign states of the Western Hemisphere through a campaign of unilateral military interventions throughout the Americas. Seeking self-interested control of the Caribbean Basin in order to surveil naval traffic in and out of the Panama Canal, U.S. forces prosecuted a series of unilateral annexations, occupations, and interventions throughout the region. Desiring the establishment of a naval base on the vital Windward Passage between Cuba and Hispaniola, the United States sought a pretext for the invasion of Haiti. That pretext came in the summer of 1915, when Haiti's President Vilbrun Guillaume Sam ordered a mass execution of political prisoners. Popular outrage led to the summary execution of Sam, his body drawn and quartered and dragged around the National Palace. The spectacle, though truthfully only slightly more graphic than politics as they had always been in Haiti, was enough for the United States to justify an invasion in the interest of "protecting American lives and business interests" in the country. The Marines landed within weeks, and the United States took over exclusive control of the customs houses, the treasury, and the organs of government. The American occupation would last nineteen years. In order to override inconvenient sovereignty issues and legal obstacles to the occupation, Franklin Delano Roosevelt, then an Assistant Secretary of the Navy, personally rewrote the Haitian Constitution, eliminating the clause that barred foreign ownership of land in Haiti and paving the way for a permanent U.S. naval base on the island.

The Marines were met with a fierce guerrilla resistance when they reinstituted slavery in the form of chain-gang labor crews, in order to build up the occupation infrastructure. Over the course of the ensuing insurgency, over two thousand Haitians were killed. The Marines left the country in 1934, amid declining popular support for the occupation at home and American congressional dismay at the failure of U.S. forces to achieve stability, assuage poverty and avoid atrocities in the country.

Such self-interested military unilateralism as typified by the Afghanistan and Haitian examples illustrates not only the human tragedy of such operations, but the long-term negative effects they have on the occupied countries' infrastructures and economies. Haiti never fully recovered from its experience with the Marine occupation, and in the case of Afghanistan, the damages of unilateral intervention are ongoing. But perhaps the worst that is illustrated by these actions is the assumption on the part of industrialized countries that it is in their rights to usurp the sovereignty, legitimacy and right to self-determination of economically less-developed and therefore weaker states for their own interests. The real tragedy such assumptions lay bare is the disproportionate suffering they cause for the civil society that invariably bears the brunt of any kind of invasion.

Self-interested unilateral state intervention in the political affairs of least-developed countries has also taken the form of industrialized-state support for the entrenchment of autocratic regimes that aggravate the desperate conditions of their citizens at the same time that they maintain friendly relations with the industrialized world. Chinese support of the Khmer Rouge in Cambodia, Belgian support of the autocratic monarchy in Nepal, Singaporean support of the antidemocratic junta in Myanmar, Soviet support of the Ethiopian dictator Mengistu, and U.S. support of the thirty-year Duvalier dynasty and the three-year Cedras regime in Haiti are all examples of the self-interested encouragement of repression, corruption, and autocracy in the least-developed nations of the world by those most industrialized. The reason in most cases for the support of these client regimes is the sympathies of the autocracies for the economic policies or the political agendas of their industrialized patrons.

SMALL-ARMS AND LIGHT-WEAPONS TRAFFICKING

The kinds of factional conflict and political instability that frequently lead to the assumption of power by autocratic regimes in least-developed countries are all too often aggravated and sustained by the proliferation of small arms and light weapons produced by and trafficked in from industrialized countries. The 2005 Small Arms Trade Transparency Barometer, an instrument compiled by the Small Arms Survey and based on the latest arms reports and 2002 customs data from U.N. Comtrade identifies the top twenty-five small-arms exporting countries, all of which are industrialized states (2005: 112). While it is true that industrialized states are also the world's primary consumers of these weapons (the United States is by far the world's most well-armed country, with nearly half of the world's small arms concentrated there), it is equally true that the majority of these weapons are not in the hands of professional armies or the police as one might expect, but in civilian possession. In fact "although few countries come close to the United States in the total number of firearms, the tendency for civilian ownership to overwhelm official stocks seems to be the norm" (Small Arms Survey 2001: 66). While this trend may be alarming, it is far more so in the countries of the least-developed world, where small arms and light weapons are at the very nexus of political instability, where they pose the greatest threat to the security of the civil society, where they are frequently the single greatest impediment to development, and where they inordinately injure and kill children. A recent study conducted by Robert Muggah of the Geneva-based Small Arms Survey found that 48 percent of all victims of small-arms injuries treated at the Canapé Vert hospital in Port-au-Prince between September 2003 and April 2004 were "students," a group representing the single largest category of gun-violence victims treated (Muggah 2005: 47).

The impact of armed conflict on development and investment in poor countries is devastating. The results of a World Bank survey of sixty-nine firms published in the 1997 *World Development Report* indicated that insecurity was ranked as the primary obstacle to investment in developing countries; this same report highlighted the small-arms violence characteristic of the "predatory" Haitian state under the Duvalier dictatorship as an example of a "recipe" for development failure (World Bank 1997: 149). Similarly a recent report by the United Nations Development Program (UNDP) on the effect of small-arms proliferation on human development notes that,

> Since the Cold War, the location and tenor of armed conflict has changed. Of the 30 to 50 conflicts occurring each year between 1989 and 1995, more than 95 per cent took place in developing countries. Most of these conflicts were largely internal affairs, rather than the proxy wars and independence struggles of the past, and virtually all of these wars were fought primarily with small arms. . . .
>
> With the number of internal armed conflicts peaking in the mid-1990s, the limits and effectiveness of development assistance in the context of widespread human insecurity and arms availability has been repeatedly tested. In Sub-Saharan Africa alone [where over half of the fifty least developed countries of the world are to be found], more than 20 per cent of the continent's population was directly impacted by civil wars during the 1990s. . . .
>
> Of the 34 lowest ranking countries on the UNDP's *Human Development Index* (HDI) in 2000, more than 20 are severely affected by conflicts (UNDP 2002: 10).

The trafficking of small arms and light weapons into least-developed countries compounds existing challenges to economic recovery at the same time that it cheapens the value of human life. Aside from the direct impact in the form of firearm death and injury, a number of indirect impacts have been documented as well. Health and education workers are more than occasionally targeted or attacked in armed conflicts, and public access to hospitals, clinics, pharmacies, and schools are frequently limited or constrained amid civil insecurity. Flight or migration away from regions of small-arms conflict accounts for most internal displacements in war zones, and also inhibits or delays refugees' decisions to return to or resettle their homes after the conflict. Trade, commercial investment, agricultural production, and even household exchanges rapidly deteriorate in the context of armed insecurity. Family and communal cohesion, gender relations, traditional exchange networks, and other forms of social capital are compromised during times of war thus undermining human development (UNDP 2002: 6–7).

The impact of armed conflict on the health and safety of children in particular has been well documented. An estimated two million children have been killed, six million seriously injured, and twenty-two million have been driven from their homes as a result of war, much of it attributable to small arms and light weapons (UNICEF 2001). And this before we consider the estimated three hundred thousand child soldiers worldwide, the overwhelming majority of whom are fighting in adult wars in the least-developed world.

Though other least-developed countries have far greater problems with firearms proliferation in the civil sector (indeed, Afghanistan and Yemen have weapons-to-citizens ratios that stagger the imagination), given the uniformity of data on the subject, the case of Haiti may be taken as illustrative of the poorest nations in general. There has been a considerable escalation of armed violence against civilians in Haiti since 2004, continuing a trend set in motion by the Cedras coup of 1991–94 during which over five thousand Haitians were killed. The findings of the Small Arms Survey indicate that "at least 700 persons died as a result of intentional firearm-related violence between September 2003 and December 2004 and three to four times that number were non-fatally injured" (Muggah 2005: 14–15). The same study also determined that in addition to gun-related fatalities, armed robbery, armed rape, armed kidnapping, and armed harassment, Haitian civilians have also endured compromised mobility, restrained access to markets and public services, and limited domestic and foreign investment as a result of the widespread civil militarism that has plagued the country with the influx of small arms and light weapons in the past decade. Here again it is children who bear the disproportionate brunt of the violence.

An assessment of the impact of the civil war in Haiti on children was conducted by UNICEF in February 2004. The survey found that

· In 15 percent of surveyed areas, children were killed in the violence;

· In more than a third of surveyed areas, children were either wounded by small-arms fire or beaten by armed gangs;

· The incidence of child rape increased dramatically in surveyed zones where small-arms violence was prevalent;

· In a third of surveyed areas, children were recruited by armed gangs;

· In over 70 percent of surveyed areas, families fled their homes for safer areas;

· In eight of ten cities surveyed, school students received death threats that prohibited them from attending classes and public events (UNICEF 2004a).

Haiti, like the rest of the least-developed world, simply cannot sustain development under these circumstances. Nor can it effectively protect its children so long as it, along with the other poorest countries, are flush with small arms and light weapons and are rife with conflict.

DEBT

At the height of the Cold War in the 1970s, the World Bank initiated a lending campaign targeting developing nations in order to both finance infrastructural projects and to serve as a bulwark against the global menace of communism. Over the course of a decade, the World Bank's stake in the economic development and political loyalties of the poor countries of the world increased fivefold (Ellwood 2004: 41). At the same time that financial aid was pouring into the developing world, so too were stockpiles of small arms and light weapons to be used in domestic conflicts against Marxist and Maoist insurgencies. Never mind that many of the governments receiving the loans and the weapons were repressive dictatorships (witness the governments of Mobutu in Zaire, Suharto in Indonesia, and Duvalier in Haiti); loyalty to the West in its struggle against the Soviet Union and its satellites was all that was required to keep the funds (and the arms) coming in. The Soviet Union followed suit, extending political, military, and economic aid to Cuba, Angola, Ethiopia, Afghanistan, and other governments of dubious reputation in exchange for their socialist devotion.

Twenty-five years after the fall of the Berlin Wall, the kleptocratic dictators of the Cold War era are all but gone, but the debt (along with tendencies toward kleptocracy and dictatorship) continue to plague the least-developed world. The World Bank's *World Development Report* for 1998–99 specifies that in six of the eight years from 1990 to 1997, developing countries paid more in debt service than they received in aid, resulting in a transfer of wealth from the developing world to the industrialized world of over $75 billion (World Bank 1999). Drawing on data from the bank's *World Development Report* for 1999–2000, Wayne Ellwood points out that the foreign debts of developing countries are currently in the neighborhood of two trillion dollars, resulting in "a debt of over $400 for every man, woman and child in the developing world—where average income in the poorest countries is less than a dollar a day" (Ellwood 2004: 48; World Bank 2000).

The magnitude of the transfer of wealth from the poorest countries of the world to the richest is exemplified in the geometric increase in the external debt of the least-developed world. From 1980 to 1995, Haiti's debt grew from $302 million to $807 million; Yemen's debt grew from $1.6 billion to $6.2 billion; Zambia's debt grew from $3.2 billion to $6.9 billion; and the debt owed by Bangladesh grew from $4.2 billion to $16.4 billion (World Bank 1997).

Since the 1980s, as the least-developed countries of the world have struggled to maintain their debt service with little plausible hope of ever repaying the principal, the World Bank, the International Monetary Fund, and the industrialized lender-states have stepped in to offer advice on the best ways for debtor nations to reorganize their economies to better compete in the global market. Invariably that advice has amounted to little more than two words: structural adjustment. The experiences of indebted countries that have taken and implemented that advice has been uniform; they have grown increasingly underdeveloped as they have turned their economies to the total service of the industrialized world.

STRUCTURAL ADJUSTMENT AND UNDERDEVELOPMENT

The legal minimum wage in Haiti today hovers around $1.70 per day. This is Haiti's "comparative advantage," its greatest economic resource. In human terms, so goes the logic of classical economic theory, Haiti's best chance for development is the marketing of itself as a source of cheap, hungry, willing workers. With an estimated 3.6 million eligible workers, 70 percent of whom are unemployed, the country has a bumper crop of cheap and starving laborers. They're still waiting for the development.

In 1982 M. Peter McPherson, then acting director of the International Development Corporation and administrator of the United States Agency for International Development (USAID), testified before the House Committee on Foreign Affairs and lobbied for funding to promote export-led development in Haiti. He predicted that closer ties between Haiti and U.S. markets would "make the prospects for Haiti as the 'Taiwan of the Caribbean' real indeed" (DeWind and Kinley III 1994: 127). McPherson's argument ultimately won, and shaped the policies of the subsequent two decades. In 1986 USAID invested $7.7 million in an Export and Investment Promotion Project "to recruit assembly contracts and attract overseas investors to Haiti" (USAID 1986; Briggs and Kernaghan 1995: 146). In 2004 the United States pledged $230 million in aid through fiscal year 2006, $22 million of which is dedicated to "Job Creation and Economic Growth"—a euphemism for export-led development. The U.S. Department of State's "Background Notes" on Haiti highlights the attractiveness of Haiti for American investment: "Benefits for both Haitian and American importers and exporters are available under the Caribbean Basin Trade Partnership Act (CBTPA)—which provides for duty-free export of many Haitian products assembled from U.S. components or materials—the successor program to the Caribbean Basin Initiative. . . . American firms enjoy free transfer of interest, dividends, profits and other revenues stemming from their investments" (U.S. Department of State 2005).

The movement of the Haitian economy toward an intensification of the export sector is consistent with the goals of the World Bank and the International Monetary Fund to integrate the economies of the developing world into the international market system through structural adjustment, or the reallocation and reorganization of capital and labor in order to bring a nation's economic structure in line with neoliberal trade policies. This specifically entails trade and exchange liberalization, privatization, deregulation, and the slashing of tariffs and import restrictions that make the developing economy favorable to foreign investment. Such policies are almost always implemented at the expense of social welfare programs and public services, leading many to the conclusion that structural adjustment is little more than a recipe for intensified underdevelopment of the quality of life of the poorest of the poor.

In the 1970s Somalia undertook a disastrous experiment in the socialist development of its economy, nationalizing its major industries and financial institutions, establishing state-owned farms, and enacting legislation designed to bring massive sources of capital under the control of the state. But the catastrophic drought of 1974–75 and the massive influx of hundreds of thousands of war refugees needing assistance in the wake of the Somali-Ethiopian war over the vast Ogaadeen region in 1977, combined with the failures of the socialist development experiment, left the Somali economy on the verge of total collapse. Billions of dollars in aid monies began flowing into the country, much of it from the United States, which saw an opportunity to hedge the Cold War geopolitics of Africa in its favor with the Soviet abandonment of Somalia in 1977 (Besteman 1999: 199–200).

Between 1979 and 1982 the International Monetary Fund and the World Bank stepped in with structural adjustment plans for the capitalist development of the Somali economy in the wake of the failed experiment with socialist self-development. Loans and other aid extended to Somalia were contingent on the devaluation of the local currency, the liberalization of trade and food pricing, the removal of obstacles to privatization, and deep cuts in public spending (Harriss and Crow 1992). The result of these policy shifts was immediate and severe. Nomadic pastoralists and sedentary farmers were hit hard by a sharp decline in selling prices at a time when Somali food production was still reeling from the devastation of the drought. The most dramatic consequence of the development program was an absolute

dependence on foreign food imports that have only escalated over the ensuing decades. The civil war, which has been raging for over ten years and
which has been exacerbated by the massive influx of military aid from industrialized countries ostensibly intended to stabilize the country, has further aggravated the food insecurity crisis.[1] With the saturation of the Somali
markets with cheap foreign cereals, domestic production has been crippled
and a cycle of starvation/cereal dumping/dependency has been set in motion.

A report on the food insecurity situation in Somalia issued by the Delegation of the European Commission in the Republic of Kenya, amplifies the
crisis and illustrates the cereal dumping connection:

> Before the war, average annual cereal production was estimated at
> 480,000 metric tonnes compared with an estimated domestic demand
> of 770,000 metric tonnes. Since the outbreak of the war, average an-
> nual production has fallen to less than 300,000 metric tonnes, while
> estimated annual domestic demand has also reduced to 600,000 met-
> ric tonnes. The gap has been primarily filled by commercial imports.
> Somalia has been a food aid recipient since the 1970s, the primary
> sources of food aid being the U.N.'s World Food Program, CARE and
> the ICRC [International Committee of the Red Cross]. (Delegation of
> the European Commission in the Republic of Kenya: 2005)

A case study of the crisis in the Haitian rice market prepared by the Trade
Environment Database describes a similar interconnection among structural
adjustment, food importation, and underdevelopment in Haiti. In 1994 the
Haitian government entered into a trade agreement with the International
Monetary Fund that mandated a structural adjustment strategy and the
implementation of trade liberalization measures, including the slashing of
tariffs on rice imports from 35 percent to 3 percent. The tariff reductions
resulted in Haiti's status as the least trade-restrictive country in the entire
Caribbean Basin. Between 1994 and 2000 domestic rice production declined
precipitously in correlation with the escalation of U.S. surplus rice imports
(Trade Environment Database 2004).

The liberalization of the rice trade between the United States and Haiti
has occurred simultaneously with other structural adjustments that have
moved Haiti toward urban-based assembly export industries. Not coinci-
dentally the decline in rice production has accelerated the collapse of the
rural economy more generally, driving newly disenfranchised farmers into
the capital where they seek limited factory work. With the highest rate of unemployment and the lowest minimum wage in the region, the overpopula-

tion of Port-au-Prince with out-of-work migrants has served foreign-owned factories in the city well. What it has not done is alleviate the conditions that contribute to child morbidity and death. The underdevelopment of the hemisphere's least-developed country is so profound as to defy exaggeration. A Haitian child dies once every five minutes from malnutrition, dehydration, and diarrhea; at least one-third of children under five suffer chronic malnutrition, which along with gastroenteritis accounts for 90 percent of child deaths (Hooper 1995). How can such suffering ever be called "development"?

All That We Know

If all we knew about the state of the world was what we knew about Haiti's poorest children, then what would we know? We would know that Haiti's poorest children are suffering in a manner familiar to children and their families throughout the least-developed world. We would know that such suffering is not a cruel twist of fate but the end result of a global system that ensures the poverty and the misery of the world's poor to the benefit of the world's most affluent. We would know that this global system of colonialism, unilateral military intervention, small-arms and light-weapons trafficking, debt, structural adjustment, and underdevelopment have established, maintained, and reproduced the miserable and violent conditions under which the poorest children in the least-developed countries of the world are living. We would know that the state of the world is defined by a set of international relations of power and capital that fuel the suffering and death of those children. Finally we would know that the persistence of these conditions is evidence that the lives of the poorest and most vulnerable in the world are sacrifices that the industrialized world is willing to make.

Paul Farmer has written eloquently of the primary challenge posed to this century's anthropology:

> The task at hand . . . is to identify the forces conspiring to promote suffering, with the understanding that these will be differently weighted in different settings. In so doing, we stand a chance to discern the *forces mortrices* of extreme suffering. A sound analytic purchase on the dynamics and distribution of such affliction is, perhaps, a prerequisite to preventing or, at least, assuaging it. Then, at last, there may be hope of finding a balm in Gilead. (Farmer 1997: 280)

If the study of street children in Haiti means anything, it means first recognizing that for all of their agency, autonomy, and will, they are suffering. If anthropology is to offer anything of substance to the global discourse on the rights of children and the difficulties under which many of them are living, then it must be willing to adopt a preferential approach to the study of the specific conditions under which children are nurtured and protected, rather than abused, battered, and exposed. Cultural rights, including education, health care, housing, work, protection against hunger and war, and other economic and social necessities are as important to the political autonomy of the child as civil and political rights, if not more so. Regularly and predictably violated throughout the least-developed countries of the world, the cultural rights of children in these regions should be at the very core of any anthropological discussion of global childhood.

The displacement of children onto the street is a cross-cultural phenomenon that finds manifestation in the least developed corners of industrialized countries as often as it emerges in the developing world. Contained within the bounds of capitalist as well as socialist economies, within nations both north and south of the equator, and from one hemisphere to the other, the stubborn persistence of the phenomenon of displaced and exposed childhood should signal that larger global machinations are at the causal root of the problem. Indeed the rapid expansion of conservative political and liberal economic policies have not eased the crises to which children are exposed, just as they have not decreased the number of children who live on the street worldwide. In fact their numbers have grown, and their lot has become more destitute and more certain. If the lived conditions of children are any indication of socioeconomic viability, then the current course of the global economy is indeed a colossal, misguided failure. If nothing else, the children who must daily carve out a social place for themselves amid the hostility and filth of the street should serve as a reminder to both anthropology and the world that in every respect, and in the words of one street boy, "*fòk sa chanje*." Things must change.

Notes

Introduction

1. See Schwartzman (2001) for an assessment of the scant anthropological literature on children in particular over the past century.

2. For example, the Center for Children and Childhood Studies at Rutgers University, Ohio University's Center for the African Child, and the Centre for Childhood, Development and Learning at the Open University (UK).

3. See also Kilbride, Suda, and Njeru (2001) for a discussion of the use of photography as a participatory approach to street-child work.

Chapter 1. *Salon Pèp*: Street Life and Society in Port-au-Prince

1. While some may debate the classification of glue as a "drug," I have chosen to define it as such here due to its effects and tendency to produce addiction after extended periods of usage.

Chapter 4. *Violenz Lari*: The Violence of the Street Economy from Below

1. A Haitian dollar is equal to five gourdes.

Chapter 5. *Lafanmi Selavi*: "The Family Is Life"

1. At the time, Aristide lived in a whitewashed manse with a swimming pool on a sprawling compound in Tabarre, just outside of Port-au-Prince. He also owns several other lavish homes in the hills of the neighboring countryside. Such things have long been the trappings of political power and influence in Haiti.

2. Aristide was reelected to his second term as president amid ostensibly fraudulent elections in 2000.

3. Though not a day over sixteen years, Ti Soni embarked on a rather determined bid to run for mayor of Port-au-Prince in 2000. While he later abandoned his candidacy (he would certainly never have been able to end up on the ticket anyway because of his age), his short-lived campaign was a curiously widespread source of bemusement throughout Port-au-Prince. Many citizens commented (though only *half*-jokingly) that Ti Soni could probably run the city better than any other politician. For whatever the triviality of his campaign, it nonetheless serves as even further evidence of the effectiveness of the Lafanmi program in stimulating children to political action.

4. A prominent Roman Catholic priest, a liberation theologian, and a close friend of Aristide, Vincent was shot and killed outside his home on August 28, 1994, presumably by FADH gunmen. The assassination prompted US State Department spokesman Michael McCurry to level a direct challenge to the Cedras coup government: "Your crimes only increase our outrage and strengthen our resolve to rid Haiti of your abuses. Make no mistake, outrages such as these reinforce the determination of the international community to take all necessary means to bring about the early restoration of democracy to Haiti." Roland Perusse (1995) points out that by "all necessary means" McCurry meant a U.N.-sanctioned intervention. Less than a month after the killing of Vincent, on September 19, 1994, the first contingent of three thousand U.S. combat troops entered Haiti as part of Operation Uphold Democracy, a U.N.-sanctioned invasion which would ultimately lead to the restoration of Aristide to the Haitian presidency.

Chapter 6. *Aprè Dans, Tanbou Lou*: After the Dance, the Drum Is Heavy

1. Title XI of Haiti's current constitution (1987) does provide for a Haitian army. In a strange and perhaps intentional oversight, Aristide did not pursue a constitutional dissolution of the army when he disbanded it by presidential decree in 1995. Rebel soldiers continue to enlist new members in Haiti today, in preparation for a full reconstitution of the Haitian army. They are growing in boldness. Following the disaster of Hurricane Jeanne in 2004, U.N. forces had to raise their weapons to disperse uniformed New Army soldiers and prevent them from seizing food aid from a World Food Program warehouse, which they said they intended to distribute to those suffering in Gonaïves. One rebel who I met in Port-au-Prince in March 2004 cited Title XI, Article 266 of the constitution in forcefully declaring the obligation of "his army"—the rebel insurgency—to "defend the country in the event of war" (subsection a) and to "lend assistance to the police when [they] are unable to handle a situation" (subsection d).

2. In a report issued during the uprising, Amnesty International warned that among those freed in rebel jailbreaks were high-ranking members of FADH incarcerated for massacres and atrocities committed during the Cedras coup d'etat. Jean-Claude Duperval, Hérbert Valmond, Carl Dorelien, and Castera Cénafils were sentenced to forced labor for life for their involvement in the 1994 Raboteau (in Gonaïves) massacre in which twenty to fifty Haitian civilians were killed by the Haitian army. Jackson Joanis was sentenced to forced labor for life for his role in the assassinations of Antoine Izméry and Father Jean-Marie Vincent, both fervent Aristide supporters. Prosper Avril was leader of the 1988 coup d'etat and indicted in the investigation of a 1990 assault on the village of Piatre by proxy strongmen hired by local landlords and FADH soldiers. Eleven were killed in the massacre that ensued, almost four hundred homes were razed, livestock were slaughtered and defiled in the fields, and crops were uprooted. The conflict originated with a disputed land tenure claim between poor farmers in the village and two absentee landholding families suspected

of having bankrolled the attack (Amnesty International 2004; National Coalition for Haitian Rights 2004).

3. Residents in the volatile Bel Air slum of the capital, an Aristide stronghold, claim to have witnessed the summary killing of thirteen people by PNH officers in October 2004. That same month, one Brazilian and one Argentine U.N. peacekeeper were shot in disarmament operations in Port-au-Prince.

Chapter 7. All That We Know: The Poorest Countries and the State of the World

1. Between 1980 and 1988 the United States contributed $163.5 million in military technology to Somalia (Besteman 1999: 15).

Bibliography

Adler, Patricia A. 1993. *Wheeling and Dealing: An Ethnography of an Upper-Level Drug Dealing and Smuggling Community*. New York: Columbia University Press.

Amit-Talai, Vered, and Helena Wulff, eds. 1995. *Youth Cultures: A Cross-Cultural Perspective*. London: Routledge.

Amnesty International. 2000. "Haiti: Unfinished Business—Justice and Liberties at Risk." AMR 36/01/00.

———. 2002. "Haiti: Political Leaders Must Reject Violence." AMR 36/016/2002.

———. 2003. "Annual Report 2003." POL 10/003/2003.

———. 2004. "Haiti: Perpetrators of Past Abuses Threaten Human Rights and the Reestablishment of the Rule of Law." AMR 36/013/2004.

Aptekar, Lewis. 1988. *Street Children of Cali*. Durham: Duke University Press.

Aretxaga, Begona. 2000. "A Fictional Reality: Paramilitary Death Squads and the Construction of State Terror in Spain." In *Death Squad: The Anthropology of State Terror*, edited by Jeffrey A. Sluka, 46–69. Philadelphia: University of Pennsylvania Press.

Aristide, Jean-Bertrand. 1990. *In the Parish of the Poor: Writings from Haiti*. Maryknoll, N.Y.: Orbis Books.

———. 1993. *Aristide: An Autobiography*. Maryknoll, N.Y.: Orbis Books.

Asad, Talal. 1992. "Conscripts of Western Civilization." In *Civilization in Crisis: Anthropological Perspectives*. Vol. 1 of *Dialectical Anthropology: Essays in Honour of Stanley Diamond*, edited by Christine Ward Gailey. Gainesville: University Press of Florida.

Bernat [Kovats-Bernat], J. Christopher. 1999. "Children and the Politics of Violence in Haitian Context: Statist Violence, Scarcity and Street Child Agency in Port-au-Prince." *Critique of Anthropology* 19(2): 121–38.

Berryman, Phillip. 1987. *Liberation Theology: The Essential Facts about the Revolutionary Movement in Latin America and Beyond*. New York: Pantheon Books.

Besteman, Catherine. 1999. *Unraveling Somalia: Race, Violence and the Legacy of Slavery*. Philadelphia: University of Pennsylvania Press.

Bourgois, Phillipe. 1990. "Confronting Anthropological Ethics: Ethnographic Lessons From Central America." In *Journal of Peace Research* 27(1): 43–54.

———. 1998. "Families and Children in Pain in the U.S. Inner City." In *Small Wars: The Cultural Politics of Childhood*, edited by Nancy Scheper-Hughes and Carolyn Sargent. Berkeley: University of California Press.

———. 1995b. *In Search of Respect: Selling Crack in El Barrio*. New York: Cambridge University Press.

Briggs, Barbara, and Charles Kernaghan. 1995. "The U.S. Economic Agenda: A

Sweatshop Model of Development." In *Haiti: Dangerous Crossroads*, edited by Deidre McFadyn and Pierre LaRamée. Boston: South End Press.

Campos, Regina, Marcela Rafeaelli, Walter Ude, Marilia Greco, Andrea Ruff, Jon Rolf, Carlos Mauricio Autunes, Neal Halsey, Dirceu Greco, and the Street Youth Study Group. 1994. "Social Networks and Daily Activities of Street Youth in Belo Horizonte." *Child Development* 65(2): 319–30.

Chevannes, Barry. 2001. *Learning to Be a Man: Culture, Socialization and Gender Identity in Five Caribbean Communities*. Barbados: The University of the West Indies Press.

Clarke, Edith. 1957. *My Mother Who Fathered Me: A Study of the Families in Three Selected Communities of Jamaica*. London: Allen and Unwin. Reprint, Barbados: The University of the West Indies Press.

Daniel, E. Valentine. 1996. *Charred Lullabies: Chapters in an Anthropology of Violence*. Princeton: Princeton University Press.

DeLauche, Judy, and Alma Gottlieb. 2000. *A World of Babies: Imagined Childcare Guides for Seven Societies*. Cambridge: Cambridge University Press.

Delegation of the European Commission in the Republic of Kenya. 2005. "Food Security Programme for Somalia." Electronic document, <http://www.delken.cec.eu.int/en/eu_and_somalia/cooperation/food_security.htm>, accessed 5 November 2005.

Desrosiers, Carril. 2000. " Haiti: Street Children Identify Themselves and Speak Out." Panos Institute. Electronic document, <http://www.panosinst.org/productions/island/ib21e.php, accessed 5 November 2005.

DeWind, Josh, and David H. Kinley III. 1994. "'Export-Led' Development." In *The Haiti Files: Decoding the Crisis*, edited by James Ridgeway. Washington, D.C.: Essential Books.

Drummond, Tammerlin. 1997. "A Constabulary of Thugs." *Time Magazine*, 17 February: 62–63.

Elie, Patrick. 1994. "Press Briefing on the Haitian Drug Trade." In *The Haiti Files: Decoding the Crisis*, edited by James Ridgeway. Washington, D.C.: Essential Books.

Ellwood, Wayne. 2004. *The No-Nonsense Guide to Globalization*. London: Verso.

Ennew, Judith. 1986. "Children of the Street." *The New Internationalist* 164: 10–11.

Farmer, Paul. 1997. "On Suffering and Structural Violence: A View from Below." In *Social Suffering*, edited by Arthur Kleinman, Veena Das, and Margaret Lock. Berkeley: University of California Press.

Fass, Simon M. 1990. *Political Economy in Haiti*. New Brunswick, N.J.: Transaction Publishers.

Foucault, Michel. 1977. *Discipline and Punish: The Birth of the Prison*. New York: Vintage Books.

Gennep, Arnold van. 1960 [1909]. *The Rites of Passage*. Translated by Monika B. Vizedom and Gabrielle L. Caffee. London: Routledge and Keegan Paul.

Glauser, Benno. 1990. "Street Children: Deconstructing a Construct." In *Construct-

ing and Reconstructing Childhood: Contemporary Issues in the Sociological Study of Childhood, edited by Allison James and Allan Prout. London: Falmer Press.

Gledhill, John. 1994. *Power and Its Disguises: Anthropological Perspectives on Politics*. London: Pluto Press.

Gottlieb, Alma. 2004. *The Afterlife Is Where We Came From: The Culture of Infancy in West Africa*. Chicago: University of Chicago Press.

Green, Linda. 1995. "Living in a State of Fear." In *Fieldwork Under Fire: Contemporary Studies in Violence and Survival*, edited by Carolyn Nordstrom and Antonius C.G.M. Robben. Berkeley: University of California Press.

Gutiérrez, Gustavo. 1995. "Toward a Theology of Liberation." In *Liberation Theology: A Documentary History*, edited by Alfred T. Hennelly. Maryknoll, N.Y.: Orbis Books.

Haitian Ministry of Social Affairs. 2000. "Report of Follow-Up on the Application of the Convention on the Right of the Child." November.

Hale, Charles. 1996. *Resistance and Contradiction: Miskitu Indians and the Nicaraguan State, 1894–1987*. Stanford: Stanford University Press.

Harriss, Barbara, and Ben Crow. 1992. "Twentieth Century Free Trade Reform: Food Market Deregulation in Sub-Saharan Africa and South Asia. In *Development Policy and Public Action*, edited by Maureen Mackintosh, Marc Wuyts, and Tom Hewitt. Oxford: Oxford University Press.

Hecht, Tobias. 1998. *At Home in the Street: Street Children of Northeast Brazil*. Cambridge: Cambridge University Press.

———. 2000. "Street Ethnography: Some Notes on Studying and Being Studied." In *Focaal: Tijdschrift Voor Antropologie* 36: 69–76.

Hooper, Michael S. 1995. "Model Underdevelopment." In *Haiti: Dangerous Crossroads*, edited by Deidre McFadyn and Pierre LaRamée. Boston: South End Press.

Human Rights Watch. 2003. "World Report 2003." New York: Human Rights Watch.

Kendall, Sarita. 1975. "Street Kids of Bogotá." *New Society* 29 (May): 117–18.

Kilbride, Philip, Collette Suda, and Enos Njeru. 2001. *Street Children in Kenya: Voices of Children in Search of a Childhood*. Westport, Conn.: Bergin and Garvey.

Kovats-Bernat, J. Christopher. 2000. "Anti-Gang, *Arimaj* and the War on Street Children." *Peace Review* 12(3): 415–21.

———. 2002. "Negotiating Dangerous Fields: Pragmatic Strategies for Fieldwork Amid Violence and Terror." *American Anthropologist* 104(1): 208–22.

Lanclos, Donna M. 2003. *At Play in Belfast: Children's Folklore and Identity in Northern Ireland*. Camden: Rutgers University Press.

Lerer, Leonard B. 1998. "Who Is the Rogue? Hunger, Death and Circumstance in John Mampe Square." In *Small Wars: The Cultural Politics of Childhood*, edited by Nancy Scheper-Hughes and Carolyn Sargent. Berkeley: University of California Press.

Mahmood, Cynthia Keppley. 1996. *Fighting for Faith and Nation*. Philadelphia: University of Pennsylvania Press.

Malkki, Lisa H. 1995. *Purity and Exile*. Chicago: University of Chicago Press.

Manigat, Sabine. 1997. "Haiti: The Popular Sectors and the Crisis in Port-au-Prince." In *The Urban Caribbean: Transition to the New Global Economy*, edited by Alejandro Portes, Carlos Dore-Cabral, and Patricia Landolt. Baltimore: Johns Hopkins University.

Márquez, Patricia C. 1999. *The Street Is My Home: Youth and Violence in Caracas*. Stanford: Stanford University Press.

Matthews, Hugh. 2003. "The Street as Liminal Space: The Barbed Spaces of Childhood." In *Children in the City: Home, Neighbourhood and Community*, edited by Pia Christensen and Margaret O'Brien. London: Routledge Falmer.

Mead, Margaret. 1949 [1928]. *Coming of Age in Samoa: A Psychological Study of Primitive Youth for Western Civilisation*. Reprint, New York: Mentor Books.

Métraux, Alfred. 1972 [1959]. *Voodoo in Haiti*. Oxford: Oxford University Press. Reprint, New York: Schocken Books.

Morton, Helen. 1996. *Becoming Tongan: An Ethnography of Childhood*. Honolulu: University of Hawai'i Press.

Muggah, Robert. 2005. *Securing Haiti's Transition: Reviewing Human Insecurity and the Prospects for Disarmament, Demobilization and Reintegration*. Geneva: Small Arms Survey.

Nagengast, Carole. 1994. "Violence, Terror and the Crisis of the State." *Annual Review of Anthropology* 23: 109–36.

National Coalition for Haitian Rights. 2004. "Piatre Massacre: NCHR Can Finally Salute an Indictment Report Fourteen Years Later." Press Release. 4 February.

Nordstrom, Carolyn. 1993. "Treating the Wounds of War." *Cultural Survival Quarterly*. (Summer): 28–30.

———. 1997. *A Different Kind of War Story*. Philadelphia: University of Pennsylvania Press.

———. 2004. *Shadows of War: Violence, Power and International Profiteering in the Twenty-First Century*. Berkeley: University of California Press.

OAS. 1997. "The Haitian National Police and Human Rights." Special Report of the Unit for the Promotion of Democracy. Electronic document, <http://www.upd.oas.org/special/hnpe.htm>, accessed 12 March 2000.

———. 2002. "The Haitian National Police and Human Rights Summary." Electronic document, <http://www.upd.oas.org/special/Haiti/resumee.htm>, accessed 7 July 2003.

Oboler, Regina Smith. 1996. "Nandi: From Cattle-Keepers to Cash-Crop Farmers." In *Portraits of Culture: Ethnographic Originals*, edited by Melvin Ember, Carol R. Ember, and David Levinson. Englewood Cliffs, N.J.: Prentice Hall/Simon and Schuster.

Olujic, Maria B. 1998. "Children in Extremely Difficult Circumstances: War and Its Aftermath in Croatia." In *Small Wars: The Cultural Politics of Childhood*, edited by Nancy Scheper-Hughes and Carolyn Sargent. Berkeley: University of California Press.

Olwig, Karen Fog. 2003. "'Displaced' Children? Risks and Opportunities in a Caribbean Urban Environment." In *Children in the City: Home, Neighbourhood and Community*, edited by Pia Christensen and Margaret O'Brien. London: Routledge Falmer.

Panter-Brick, Catherine. 2001. "Street Children and Their Peers: Perspectives on Homelessness, Poverty and Health." In *Children and Anthropology: Perspectives for the 21st Century*, edited by Helen B. Schwartzman. Westport, Conn.: Bergin and Garvey.

Perusse, Roland. 1995. *Haitian Democracy Restored: 1991–1995*. Lanham, Md.: University Press of America.

de Regt, Jacomina P. 1984. "Basic Education in Haiti." In *Haiti—Today and Tomorrow: An Interdisciplinary Study*, edited by Charles R. Foster and Albert Valdman. Lanham, Md.: University Press of America.

Reynolds, Pamela. 1995. "Youth and the Politics of Culture in South Africa." In *Children and the Politics of Culture*, edited by Sharon Stephens. Princeton: Princeton University Press.

Riches, David. 1986. "The Phenomenon of Violence." In *The Anthropology of Violence*, edited by David Riches. Oxford: Basil Blackwell.

Riesman, Paul. 1992. *First Find Your Child a Good Mother: The Construction of Self in Two African Societies*. Camden: Rutgers University Press.

Rizzini, Irene, and Irma Rizzini. 1991. "Menores Institucionalizados e Meninos de Rua: Os Grandes Temas de Pesquisas na Decada de 80" [Institutionalized Minors and Street Youth: The Great Research Topics of the 80s]. In *O Trabalho e a Rua: Criancas e Adolescentes no Brasil Urbano dos Anos 80* [Work and the Street: Children and Adolescents in Urban Brazil during the 80s], edited by Ayrton Fausto and Ruben Cervini. São Paulo: Cortez.

Robarchek, Clayton, and Carole Robarchek. 1998. *Waorani: The Contexts of Violence and War*. Fort Worth, Tex.: Harcourt Brace.

Robben, Antonius C.G.M., and Carolyn Nordstrom. 1995. "The Anthropology and Ethnography of Violence and Sociopolitical Conflict." In *Fieldwork under Fire: Contemporary Studies of Violence and Survival*, edited by Carolyn Nordstrom and Antonius C.G.M. Robben. Berkeley: University of California Press.

Scarry, Elaine. 1985. *The Body in Pain: The Making and Unmaking of the World*. Oxford: Oxford University Press.

Scheper-Hughes, Nancy. 1992. *Death Without Weeping: The Violence of Everyday Life in Brazil*. Berkeley: University of California Press.

Scheper-Hughes, Nancy, and Daniel Hoffman. 1997. "Brazil: Moving Targets." *Natural History* (July/August): 34–43.

———. 1998. "Brazilian Apartheid: Street Kids and the Struggle for Urban Space." In *Small Wars: The Cultural Politics of Childhood*, edited by Nancy Scheper-Hughes and Carolyn Sargent. Berkeley: University of California Press.

Scheper-Hughes, Nancy, and Carolyn Sargent, eds. 1998. *Small Wars: The Cultural Politics of Childhood*. Berkeley: University of California Press.

Schwartzman, Helen B. 2001. "Children and Anthropology: A Century of Studies." In *Children and Anthropology: Perspectives for the 21st Century*, edited by Helen B. Schwartzman. Westport, Conn.: Bergin and Garvey.

Shiraishi, Saya S. 1995. "Children's Stories and the State in New Order Indonesia." In *Children and the Politics of Culture*, edited by Sharon Stephens. Princeton: Princeton University Press.

Siméon, Nicole. 2002. "The Situation of Haiti's Street Children: Diagnosis of a Large-Scale Problem." Panos Institute/MediaNet Bulletin, December. Electronic document, <http://www.panosinst.org/Haiti/h12-02e.shtml#elab>, accessed 7 July 2003.

Simmel, George. 1955. *Conflict and the Web of Group Affiliations*. Glencoe, Ill.: Free Press.

Sluka, Jeffrey A. 1990. "Participant Observation in Violent Social Contexts." *Human Organization* 49(2): 114–26.

———. 1995. "Reflections on Managing Danger in Fieldwork: Dangerous Anthropology in Belfast." In *Fieldwork Under Fire: Contemporary Studies of Violence and Survival*. edited by Carolyn Nordstrom and Antonius C.G.M. Robben, 276–94. Berkeley: University of California Press.

Sluka, Jeffrey A., ed. 2000. *Death Squad: The Anthropology of State Terror*. Philadelphia: University of Pennsylvania Press.

Small Arms Survey. 2001. *Small Arms Survey 2001: Profiling the Problem*. Geneva: Small Arms Survey.

———. 2005. *Small Arms Survey 2005: Weapons at War*. Geneva: Small Arms Survey.

Stephens, Sharon, ed. 1995. *Children and the Politics of Culture*. Princeton: Princeton University Press.

Stoll, David. 1993. *Between Two Armies in the Ixil Towns of Guatemala*. New York: Columbia University Press.

Swart, Jeane Margaret. 1988. "An Anthropological Study of Street Children in Hillbrow, Johannesburg, with Special Reference to their Moral Values." Master's thesis, University of South Africa.

Sykes, Karen. 1999. "After the 'Raskol' Feast: Youths' Alienation in New Ireland, Papua New Guinea." *Critique of Anthropology* 19(2): 157–74.

Tambiah, Stanley Jeyaraja. 1992. *Buddhism Betrayed?: Religion, Politics and Violence in Sri Lanka*. Chicago: University of Chicago Press.

Theis, Joachim. 2001. "Participatory Research with Children in Vietnam." In *Children and Anthropology: Perspectives for the 21st Century*, edited by Helen B. Schwartzman. Westport, Conn.: Bergin and Garvey.

Toler, Deborah. 1998. "The United States in Haiti: Harvest of Hunger." Foodfirst Research Report. Oakland, Cal.: Institute for Food and Development Policy.

Trade Environment Database. 2004. "Trade and the Disappearance of Haitian Rice." TED Case Studies Number 725. June. Electronic document, <http://www.american.edu/TED/haitirice.htm>, accessed 4 November 2005.

Trouillot, Michel-Rolph. 1990. *Haiti: State against Nation*. New York: Monthly Review Press.

Turner, Victor. 1967. *The Forest of Symbols*. London: Cornell University Press.

———. 1969. *The Ritual Process: Structure and Anti-Structure*. Chicago: Aldine Publishing Company.

U.N. Commission for Human Rights. 1994. "Situation of Human Rights in Haiti." Report to the Special Rapporteur. E/CN.4/1994/55.

———. 1995. "Situation of Human Rights in Haiti." Report to the Special Rapporteur. E/CN.4/1995/59.

———. 1996. "Situation of Human Rights in Haiti." Report to the Special Rapporteur. E/CN.4/1996/94.

U.N./OAS International Civilian Mission in Haiti. 1993. "Report on the Situation of Democracy and Human Rights in Haiti." A/48/532.

UNDP. 2002. *"Development Held Hostage": Assessing the Effects of Small Arms on Human Development*. New York: United Nations Development Program.

UNICEF. 1989. *Convention on the Rights of the Child*. 20 November.

———. 1999. "Haiti Faces Major Education Challenges." CF/DOC/PR/1999/19.

———. 2001. "No Guns, Please: We Are Children." Fact sheet.

———. 2004a. "Les Enfants d'Haïti Face a la Crise: Situation et Realites Evaluation Rapide de l'Impact de la Crise Actuelle sur la Situation des Enfants en Haïti."

———. 2004b. "State of the World's Children 2004: Girls, Education and Development." New York: UNICEF.

———. 2005. "State of the World's Children 2005: Childhood Under Threat." New York: UNICEF.

USAID. 1986. "Haiti: Project Paper/Export and Investment Promotion." Project Number 521-0186. August 8.

U.S. Department of State. 1995. *Human Rights Report: Haiti*. Washington, D.C. March 1995.

———. 1999. *Haiti Country Report on Human Rights Practices for 1998*. Washington, D.C. 26 February.

———. 2005. *Haiti Country Report on Human Rights Practices for 2004*. Washington, D.C. 26 February.

———. 2005. "Background Notes: Haiti." Electronic document, <http://www.state.gov/r/pa/ei/bgn/1982.htm>, accessed 3 November 2005.

Warren, Kay B. 1993. "Interpreting *La Violencia* in Guatemala: Shapes of Mayan Silence and Resistance." In *The Violence Within: Cultural and Political Opposition in Divided Nations*, edited by Kay B. Warren. Boulder, Colo.: Westview Press.

Wolf, Eric. 1982. *Europe and the People without History*. New York: Columbia University Press.

World Bank. 1983. *Country Program Paper: Haiti.* Quoted in Josh DeWind and David H. Kinley III, *Aiding Migration: The Impact of International Development Assistance on Haiti.* Boulder, Colo.: Westview Press, 1988.

———. 1997. *World Development Report 1997: The State in a Changing World.* New York: Oxford University Press.

———. 1999. *World Development Report 1998/1999: Knowledge for Development.* New York: Oxford University Press.

———. 2000. *World Development Report 1999/2000: Entering the 21st Century.* New York: Oxford University Press.

World Health Organization. 2000. *Working with Street Children: A Training Package on Substance Use, Sexual and Reproductive Health including HIV/AIDS and STDs.* Geneva: World Health Organization.

Index

J. Christopher Kovats-Bernat is assistant professor of anthropology at Muhlenberg College in Allentown, Pennsylvania. He has been studying street children, political violence, and Vodou in Haiti since 1994.

Breinigsville, PA USA
24 January 2010
231281BV00002B/43/P